MANOLOGY

Secrets of Your Man's Mind Revealed

TYRESE GIBSON

and

REV RUN

WITH CHRIS MORROW

A TOUCHSTONE BOOK

Published by Simon & Schuster

New York   London   Toronto   Sydney   New Delhi

Touchstone
A Division of Simon & Schuster, Inc.
1230 Avenue of the Americas
New York, NY 10020

First Touchstone paperback edition January 2014

TOUCHSTONE and colophon are registered trademarks of Simon & Schuster, Inc.

For information about special discounts for bulk purchases,
please contact Simon & Schuster Special Sales at 1-866-506-1949
or business@simonandschuster.com.

The Simon & Schuster Speakers Bureau can bring authors to your live event.
For more information or to book an event contact the
Simon & Schuster Speakers Bureau at 866-248-3049
or visit our website at www.simonspeakers.com.

Designed by Ruth Lee-Mui
Cover photograph © Tommy Garcia

Manufactured in the United States of America

1   3   5   7   9   10   8   6   4   2

Library of Congress Cataloging-in-Publication Data
Tyrese.
Manology : secrets of your man's mind revealed / by Tyrese Gibson and Rev Run.
        pages   cm
1. Man-woman relationships.   2. Men—Psychology.   3. Interpersonal relations.
        I. Simmons, Joseph.   II. Title.
        HQ801.T97   2013
155.3'32—dc23   2012047118

ISBN 978-1-4516-8184-0
ISBN 978-1-4516-8185-7 (pbk)
ISBN 978-1-4516-8186-4 (ebook)

Rev Run:

I'd like to dedicate this book to my wife, Justine;
and to all my children, whose unconditional love continues
to inspire me to be the best husband and father I can be every day.

Tyrese:

I want to dedicate this book to both of my beautiful
grandparents, who recently transitioned into heaven.
Bobbi Gibson, the original Gibson; and my grandfather
Rev Ellis. I hope I continue to make you both proud
and honor you both by carrying the family name.
May God rest your souls in heaven. We as a
family love you and miss you dearly!

A JOINT PRAYER FROM REV RUN AND TYRESE GIBSON

Father God, we pray that this book will touch lives and relationships of men and women who are seeking to be healed and restored. We know in order for this to take place, fears will have to be shed and a boldness obtained. Understanding with boldness lies an undertaking of courage, risk, and bravery. Lord, we pray that you would put the anointing of inspiration on the words that have come forth from us.

Our prayer is that women that are hurting and disillusioned are able to find beauty in self. We pray that you heal those broken hearts one piece at a time and re-spark the healthy relationships that they're looking for.

As it is written in Corinthians 13:4–7, "Love is patient, love is kind. It does not envy, it does not boast, it is not proud. It does not dishonor others, it is not self-seeking, it is not easily angered, it keeps no record of wrongs. Love does not delight in evil but rejoices with the truth. It always protects, always trusts, always hopes, always perseveres."

In reading this book, we thank God that you have decided to put your pride and ego to the side. You have chosen to explore growth, new concepts, ideas, perspectives, views, and new understandings. For that, we are grateful. As you embark on this journey, we hope that you walk away feeling like every page was worth your time.

We thank God in advance for any clarity this book might provide. We have learned over the years that you cannot be frustrated, sad, depressed, and miserable walking around this earth in a state of confusion over things that you have clarity over. We ask that you use us as a conduit to deliver a message.

God, may your love go before us to lead us, beside us to protect us, behind us, to push and encourage us, above us to cover us, beneath us to sustain us, and may your love be in us, to fill us with your joy, and your power that our lives might bring glory and honor to you. This we pray in the matchless name of Jesus the Christ. Amen.

CONTENTS

Contents

Contents

Contents

INTRODUCTION

TYRESE

As I write this, my daughter Shayla is five years old. She's a beautiful, intelligent, inquisitive, and vivacious little girl, full of life and love. Without a doubt, she is, and always will be, the love of my life.

When I put her to bed, I have her say the following affirmations with me:

"Who's the greatest little girl in the whole world?"

"Shayla," she responds.

"Who can be anything they want to be when they grow up?"

"Shayla."

"Who loves you unconditionally more than anything in the world?"

"My daddy!"

I have Shayla repeat those words not only because she is beautiful, and she is the greatest (at least in my admittedly biased eyes), and she can be anything she wants to be when she grows up, and I do love her more than anything, but also because I know that if I don't reenforce those facts in her mind, eventually certain people she meets or certain things that she may be exposed to or experience in the world might trick her into thinking otherwise.

Or more specifically, men will.

I believe that almost all little girls start off believing that they are smart and beautiful and can accomplish anything, but far too many have much of that beauty, confidence, and optimism stolen by some of the men they encounter.

Maybe it's a daddy who leaves one day and then never comes back. Maybe it's an uncle or preacher who steals not only their innocence but much, much more. Maybe it's a teenage lover who whispers sweet nothings in her ear but then steps out behind her back. Maybe later on it's a boyfriend who'll never commit, or a husband who does but then still doesn't want to stay at home.

No matter what the situation, it seems like in a blink a beautiful, confident young girl can be transformed into a self-doubting and despairing woman, not because there is anything inherently wrong with her but because she could never figure out the men in her life.

That's why this book is about stopping that slide and helping women regain that confidence and positive outlook.

Not because all men are cheaters, manipulators, or pimps. No, as Reverend Run and I hope to show you, there are plenty of good men out there.

Instead, the truth is that no matter what heights your relationships have soared to, or depths they've sunk to, there is always more you can learn about the men in your life. Unfortunately, in this society we tend to stunt that growth by not confronting some very basic, and sometimes raw, truths about men and their relationship to women.

As you'll see, I happen to *love* confronting truth. When I pray at night, the number one thing I ask to be blessed with is clarity, no matter what it reveals. As was mentioned in the opening prayer, it's impossible to be stressed or depressed about situations and relationships that you have clarity on. Having grown up around people who hid from the truth and spent their lives confused and unclear, I never want to live like that.

I grew up in the Watts section of Los Angeles, in a house dominated by dysfunction. Where there was no father. Where when a man did show up, violence usually wasn't far behind. Where addiction, depression, and, sadly, even abuse became the norm. The adults in the house never really confronted or challenged the situation, and as a result, nothing ever really changed. In a house where truths were under the rug, I wanted to take that rug out to the front yard, shake it up and down and beat it with a broom until every one of the nasty, dirty little realities came falling out and scurried away from me.

I'm blessed to have experienced a level of success I never even dreamed of coming up in the ghetto. Two movies I was featured in, *Transformers: Dark of the Moon* and *Fast Five,* broke box office records worldwide and collectively went on to gross $1.7 billion. Several years ago I decided I was "done" with the music industry, but at my fans' urging last year I released an album called *Open Invitation-Reloaded,* which was number one for two weeks and featured a single, "Stay," that itself was number one for eleven weeks. Every day I think, "Thank God I listened to my fans!"

I also wrote a *New York Times* bestselling book called *How to Get Out of Your Own Way,* and one of the biggest thrills of my life was standing onstage with Oprah Winfrey and Stevie Wonder in Chicago during the taping of Oprah's final show and having her tell me, "Tyrese, oh my God, I read your book and it was powerful."

But the only reason that child who never imagined a life beyond the streets was able to make his way to the big screen and stand onstage with Oprah was that I wasn't afraid to look past my circumstances and address the unfamiliar. I know how hard it can be to change your perspective and attitude. I also know just how rewarding those changes can be when you finally do make them.

In *Manology* I want to encourage you to look past what you think you know about men and consider some of the insights Reverend Run and I are going to share in this book. It isn't always easy to share some of the less flattering aspects of your past, but if this book can bring clarity to even one woman, then it will all be not only worthwhile but perhaps even the most important thing I've ever done.

I know I can make a difference because men are one subject I happen to be extremely knowledgeable about—specifically, what's going on in our minds. Having made that journey from the hood to Hollywood, I've witnessed the full range of the male spectrum. I've seen what men do and think when it seems like they don't have any future beyond their block, and I've seen what they do and think when suddenly there aren't any barriers between themselves and their fantasies—when the true depths of their desires, for better or worse, are not only tolerated but celebrated.

And those truths that I'm going to share with you will often be raw, and parts may even make you uncomfortable. But that's how I give it to my friends, and if you're reading this, then I consider you a friend too.

Each time you start to pick up this book you should hesitate just a little, because what I'm saying is hitting so close to home. If I'm not striking that nerve, then I'm not being a good friend. Because in these pages I'm peeling back all the layers and revealing MY complete truth. Unapologetically.

I'm OK with not everyone appreciating my perspective or my honesty. My goal for this book is to promote a dialogue in which we can really talk about what's going on with your relationships and expectations. When you're finished reading, hopefully there will be some fundamental shifts in how you view men.

Instead of basing your life on how you've been taught things ought to be, you can make rational, controlled decisions on how we actually ARE. For better or worse.

Obviously every time we say, "Men do this" or "Men think that" there are going to be exceptions to those rules. You don't need to look any further than Rev and me to see that not all of us are alike.

Also, I need to stress that just because I have insight into the behavior and motivations of men, I am still very much a work in progress as a man myself. I'll tell you right now that I'm in therapy for some of the things I experienced and witnessed during my childhood, and while I'm making great progress, I don't consider myself all the way home yet.

I'm honored to be sharing these pages with Rev Run, but I want to stress to you that there's no "Reverend" before *my* name. I'm still just plain old Tyrese Gibson, and trust me, Rev and I have very different views and perspectives, not to mention different types of language we use to express our views.

Respectfully agreeing to disagree is one of the foundations of Rev's and my friendship. In fact, our friendship was actually born out of a disagreement!

THE CONFLICT THAT SPARKED A DIALOGUE

It all started several years ago after I received one of Rev's "Words of Wisdom" emails: You know! Those inspirational emails you saw him writing while he sat in that bubble bath at the end of every *Run's House.*

At that time, my perception of Rev was probably the same as most people's. I knew that he was one of the greatest rappers of all time and that his group, the legendary RUN DMC, was perhaps the most influential in the history of hip-hop. But I also knew him as the star of *Run's House,* as a man who managed to navigate the turbulent seas of celebrity through finding God and then used that faith as a foundation on which to build a beautiful family. Like a lot of men, especially African-American men, I was extremely inspired by what Run had created. When the show finally ended, I was still searching for that inspiration, which is why I ended up subscribing to his "Words of Wisdom" emails.

While I loved receiving those emails, one day I got one that I just couldn't cosign. I can't remember exactly how it was worded, but essentially Rev was saying that once you're married, there's zero room for infidelity or misbehaving. Not because you don't want to anger your wife but because you don't want to anger God.

I respected what he was saying, but I also felt that even after invoking God's name in their marriage vows, most men will refuse to stay faithful if the sex is bad. Just on impulse, I sent him a short note explaining my views, assuming that would be the end of it. In my mind, there was no way that Run was actually sending these messages out from his own email account. I was content just to float my thought out into the universe and never expected it to go any further than that.

So imagine my surprise when several minutes later I got a reply back saying, "Is this really Tyrese? The singer? If so, call me back at this number. Rev."

Huh? I was shocked, but I collected myself and called Rev immediately. After a little bit of small talk, we got into it and started arguing about cheating. And arguing. And arguing. We ended up staying on the phone for several hours until we finally decided that we'd just have to "agree to disagree." But despite our differences, the conversation had been stimulating and inspiring. We could both tell that a great new friendship had emerged.

Some people might call it a mentor/protégé thing or a "bro-mance," but we started saying that Rev was my "MAN-tor," which, as we'll explain, is a term we coined for a man who teaches another man how to mature and evolve. However you want to label it, it was clear to me after a few more conversations that Rev had quickly emerged as one of the major forces in my life. Any man who not only talks but also "walks" the word of God is my hero.

Soon we began talking almost daily, chopping it up about everything under the sun—the music industry, films, our kids, fame—but particularly relationships, a subject I really respect his opinion on. It's been said before, but I really felt like Rev was a hip-hop Bill Cosby. So when he talked about what it took to be a man of God and raise a family with respect, spirituality and integrity, I had to listen.

Whenever we spoke, I would try to get his opinion on not only what was holding me back but also what was holding men and women back in general. Because everyone—at least everyone I know—wants something similar to *Run's House* in their own lives. Maybe not down to the last detail, but a similar mix of regality and ghetto love.

As Run will share, those conversations were incredibly healthy and motivating for him too. While he's evolved so much over the years, he still has room to grow and speak. Speaking with me gave him the energy to keep pushing in that direction. When I would press him to go deeper into his truths, it forced him to reexamine his own life.

We started calling this process "iron sharpening iron." Because just as only iron can sharpen iron, often it takes two intelligent, inquisitive, strong-willed individuals to sharpen each other. If you just sit back and become comfortable with what you've got, you're never going to stay sharp. But if you have someone else who's always pushing and challenging you, then the growth in your life and career will always be that much greater!

We both live our lives in the spirit of "People who know better should *do* better." Our hope is that by learning the inner workings on your man's mind, you're going to know what you're really dealing with in a relationship. And armed with that knowledge, you're going to do so much better at finding the happiness and fulfillment you deserve in your relationships.

OK, I've said my piece. So now I want to let my partner Rev Run have his chance to speak.

Rev Run

Since Tyrese just said that this book should be about raw, honest truth, let me start by sharing some of my own:

I wasn't a big fan of Ty the first time I met him.

The story (and it's one that I didn't even share with Tyrese until we started working on this book) of how our relationship started off on the wrong foot is this:

Back in the early 2000s, RUN DMC agreed to perform at Watts Day, a charity event Tyrese was throwing in his old hood. I didn't know him personally; we only did it because Jam Master Jay liked Tyrese and wanted to help him out.

When we arrived to perform, Tyrese was nowhere to be found. Still, we took the stage and launched into a set of some of our greatest hits: "Rock Box," "Sucker MCs," "Peter Piper," and "Jam Master Jay." Songs that never failed to get a crowd hyped.

Just as we launched into "Run's House," Tyrese pulled up in a tricked-out truck. He jumped out, and immediately the crowd gravitated to him.

But as soon as "Run's House" was over, Tyrese gave everyone a wave, hopped back in his truck and drove off. He had listened to all of *one* of our songs and then broken out. *This little punk is going to leave during the middle of a RUN DMC set?* I thought to myself. *When we're playing for free at HIS charity event. Oh, hell naw!*

From then on, whenever I'd see Tyrese on the TV, or hear one of his songs on the radio, I'd get a little annoyed. "Little Tyson Beckford pretty boy wannabe," I'd say under my breath. As much as I'd like to think I was above that sort of behavior, the truth is I had let my insecurities get the best of me.

So when he suddenly emailed me out of the blue that morning,

I was shocked. But as I reread his message, I could tell he probably didn't even remember the incident at Watts Day. (Not only did he claim not to remember it when I finally brought it up but he claimed it didn't even happen. Trust me, it happened.)

Even though he was writing to challenge something I had said, there was a tone of respect in his email. Rather than hold on to an old grudge, I thought to myself, *Wow, dude actually reached out to me. Let me hit him back and see what he's about.* And as he just related to you, we immediately launched into a heated debate over what I'd written.

"I can't believe you want to tell women that cheating is inevitable," I told him after he explained his position. "You can't tell a woman that. It's not right. Man, you just want to run amok on the earth, but still have a woman in some sexy Victoria's Secret thing waiting to rub your feet when you get home at night. Sorry, it doesn't work like that. You better go take out the trash and tell your woman you love her on your way out to the garage."

Though that was just the first of many disagreements we would have, I could see that Tyrese had some important ideas to share, with both me and the world. We've been best friends since that first conversation and talk on the phone at least once, if not more, every day.

Looking back, Tyrese reached out to me at the perfect time in my life. His friendship was like a breath of fresh air being blown into my home. Though I was incredibly grateful for the success of *Run's House,* I noticed afterward that my friends didn't want to hang out with me quite as much. It was as if my life looked too shiny, too perfect to them. I was feeling more like a monument to a certain ideal than a living, breathing man.

The irony was that even though I don't drink, smoke, or chase women anymore, I wasn't looking to separate myself from people who still did have a little bit of that wildness in them. What would be the point of me having gained some wisdom if I wasn't willing to share it with people who could use it? As you'll read, I believe the best way to help a man change for the better is actually through a type of relationship I call "MAN-torship"—where one man can lead his friend through example, rather than just preaching down from that mountaintop at him. That's the kind of relationship that helped turn my life around, and it's the type of relationship I was looking to share with someone else who might be in need of some direction.

Thankfully, rather than being intimidated by my reputation, Tyrese was receptive to being MAN-tored. And truthfully, he was not only eager to find out what sort of wisdom I could share with him but he helped push me in a new direction too.

If our conversations have helped *sharpen* him up, they definitely helped *loosen* me up. Tyrese reminds me not to take myself so seriously as "Rev Run" and instead to have fun with my marriage and my reputation. He's brought a lot of new energy into my life and helped me begin to have a much greater appreciation for my blessings.

One of our primary hopes for this book is that it can help sharpen you up too. If you keep falling for the same type of guy without ever finding true love or happiness, we're going to show you how to avoid falling into that trap and start meeting men who are actually better suited for you. Or if you keep having men walk all over you, we're going to teach you how to establish a bottom line when it comes to your relationship and actually enforce it. You know how countries impose "no fly" zones over certain territories? Well, we're going to show you how to enforce "no walk" zones over yours.

For others, *Manology* will help loosen them up when it comes to the men in their lives. For instance, if you're obsessed about changing your man into something "better," we're going to teach you to let go of that energy and instead become a facilitator of his evolution, an approach that will earn his appreciation and respect instead of his resentment.

If you've been having trouble communicating with your man, we're going to teach you when are the best times to talk to him.

If you're having a difficult time getting your man to see what a great thing he already has right in front of his face, we're going to teach you how to correct the condition that plagues too many relationships: Male pattern *blindness*.

Ultimately, while *Manology* will help demystify the men in your life, the most fundamental message to be found in this book ain't even about them. No, at its core this *Manology* is about helping women feel good about themselves.

Tyrese and I might disagree on a lot of topics—in fact, our original title for this book was *I Beg to Differ*—but there's one goal that we're in rock-solid agreement on: we want to help women stop getting tripped up by the men in their lives and start empowering themselves.

As fathers ourselves, Tyrese and I have a vested interest in creating a more leveled playing field between men and women. Remember, Tyrese has a daughter, and I've got three of them: Vanessa, who's approaching thirty; Angela, who's in her midtwenties; and five-year-old Miley. It would break our hearts to see a daughter of ours get tangled up with a man who didn't treat her with respect or have her best interest at heart. Just as we would never want to watch one of our daughters become joyless just because she was boyless (a condition I'll speak on later).

If I could venture a guess, some of what Tyrese has to say in this book will strike you as pure craziness. Don't worry, ladies, I will be here to put a foot on his tail when he goes overboard or gets too far out of bounds on a particular subject. But even if we don't always agree with what Tyrese is saying in these pages, we can't tune him out. To do that would just be a dance *around* the truth. To truly change your life, you've got to dance *with* the truth. Because without the truth you're always going to be living a lie.

Frankly, at times it's going to seem like both of us are promoting or defending the self-centered, egotistical stuff that men do. So let me say one thing to all the women reading this book: the core of *Manology* is sharing the secret thoughts of men. Not justifying their actions.

Again, with emphasis:

This book is about *sharing* men's *secrets.*

Not *justifying* their *actions.*

That means that even though we might ask you to try to understand some of the sexist, selfish, inconsiderate, annoying, thoughtless and misogynistic things that men do, we're not suggesting it's right for men to do them.

We're simply trying to help you identify the needs, desires, concerns, and insecurities that those actions arise from so you can figure out how to deal—or not deal—with them. So that when you look at your man, your lenses won't be clouded by fear, insecurity, confusion or even love. You'll be able to look at him clearly and say, "He's the one for me" or "I loved him, but it's never going to work the way I need it to. It's time to say good-bye."

Finally, I want to address the role that God plays in both my life and this book. Obviously, as a reverend, my relationship with God is the most important one in my life. It was God who helped me evolve from the swaggering rapper who "meet this little girl/hair was kinda curly/went to her house/to bust her out/I had to leave early" to the husband who tells his wife, "I never want to leave your side."

Just as it was God who made me not only a better husband to my wife but a much better father to my children as well. Yes, it's been

God who pulled me out of the darkness that had enveloped my life and helped me see just how beautiful life can be. It's a role God can play in your life too. In fact, one of my favorite Tweets to send out is this quote from Max Lucado: "A woman's heart should be so hidden in God that a man has to seek Him just to find her."

While I really do believe a woman should hide her heart with God, I don't ever want it to feel like I'm being too rough or strict with my interpretation of His word. If anything, I'm actually pretty lenient in how I try to translate my understanding of God's teachings into everyday realities.

No, I envision this book being applicable to everyone's lives, whether they're Christian or not. The blueprints for success that I'm going to lay out are the ones that I've learned through the Bible, but they can be applied to any life or situation.

The reason I'm not so strict is that if there's one thing I've learned over the years about relationships, it's that they're rarely ever perfect, but they're always precious. Try to move through life understanding that no matter how hard you work, or no matter how closely you follow the blueprint, you're probably never going to experience a "perfect" man.

And that's OK.

What isn't OK is wasting your time with a man who not only isn't "perfect" but doesn't treat you as precious either. *Manology* will help you find the clarity to make the right choices in your relationship and move closer to the happiness that you deserve.

CHAPTER 1

THE MAN-IPULATOR

TYRESE

It was 1999 and I was performing onstage at the House of Blues in Houston, Texas. She was standing in the front row, her thick body poured into her tightest dress, reaching out to me and screaming my name.

Staring back at her, I began singing my hit that was burning up the airwaves.

> *Sweet lady, would you be my*
> *Sweet love for a lifetime?*
> *I'll be there when you need me*
> *Just call and receive me.*

That's what I was *saying* to her.

MANOLOGY

Now what I was *thinking* was a little different.

Stop screaming and save your energy, baby girl. Just let me focus on these lyrics, these dance steps and the mark; I'm supposed to be on when the fireworks go off. And when I'm done with all that, me and you gonna get together in a different kind of way.

And true to my word, I did stay focused for the rest of the show. I sang my heart out, danced my butt off and hit every last one of my marks.

Just before the final song, she felt a light tug on her arm from a big dude who had suddenly materialized beside her. "Excuse me, miss, I'm Tyrese's security," he explained. "Tyrese sent me out here to invite you and your girls to meet him backstage after the show."

She accepted the invitation. Backstage we exchanged some small talk, and she ended up coming back to my hotel with me. Then well, you know things got real interesting. . . .

Now, was that a special night? A once-in-a-lifetime moment. Nah.

For me, that scene played out so many times. It was almost like living in a world within a world, where there were no rules, just you and whoever you want to do it with, wherever you want to do it.

Now before some of y'all start thinking, "It's only the first chapter and already it seems like Tyrese's ego is out of control," let me also say this.

As much as that ego might have liked to believe it, in my heart I knew those women weren't buying tickets, jockeying for position, and screaming their lungs out just for *me*.

They were also screaming for their dream.

The dream of having a man stare into their eyes and ask, "Would you be my sweet love of a lifetime?"

The dream of having a lover call them out of the blue just to ask, "Have I told you lately that I love you?"

The dream of a man taking them by the hand and saying, "Girl, I want to take the time and thank you for putting up with me. . . . Even though I made you cry, I want to make it right."

But since women rarely, if ever, hear those words from their own man, they make sure that they're going to get close up to that stage and hear them from me.

The irony, of course, is that even though I've always delivered those songs from the bottom of my heart, for many years my actions were constantly singing a different tune.

Even though I knew most women were searching for that "love of a lifetime," I wasn't thinking much past the "love of a nighttime."

Today, I'm so grateful that I've graduated from that season of my life and moved on to a much healthier place. Back then, I was living a lifestyle that could have easily spiraled out of control. Sometimes, when I reflect back on those days, I'm so thankful that I never drank or did drugs, because if I had, there's no question that my life would be a lot different than it is now.

Today, I'm in a place where I can finally be honest about what I want out of a relationship. A place when I can tell my woman, "Just give me some time to make it right; I'm being completely sincere."

Not that I didn't mean it before, because I did. It's just that for a man, often there's a gap between saying something and actually having that confidence that he can live that way too.

But if you are going to truly understand how a man thinks, how he's constantly looking for ways to defer your dream of a healthy relationship, then I need to take you back to those early days, even though I'm not proud of how I was living back then.

In fact, when Rev and I initially started discussing this chapter, I was resistant to the idea of pulling back the curtain on my old ways and exposing them to the world.

I knew that some women would be turned off by my behavior, even if it was in the past. I understood that my mind-set would sound arrogant at best and downright exploitive at worst.

I can live with that perception, provided that it helps women gain some clarity about the men in their lives.

My biggest fear was that I didn't want to make it sound like I was glorifying that old behavior. I wouldn't want a man to read about those days and say, "Ah, so that's how a real boss puts it down."

My pimpin' past is not one that I would endorse to other men. It would have a negative effect on the women in their lives, and, as Rev will break down later in the chapter, it would also hurt those would-be pimps.

Which is why despite my initial reservations, I ultimately decided that you do need to meet the old Tyrese. Because unless I share my raw truth, there's no way that I can truly help people.

Specifically, I need to address just how deceitful and conniving men can be when dealing with women. Or, as Rev and I like to call it, MAN-ipulative.

We celebrate men who demonstrate Machiavellian tendencies when it comes to politics or business, but we still like to pretend that they're the ones getting strung along when it comes to personal relationships. We need to face facts on just how

MAN-ipulative men can be in their relationships. We need to own up to and address the fact that men can be just as calculating, controlling, and cunning in the bedroom as they are in the office or hustlin' out on the streets.

Back in my old days, my MAN-ipulation game was serious. I had been dealt the fame and wealth cards quick and fast, and I was not shy about playing them. At all.

Granted, most men don't have that advantage when dealing with women. But I believe that my playing from such a strong hand makes my story even more relevant.

I want you to get inside the mind state of a man when he thinks *anything* is possible, when he's simply following his ego instead of the so-called rules.

I want to expose you to the standards of trickin' that I saw set in Hollywood. So that no matter what level you encounter it in your own life, whether it's Hollywood or the hood, Sunset Strip or the suburbs, you'll be prepared.

THE MAN-GICIAN

I see similarities between what professional magicians and professional MAN-ipulators do. Magic is all about creating distractions. For instance, notice the way a magician speaks when he's onstage. It's always very theatrical, with a lot of hand movements. That's to create a distraction. He might wear a bright red handkerchief, or be assisted by beautiful women, for the same reason. To create a distraction. Everything a magician says and does is intended to distract you from what he's really doing. He wants you to get so caught up in the loud voice, hand motions, colors and smoke that you never notice him pulling that card out of his sleeve.

How I went about dealing with women was no different. I was a MAN-gician who had mastered the art of distraction. But while a magician tries to distract his audience from something that's intentionally concealed, I was a MAN-gician trying to distract women from the truth that was hidden in plain sight:

And that truth was that they weren't happy in their relationships with me.

Now just so you don't get the wrong idea, they weren't unhappy because I was a bad guy, treated them poorly, wasn't fun to be with or didn't know how to love them right.

No, I was a good dude who treated them well, showed them an incredible time and always put it down in the bedroom (if I may say so myself).

Yet despite all that, they were often unhappy being with me. Despite all the incredible things happening on the surface of our relationship, deep down they could sense that I'd never be as committed to it as they were.

And they were right, of course. Yet rather than address my lack of commitment, I'd try to buy time with distractions.

The first things I'd pull out of my MAN-gician's bag of tricks (hey, why do you think they call it trickin'?) were simple diversions like money or gifts. In other words, if I sensed that a woman was getting hip to my runaround, I might surprise her with a new handbag. Or perhaps I'd let her hold one of my credit cards (only the ones with a set limit, of course) and send her off to the mall. Or if I was going to be "busy in the studio" (my old euphemism for seeing another woman) that weekend, then I'd give her a couple of airline tickets so she could go visit her friends in Miami.

All those gestures were made under the guise of love, but in reality they were just so many clouds of smoke meant to distract her from the fact that our relationship wasn't really going any-where.

Eventually she'd start to see through the smoke. Instead of saying, "Thanks, Boo" and running off to the mall or jetting down to Miami, she'd shake her head and say, "No, Rese, we need to talk. We need to figure out where this thing is going."

When those moments came, do you think I surrendered and said, "OK, baby, let's talk about this"? Of course not.

Instead, when it was time to face the music, I'd just turn up the distractions instead. And the loudest distractions that I had at my disposal were elaborate romantic gestures. That's right, when-ever plain old trickin' just wasn't getting the job done anymore, I would go out of my way to stage something *extremely* elaborate and sexy.

One of my favorites would be to tell my girl to be ready to go out at eight, but then insist on keeping the rest of the night a surprise. At eight o'clock on the dot a white limousine would pull up to her house and take her to a five-star hotel, where a bellhop would be waiting for her at the entrance. He would escort her up to the penthouse suite, where I'd be waiting for her. His and hers massage tables would already be set up, and we'd spend the next two hours getting mind-blowing massages together. After that, I'd have a full-course meal delivered to our room, which we'd eat while lounging in our bathrobes. After that . . . well, you know the rest. I don't even have to say it. Not only did we enjoy an incredible night together but I'd also just MAN-ipulated my way into several more months of not having to address my lack of commitment.

Believe it or not, there were some cases where I had to step my game up even higher than that. There's a rumor on Twitter, which I can neither confirm nor deny, that me and a young lady once made love with a live violinist and Spanish guitar player serenading us in the bedroom.

I can't lie, there were some women who seemed immune to my trickin', even when I brought it on at that all-star level. I remember I met a beautiful, supersmart attorney just as she was coming off a bad breakup. She decided she was going to be celibate until she got her head together, and despite the connection we both felt, she told me in no uncertain terms that sex was not going to be on the table anytime in the near future. She didn't say it in a snide or threatening way but rather made it clear that she was going through a tough time and would appreciate my respect and patience.

I know women think all men are always in a rush for sex, but the patience part was actually easy for me. Respecting her wishes was a different story.

Even though I did care about this woman and appreciated what she was going through, I still tried to flip it on her. After she told me about her celibacy, I told her, "Hey, you're not going to believe me, but I've been thinking about laying off sex for a while myself." I explained my rationale: after years of moving around, I just needed a break. I understood where her head was at, and it was actually a relief for me to not have to worry about sex. I was happy to just spend time with her.

True to those words, for several months I never made even the slightest move toward sex when we got together. At first she was skeptical, but after a while she was impressed and decided I had in fact been telling the truth.

My boys used to ask me, "How the hell do you hang out with such a sexy lady without trying to go there?" I told them, "Hey, it's easy to turn down a slice of really good cake when you've been snacking on potato chips all day. It's only hard when you're hungry."

And I definitely wasn't hungry. Anytime I wasn't with my attorney I'd be creepin' with someone else who was more than willing to satisfy my sexual desires. It feels foul to admit this today, but I can even remember calling her from a hotel room with another woman in the bed with me. I put on my sleepy voice and told her, "Hi, baby, I'm about to go call it a night, I'm sooo beat from this tour. I just wanted to hear your voice before I went to bed." All the while I'm giving this other woman the "Shhh, don't say nothin'" signal as she lay next to me naked.

It's sad to say, but when a man is in that MAN-ipulative mind state, you can't even rest easy knowing that he just said, "Good night, I love you, baby," over the phone. Unless you're lying right there next to him, you can never assume that someone else isn't. Sorry, but that's just how so many of us get down.

After a few months of alleged good behavior on my part, the attorney finally started to let her guard down just a tiny bit. We started going on little weekend trips together, even sharing the same bed. But even then, I still wouldn't make a move. Which just made her fall harder and harder for me.

She was a beautiful, intelligent, successful woman that guys were constantly trying to seduce. The fact that I was content simply spending time with her got her mind twisted. She found herself in uncharted territory and started to question herself. When I first met her, she was unwavering about her decision. Now her plan was coming apart at the seams. She had always been supremely confident, but now she began to worry that she might lose me if she didn't give all of herself to me.

One night we were sitting in my car outside her house, having one of those magical conversations about our lives, our pasts, our dreams and our fears. After hours of intense conversation, I finally said good-bye. Not even a peck on the cheek. But before I could even unbuckle my seat belt, suddenly she was on top of me, insisting that I take all of her. Forget about having to convince her—I didn't even have a say in the matter. I had MAN-ipulated her so thoroughly that she threw all her plans and principles out the window in a passionate moment. I had MAN-ipulated her right into my bed (or in this case, my backseat).

The only problem was that once I had her, I didn't want to keep her. As men, we'll go to incredible lengths—even feigning celibacy for months—if we think it will aid our pursuit of a woman. Once we catch them, however, all that interest and intensity start to rush out of us like air out of a popped balloon.

Now before I break down why men are much more interested in catching than keeping women, I need to address what some of you might still be thinking right now: *Please, the type of MAN-ipulation or whateva you talkin' about, that's a game that only somebody famous can run. Ain't no way in hell that an Average Joe can get away with that type of mess.*

Even Rev has told me, "I don't think you understand that most people don't live like that. I'm in the business, and I've only heard of two or three other dudes who are running the same kind of games that you do. What you're doing is on a whole other level."

But I believe that no matter where you are, you are going to encounter plenty of men who have the same issue. It could be on a college campus, in a housing project, in a trailer park, hell, even

---

a nursing home (don't sleep, Viagra has got those places poppin'). It really doesn't matter.

So while my situation might not have been exactly the same as your man's, understand that those dudes still have that MAN-ipulator in them. As I said earlier, my lifestyle back then represented a man's natural tendencies taken to their most extreme level. If I had the opportunity to MAN-ipulate four or five different women a day, I wouldn't hesitate to take advantage of that opportunity. Some men might have to wait six months for one opportunity, but they're still going to pounce on it.

I might have been creating smoke with the type of elaborate pyrotechnics you'd see in a Hollywood movie, while a dude from the hood might have to sit there and rub two sticks together like a caveman to create his smoke. But no matter how hard he has to work, he's still going to do what it takes to create distractions.

So rather than worry about whether every man can run the same games that I did, the bigger question is, why do men in general spend so much time trying to MAN-ipulate rather than just be up-front about their intentions?

Wouldn't it be easier for me to just tell a woman that I'm not ready to settle down than to spend so much time, brainpower and money cooking up elaborate ways to stall?

Of course it would. But our insistence on concealing our true feelings is one of the great ironies of the male mind state.

SO BOLD

In almost every aspect of their lives, men have very little trouble articulating how they're feeling. In fact, we take pride in being very bold, very forthright and aggressive with our truth. We like to fancy ourselves generals marching at the front of an army. We want everyone to know where we're at and what we're planning to do. Except for when it comes to our relationships. Then, instead of that general, we tend to act more like thieves in the night.

I used to be a classic example of this kind of Jekyll and Hyde behavior. In my professional life I've never been shy about articulating my truth. If I think a promoter is jerking me, I'm going to get right up in his face and let him know that he'd better correct the situation ASAP. I'm not going to sulk or wait for the "right moment" to discuss the issue. No, the situation is going to get addressed immediately.

If I think a director needs to cast me in his new film, I'm going to get on the phone and make my pitch to him *directly*. Forget about hoping my agent can seal the deal. If I can get his number, that director is going to hear from me about why I would be great in his film!

Or let's say I think I deserve the cover of a magazine. Then I'm going to get on Twitter and make my case as loudly as I possibly can. I'm even going to ask my fans to write to that magazine and tell them that they want to see me on the cover too.

That's right. I've always been *bold* with my truth.

Except for when it came to my relationships with women.

Why did I feel the need to obscure my true intentions with so many women? Why did I always try to hide behind the smoke rather than walk out into the light?

Thankfully, today I'm able to give you an answer. But it's one I'm able to share only because I demanded one of myself.

Even though my lifestyle might have represented every man's

fantasy, I couldn't stand the way I was living back then. I was never truly comfortable playing with women's emotions, especially women who deserved so much better. Women who gave me so much love and honesty but got nothing but distractions and smoke back in return.

On a physical level, I became afraid I was going to catch AIDS and die. I'm not exaggerating when I say that being with multiple women every week, sometimes every day, was *normal* behavior for me.

For many years, I wore that promiscuity as a badge of honor. But in the back of my mind I also knew that it was only a matter of time before it caught up with me. That possibility started looming very large in my mind following a conversation I had with the rapper Kurupt, who told me about visiting Eazy-E of N.W.A. as he lay in a hospital bed dying of AIDS. "Rese, this situation is very real," he warned me. "My man E was here chillin' one week and is about to be gone the next. The Monster doesn't care if you're famous or not. If you're not careful out there, it's going to get you."

His words and actions made a real impression on me. After seeing what happened to Eazy, despite being out on the road with rappers like Snoop Dogg, Kurupt stopped having casual sex. I didn't change my lifestyle right away, but in my mind I always told myself, *Man, if you don't slow this thing down, The Monster is going to catch you.*

Now before you think I was too out of control, I should say that when my ex-wife and I conceived our daughter, it was the first time I'd ever gotten a woman pregnant. Still, that fear of dying from the monster was one of the main reasons I embraced

Rev's MAN-torship so strongly. It's also why I decided to try therapy (something, as I'll discuss later, too many African-American men are unwilling to do) and see if I couldn't come up with some answers for why I had let my lifestyle spiral out of control.

Through talking to Rev, as well as my therapist, the most basic answer I came up with was that I was scared. I was afraid that even though I seemingly had the world at my fingertips, it was only a matter of time before it would all slip out of my grasp.

FAR FROM SEXY

You must understand that when I was doing all that running around, in my own mind I was still a black little ghetto kid from Watts who had been thrust into the music industry and fame without really knowing what was going on.

Yes, I was getting *called* sexy, but I still felt like that ashy little nigga who nobody was checking for. The guy who never heard the word *handsome*, let alone *sexy*, until I got on TV. Believe me, if some girl had said, "Hey, sexy" when I was growing up, I would have turned around like, "Who the hell you talkin' to?" Even when I did start getting attention, I still felt that I was only borrowing it.

So while I might have been sitting on top of the charts, inside my mind I was constantly worrying about falling off. I might have seemed as confident as they come on the outside, but inside I was scared out of my mind.

Why was I scared?

Because I was convinced that the lifestyle I was living was too good to be true. Since there were no reference points in my background for all the money, power, luxury, and sex I was experiencing, I had no reason to believe they would last.

And like many men, instead of being cautious and taking things slow, I threw myself headfirst into the lifestyle. It became an all-or-nothing thing with me. Why not dive right in? I figured, *If it's all going to be gone tomorrow, why not enjoy what I can now?*

Another one-night stand? Not a problem. Another club, another party, another shopping spree, another limo, another flight for my boys and some sexy chicks? Absolutely!

I felt like a male Cinderella. Since I was sure someone was going to come to take away that glass slipper, I might as well get it all in now before the clock strikes midnight!

Please don't get it twisted—I am not looking for *any* sympathy here. I wouldn't trade my situation for anything, and I wake up every day thanking God for showing such favor on my life.

And outside of my daughter, one of my greatest blessings is still to be able to enjoy the high I get from sharing my music with my fans. I've been in some box office smashes, but even being up on the silver screen doesn't compare to standing behind a curtain and listening to the host introduce you while all the women in the audience scream. Just knowing how they want to touch you and hear your voice sing the songs that they've made love to, even had children to, is such a blessing. Knowing that they can't wait to hear you sing those songs that gave them comfort and helped them heal during some of their toughest stretches; man, nothing compares to that.

It's a beautiful, uplifting kind of power. Unfortunately in the beginning I didn't know how to wield it correctly. Because I didn't believe that power would last, I used it to trick and MAN-ipulate women instead of to help bring them joy.

Which is why, for this chapter, it's critical that women understand that even the sexiest, most successful, and seemingly confident men are often extremely insecure about themselves.

Maybe, like myself, they grew up feeling ugly.

Maybe, like myself, they grew up without a father's love and direction.

Maybe, like myself, they had a mother who blamed them for her unhappiness.

Maybe, like myself, they were taken advantage of by someone who should have been protecting them.

Again, I'm not inviting you to a pity party here. I just need to remind you that instead of falling for the distractions, you have to blow away the smoke and try your hardest to see what's really going on with a man.

Hopefully you'll be happy with what you find after you take a deeper look. The good news is that if someone who was as lost as I was can get back on track, then *any* man can.

Some men don't even need changing. There are plenty of guys out there who grew up in good families, surrounded by strong role models, and aren't tripped up by the kinds of insecurities that haunted me.

If you're lucky enough to have one of those guys, chances are the next time he brings you flowers, he really is just trying to apologize for getting short with you the other night. Or if he arranges a romantic dinner, then he really just wants to demonstrate his love for you.

I don't want anyone reading this to automatically catch an attitude with her man the next time he brings her flowers. I don't want you to fly off the handle and say, "I know what you're up to.

This is just you trying to blow smoke...." No, there are guys out there who are stand-up MEN. Not low-down MAN-ipulators.

Unfortunately, while those kinds of guys do exist, they are also in the minority. Which is why I now want to share some concrete steps that you can take when dealing with that MAN-ipulative majority.

SHARE SLOWLY

Whenever you're dealing with a *new* man, one of the first things you must do is exercise extreme discipline in controlling the amount of information you give him about your *old* man.

The truth is that while a man might *appear* sensitive and caring, you can't trust him not to try to exploit the vulnerabilities and fears you confide to him.

I've met many women who opened up to me very early in our relationship. There was one who suddenly blurted out after only a couple of dates, "This is really hard for me to admit, but I caught my fiancé in bed with one of my best friends. And after I confronted them, it came out that they'd been having an affair, he'd gotten her pregnant and she'd gotten an abortion. It was really devastating, and at first I postponed the wedding while I tried to figure out if I could get past it, but I finally decided that I just couldn't go through with it...."

I responded by saying, "What a dog, I can't believe he'd do something like that. A man would have to be crazy to disrespect a woman as incredible as you. You did the right thing, baby."

But in my *mind* I was thinking, "OK, this one is very insecure. She caught the dude with her best friend, but she still didn't walk on him that *moment*. She tried to make it work, even after she found out he got her homegirl pregnant too. If she was willing to put up with that from him, then that means I'm going to have *a lot* of working room . . ."

That's just how my mind was working back then. Today, I am in a much different place. In fact, one of the things that attracted me to my current girlfriend was her honesty about her past relationships. When she opened up to me about how an old boyfriend cheated on her with multiple women and constantly took her love for granted, my mind didn't switch into MAN-ipulation mode. I didn't start to make mental calculations about what I could get away with. Instead, those revelations made me feel even more protective of her. I couldn't stand how an old dude had smashed her heart with his cheating, and I vowed to myself that I'd *never* do something like that to her.

If she had given me that degree of information back in the day, however, you can believe I would have done what her ex did to her and then some. Because once I knew what a woman was willing to tolerate, then I would know what I could get away with. I would know all the buttons to push and all the strings to pull that would allow me to keep the upper hand in the relationship.

That's why I'm begging you ladies to please be extremely cautious and judicious when sharing information about yourself at the outset of a relationship. I know that after you've had a couple of glasses of wine and the vibe is feeling right, it's easy to think, "I just want to tell this man about myself. I want to unburden myself of all this pain and drama I've been carrying around with me. . . ."

Sharing your fears can be very therapeutic in the right setting, but a bar or a bedroom isn't one of them. So when you start feeling the need to share, please catch yourself and reel your emotions back in.

Whatever you do, don't feel that you run the risk of losing a man if you don't open up to him physically and emotionally. If there's a real connection, it's not going to matter when you share your story. That guy is going to be around for a long time. But if that vibe you're feeling is really just part of a smoke screen, then you're just going to be giving a MAN-ipulator the ammunition he needs to keep you off balance and second-guessing yourself.

No matter how strong the connection initially feels, give yourself six months before you reveal any of your vulnerabilities to a man. I'm not saying don't go out with him, don't have sex with him or don't love him. Do all of that if it feels natural.

Do not, however, give him access to those emotional parts of yourself until you really know what season he's in. Is he a man who's going to rip your heart into a thousand pieces? Or is he the man that's going to cherish and protect your deepest feelings?

Give yourself time to be able to make an educated, informed decision. But until then, guard your fears. Because if they fall into the hands of a MAN-ipulator, it will take you a lot longer than six months to get your selfhood back again.

BEWARE OF GODLY MAN-IPULATORS

I also want to caution you about some of the most dangerous, insidious MAN-ipulators out there, the so-called men of God. (Sorry, Rev. I know you won't like this, but it's how I feel.) I can't tell you how many of these men use their status and "spirituality" to really mess a woman up. We hear a lot of talk like "Girl, you need to watch out for those ballplayers" or "Don't get caught up with those musicians," but I believe that we need to add a lot of men of God to that list.

I might have been a master MAN-ipulator back in my day, but I didn't have a thing on some of these preachers. They have such a way with words that they could read a nursery rhyme to you and make it sound like the greatest novel ever. You could become enraptured just listening to them talk about going grocery shopping.

As a preacher, that man is able to create an immediate comfort zone where you feel like it's fine to let your hair down. Wait six months before opening up? A preacher is going to have you unburdening your insecurities on him in six minutes. Why wouldn't you? Helping people sort through their issues is his job, his calling. Plus, your momma loves him and keeps pushing you closer to him. "Go talk to him, honey," she'll say with the best intentions. "He can help." Yes, he can help. He's going to help himself to some of you. While he's a man of God, he's still a man first.

To be clear, I'm not only talking about actual preachers and pastors here. I'm also talking about men who might not have an actual position in the Church but still try to use God to their advantage. Men that pretend they are "praying for" women but are really "preying on" them. A good friend of mine decided that she was done with her lifestyle of messing with athletes and entertainers out in the clubs. She started going to church consistently and making God a priority in her life.

After a while she started catching feelings for another member of her congregation, a man who seemed to be undergoing a similar transformation. He happened to be an athlete, but he told her that he was different from the others she'd met. He said he was celibate and that he was more focused on God's plans for him than a sexual relationship. He also confided his supposed weaknesses to my friend, telling her that he was very insecure about his looks and that he felt uneasy around women (even though by all accounts he was a very good-looking guy).

My friend felt a strong connection with this man and quickly fell in love. She opened up about all of her issues and insecurities, including her own decision to be celibate. At first he seemed respectful of what she had shared.

But in time he wore her down and they began having sex. Not surprisingly, soon after that things began to change. The man who had claimed to be insecure around women began to reveal himself as quite a flirt. The man who had claimed that he was only focused on God's plan started going to church less and less. The man who had claimed he wasn't worried about sex seemed to want lots of that, but not much else. My friend told me, "Rese, it got to the point that I really didn't recognize him anymore. Once he got what he wanted, it was like he changed right before my eyes."

What I need women to understand is that men from all walks of life and from all different backgrounds can be MAN-ipulators. Again, this is not pastor-specific. I'm sorry if that's sounding repetitive, but I really need to drive this point home. An R&B singer might croon a love song, or a preacher might praise God, or a churchgoer might seem like the most sensitive soul on earth, but you need to understand that inside their minds they are making calculations. They are looking for weaknesses. They are seeking vulnerabilities they can exploit.

If they end up prying that information out of you, then there's not much you can do. Please don't just give it away to them. The betrayal of a godly MAN-ipulator cuts very deeply and takes a long time to recover from.

Rev Run

Let me start by addressing what Tyrese just wrote about men of God. I know he has the best intentions in sharing that information, but I think he is presenting them to be a much greater danger than they actually represent.

Listen, are there a few bad (OK, rotten) apples out there abusing the word of God? No doubt. It's very difficult for me to hear about it, not only as a man of God myself but especially as someone who has gained so much through the MAN-torship of my own pastor.

So while Tyrese thinks you have to be more careful around religious men, I disagree. Instead, I believe that men who pursue spiritual lives are actually *less* likely to be MAN-ipulative than those who don't. I've found that to be the case with men I've met through the church, but I have no doubt that it's true of men who go to mosque or synagogue or practice Yoga too. As a rule, men receiving guidance and MAN-torship are at the very *least* going to be pointed in the right direction, even if it takes a while for them to set off down that path.

I'll put it like this: Who would you rather take a chance with—a guy who hits the club three nights a week, or a guy who's in church three nights a week?

A guy who's holding a cold Heineken the first time you meet him? Or a guy holding a worn Bible?

I thought so.

To put it in perspective, let me share a story that a good friend just told me. It was time for his daughter's first vaccinations and he was nervous about getting them, since he'd read articles about how they might lead to autism.

When it was time to get the shots, he came to the appointment armed with several of the articles. He asked the doctor whether she thought his daughter should still get the shots, given all the concerns that people had. The doctor heard him out and then very evenly told him, "I can't tell you that there aren't concerns out there. All I can tell you is that these are the same vaccines I gave to my own children."

My friend had been expecting to get into a big debate over vaccines, but there wasn't much more to say after that. When someone tells you "This is what I did for my own kids," that's the ultimate endorsement they can give.

When it comes to dating men of God, I'm giving a similar endorsement. I've always encouraged my daughters (and my sons) to try to connect with people who put God first. Sometimes they've followed my advice and sometimes they haven't. And that's fine; as a parent, you can't do much more than point your child in what you perceive to be the best direction and hope they walk a straight line.

In giving that endorsement, I'm not suggesting that you should blindly accept everything a guy with a Bible tells you. No, a man holding a Bible is still a man, and you should exercise caution until you can fully ascertain where his head and heart truly rest. And in coming chapters I'm going to share some strategies on how you can make that judgment.

Just don't be one of those women who hears about how such and such preacher abused his power and then decides, "These Church dudes are full of it. I'm not messing with them anymore."

When you take *on* that attitude, you are taking yourself *out* of what I believe is the best possible position for finding a good man. I know from firsthand experience that the Scripture is a road map toward experiencing lasting happiness through commitment and family. The Bible might not be the only map that can lead you there, but I'm pretty confident that it's the one that takes you there with the least amount of detours or roadblocks.

MEN WANT TO BE MARRIED (EVEN IF MOST DON'T KNOW IT)

I'm proud of Tyrese for having the guts to reveal that part of his life with you. Some people might not understand what's courageous about his admitting that he used to trick women into staying with him when they weren't happy or having sex when they wanted to be celibate, but I know it took strength. Because as both a friend and a MAN-tor, I've witnessed just how hard Tyrese has worked to move out of that space. Going back to it, even if only on the written page, can be challenging.

But I gotta say that as far as Tyrese has come, listening to him discuss his MAN-ipulative ways with women reminds me of a quote I once heard: "A boy brags about having sex with a thousand women, but a man is happy to have one woman and a thousand positions to sex with."

I've shared that quote with Tyrese many times, not to diss him by calling him a boy but rather to keep reminding him that if he can grow up a bit and embrace what's on the other side of maturity, so many beautiful things are going to open up for him.

I try to constantly be in his ear, whispering, "I love my marriage." Telling him, "Nothing could *ever* be better than spending the rest of my life with my wife." Letting him know, loudly if need be, "I can't think of *anything* that brings me more happiness than my family."

I want you to know that those words were written with complete humility and gratitude. Just as Tyrese wasn't trying to brag by talking about all the women he slept with, I'm not trying to brag by saying I'm happy in my marriage. I'm not trying to rub my situation in your face if you're feeling unhappy or unfulfilled in your relationship. Just the opposite, in fact.

No, the reason I want to stand up on my tippy toes and shout

24

"I love married life" is that chances are your man hasn't heard other men say that *loudly enough.*

You see, even though most men seem very confident about what they think will make them happy in life, they often don't have a clue what real happiness is.

As a society, we've tricked men into believing that promiscuity is an amusement park you want to visit as often as possible, while marriage is a jail you want to stay out of by any means necessary.

That's why I want men to know that I view marriage as far from being a jail; it's an amusement park, full of laughter and excitement. Are there a couple of moments when your stomach might drop like you're on a roller coaster? Sure. But those moments pass.

It's critical that you, as a woman, hear me say that, because you must have confidence that men do love their marriages. That deep down they do understand that nothing is going to bring them more pleasure than having a wife and a family.

The problem is that while they are aware of this deep down in their hearts, up on the surface they've become convinced that pure pleasure lies somewhere other than in commitment.

That's dangerous, because men are always going to pursue whatever they perceive to be the most pleasurable option. It's just in our nature.

Which is why as a woman, you must never try to stand between your man and his pursuit of pleasure.

That might go against your best instincts, but please trust me: trying to deny a man pleasure is not a fight you want to wage.

Instead of denying him pleasure, your efforts should be focused on reminding him that despite what he thinks, the most pleasurable thing he can do with his life is spend it with *you*! That the most fun he can possibly have is raising a family with *you*. As Ben Franklin put it over two hundred years ago, "Marriage is the most natural state of man, the state in which you will find solid happiness."

You're not asking your man to learn anything he doesn't already know. You're just asking him to look past all the distractions and remember it.

I realize that some of you might be saying, "Whatever, Rev. I'm happy you feel that way, but I'm never going to convince my man that family life is like Disney World."

But before you reject my thesis, understand this: you don't necessarily even have to convince your man that married life is going to be like visiting Disney World. Initially, you just have to help him see that the rolling stone lifestyle that he's clinging to is actually the one that feels like jail.

Doing so might seem like a daunting task, but it's not nearly as hard as you'd imagine. The truth is, most men don't enjoy the playboy lifestyle as much as they'd have you believe. Sure, they like to talk about needing their "freedom" (especially around their male friends), but here's a little secret: they don't truly "love" that freedom.

If you could give all those playas a truth serum, these are the sentiments that would probably come pouring out of them:

"I'm not happy waking up to a strange woman in my bed every morning."

"I'm lonely."

"I need a steady, supportive presence in my life."

"I spend hours dreaming about what my life with my wife and kids is going to be like. I imagine houses we're going to live in, names we'll give our kids, teaching my son how to play basketball and driving my daughter to practice ballet."

"Most of the time I can ignore my loneliness, but every holiday it kills me not to have a family to celebrate with."

Believe me, I've experienced both kinds of "pleasure," and there is zero doubt in my mind that I'd much rather be a rock gathering moss inside *Run's House* than a stone rolling around out there in the single world.

Even as a young man, I knew that the rock-star lifestyle left me feeling hollow and depressed. But rather than look for an alternative, I figured my problem was that I simply hadn't indulged *enough.* If sleeping with two strange women every week wasn't making me happy, then I figured I needed to sleep with three. If having a side piece in Philly wasn't enough, I figured I needed one in Dallas and Chicago too.

So many men fall victim to that sort of twisted logic. Instead of slowing down when they start to feel out of control, they speed up and actually drive even deeper into the mess they've created. They've been exposed to so many voices telling them that they need more sexual freedom and more debauchery that they can't hear their own truth anymore.

I had to hit rock bottom before I finally set out to find a new source of happiness. I've told this story before, but it bears repeating because it demonstrates the lengths men will go to in order to chase that pleasure.

My moment came at the height of our success, when we were out on tour and I was pushing the rock-star lifestyle to the limit. One day I was sitting in a hot tub in the penthouse suite of a five-star hotel. In addition to soaking in the tub, I was also eating a plate of pancakes *and* smoking a joint *and* getting my hair trimmed by my barber. The phone was sitting on the edge of the hot tub because I was expecting some call girls to ring me once they got to the front desk, and I definitely didn't want to miss that call.

Being zoned out from the weed, I was startled when the phone eventually rang. In my rush to answer it, I accidently knocked the ash from my joint into my pancakes. I still had plans for those pancakes, though, so I tried to blow away the ash, which had gotten stuck in the syrup. But as I leaned over, some hair from my barber's clippers fell into the syrup and got stuck in the ash too. I started trying to pick the hair and ash out of the pancakes, but since I was also trying to keep the joint dry it was all too much, and I just ended up knocking the pancakes into the water.

Sitting there in the hot tub, watching pieces of soggy pancake mixed with bits of hair and ash float past me, I felt a wave of revulsion pass through my entire being. In that mess I'd created, I finally saw just how nasty I'd allowed my whole life to become.

I knew right then and there that I couldn't live that way anymore. That if I continued down that path, I'd end up killing myself. Maybe passively through drugs or a sexually transmitted disease, or even directly, by my own hand. That's how empty I felt in that moment.

Thankfully that wave of emptiness was ultimately what pushed me *out* of that self-destructive mind state and *toward* God's embrace. I wasn't able to get there by myself—it took the guidance and MAN-torship of a very spiritual man to lead me all the way out of my darkness.

Men are not happiest in that proverbial hot tub. They might be happy, but they're not *happiest*.

Notice I didn't say "some men" or "most men." No, I'm going to make a sweeping statement and say that at the end of the day, even the rollingest stone wants to settle down and gather some moss.

For example, let me share a conversation I once had with a famous rapper I'm friends with. I've known a lot of stars in my day, but none of them have embraced that lifestyle like this guy has. If there was ever someone who'd seem like he would be happy to keep on rollin' for the rest of his days, it would be him.

Yet one day I was teasing him about all the one-night stands he had on the road, telling him he had to stop breaking so many women's hearts. He just rolled his eyes and then, under his breath, said, "What about me? I'm hurting *myself.*"

Hearing him say that really cemented my belief that no men are *truly* happy leading a MAN-ipulative lifestyle.

If they had a Mount Rushmore for MAN-ipulators, there would be a rapper and an R&B singer up there. So if even rappers, rockers and singers all tired of one-night stands and groupies, then it's safe to say that your man wants something healthier and more satisfying too, no matter how he acts or what he might say.

This is why, despite all the smoke and distractions he might try to create, you should never, ever lose sight of this truth: you and your man share the same dream.

We're going to cover a lot of difficult terrain in the upcoming pages—lust, miscommunication, infidelity and marital discord. There will probably be moments when you think to yourself, *The gap between what my man is thinking and where I need him to be is just too wide. I don't think this is ever going to work. . . .*

But have faith that even though it won't be easy, you and your man ultimately want to end up at the same place. Never let that truth out of your grasp.

CHAPTER 2

MANOLOGY AFTER DARK

Tyrese

I'm someone who's passionate about communication and conversation, so it's probably no surprise that I've really taken to Twitter. I love connecting and getting into whatever I'm doing, thinking and feeling during my day.

I enjoy getting into all sorts of topics, but one of my favorites is a little something I call #TwitterAfterDark.

If you follow me, then you already know I'm a night owl. My brain doesn't really get firing on all cylinders until 2:00 or 3:00 a.m., when most of my deepest thoughts seem to occur.

Especially about sex.

It's really no surprise that I'm up thinking about sex so much. I don't smoke. I don't drink. I don't do drugs. Sex is one of my only outlets from the stresses and responsibilities of life.

So if I'm not actually doing it, then I have to at least be talking about it.

Whenever I feel the need to share something on that topic, I'll start by sending out a little warning Tweet.

"Welcome to #TwitterAfterDark. Kids go to sleep. I'm on my grown man tonight." And then I'll go in.

We have the type of conversations that grown folks should be having about sex but often don't.

And on those rare occasions when they do, it's usually with their own genders.

Think about it. The physical act of sex takes place between a man and a woman, but *conversations* about that act generally take place between members of the same sex.

You might sleep with men, but don't most of your conversations about sex take place between you and your girls? Or if you do talk about sex with men, isn't it usually either guys that you've put in the friend zone (more on them later) or your gay guy friends? As for the guys you've actually been intimate with, it's probably been hard to have in-depth sexual discussions with them. So instead you turn to the people you're more comfortable with.

That's certainly how it happens with most guys. The vast majority of our conversations about the details, concerns, mysteries and pleasures of having sex with *women* take place with other *men*. Which, unfortunately, are not usually conversations that yield a lot of helpful information.

That's because when dudes talk to each other about sex, they're usually more concerned with trying to inflate their own egos than actually telling the truth. At least when women talk about sex, they tend to be honest about what they experienced or what their issues are. With guys, all you hear are the same stories over and over again: "Yo, you should have seen how I hit that last night" or "Man, I almost smashed this girl's life away last night. Now she won't stop textin' me."

What you won't normally hear, however, is a guy telling his friends, "Wow, I got so excited just touching her that I couldn't hold out, I barely made it two minutes" or "I really liked her, but I was so nervous that I couldn't get anything going."

As you ladies can attest, the last two scenarios happen just as frequently, if not more so, than the first two. Yet you will hardly ever hear guys talk about them. Nope, all that information gets swept under the rug in a man's mind, so that even on those rare occasions when a man and woman do have a frank and honest discussion about their sex life, he doesn't even have access to his own truth. He's so used to bluffing and bragging that he can't even talk openly about what he's feeling when he has a chance to with the very person he's sleeping with.

We need a real dialogue about sex between men and women—conversation in which guys don't just brag with each other, or women giggle over a bottle of wine with their homegirls, but one in which men and women really open up and share with each other about what's going on in the bedroom.

Communicating about sex can be hard, but it's so necessary. This is because great sexual chemistry doesn't always just happen. Sometimes, as in an actual chemistry lab, time and effort must be spent conducting experiments until the right formula is discovered. If you have two scientists in the lab experimenting without communicating with each other, it's going to be extremely difficult for them to develop that formula.

✦ Don't get me wrong; natural, spontaneous and effortless sexual chemistry can be amazing. But when you rely exclusively on chemistry "just happening," you are severely limiting the potential pool of people you can build relationships with. Even worse, relying on natural sexual chemistry might mean you always wind up with the same sort of guy even though all other aspects of the relationship are terrible.

✦ If you find yourself with someone and everything *but* the sex is right, don't give up on that relationship too quickly. You can create incredible sexual chemistry where none existed before. I know this because I've been there. Yes, I've been in several relationships, as I'll share, where the sex was just not right at first. In fact, initially I even had an awkward chemistry with my current girlfriend. But instead of letting that get between us, we worked at it. Today, ours is the greatest relationship I've ever been in. Emotionally, spiritually, *and* sexually.

Just as I found a way to overcome those slow starts sexually, you can too. You just have to be extremely open and frank in discussing sex with your man.

IS SEX MORE EMOTIONAL OR PHYSICAL FOR A MAN?

Before I get into the technical issues, I need to address the most frequent sex-related question I get by my female followers on Twitter. For them, sex is as much emotional as physical, and they want to know if men feel the same way.

The answer is no, though I should amend that to "At least not at first."

If you had asked me that question even just a few years ago, I would have said no unequivocally. I believed that for a man sex is *always* going to be primarily physical.

Thankfully, now that I've matured, what I've learned is that men *are* capable of having both a physical and emotional connection with sex. And that when emotions are added to the equation, they take a relationship to heights I didn't even know existed before.

But as a woman, you must understand that many men have not reached that maturity level yet. Personally, I had to evolve a great deal in order to experience the emotional dimension of sex. Until that evolution takes place, man's perception will be that sex is a purely physical act.

For y'all, it is so different. As a female friend once put it very succinctly, "Sex is something that begins, and sometimes ends, between my ears. It never starts between my legs."

For most men, however, sex is a physical act that always starts between their legs. It's a physical itch that they have to scratch.

That means if a man is driving in his car and starts feeling horny, he's going to look to act on that arousal. He might call up his girlfriend and see if he can arrange a quickie. Or maybe, if he's nasty, he'll pull over on a side street and take care of himself. If he really lacks self-control, he might even start cruising around looking for someone he can pay to take care of his situation.

More often than not, a man is going to be in such a rush to address the physical urge of sex that it will never have a chance to travel up to his mind. For most men, sex stays stuck between their legs. I know, because I was stuck in that stage for a very long time.

The truth is, I wasn't really able to experience sex on both a mental and physical level until I engaged in an open and honest sexual dialogue with my current girlfriend. It's in the spirit of that transition that I now want to invite you to *Manology* after Dark.

ONE-MINUTE MEN

One topic that always generates a lot of conversation is a man's sexual stamina. Or in many cases, a lack thereof.

You know who I'm talking about: The one-minute men!

We all had a lot of fun when Missy Elliott and Ludacris sang about them back in the day, but it's no laughing matter for a lot of folks. Premature ejaculation has taken the air out of a lot of relationships before they've ever really had a chance to grow.

I won't front, I have had moments when I've tapped out a littler earlier than planned. Not in the first round, but certainly not as late as I had been looking forward to either. And it should be noted that those moments took place almost exclusively when I was *really* into a woman.

Today, I'm deeply in love with a beautiful and amazing woman. We've had sex hundreds, if not thousands, of times, but the thought of being with her still makes me incredibly excited, to the point where sometimes I wonder if I'll even make it through the first round.

I haven't quite gotten to this point myself, but I have a friend who, if he senses that he's on the verge of a great sex bout, he'll sometimes borrow a page out of *There's Something About Mary* and "clean out his pipes" first. That's right, before he and his girl get in bed, he'll take a shower and discreetly get that first nut out of the way so he can be sure that the second one is going to last properly. (Sorry if that was too much information for some of you, but I told you I was going to keep it real with you in this book!)

As a mature man in a relationship, that wasn't a big deal to admit. He loves his lady and sometimes wants to take an extra step to ensure that the night is going to be a long one.

Suppose, however, that you end up with a man who isn't quite as secure in his situation. Perhaps you two meet at a party. You share several dances, have incredible conversation and can both feel the chemistry building.

You invite him back to your place, one thing leads to another, and soon you two are undressing each other and jumping right into bed. You just *know* this is going to be an incredible night. He puts on a condom, starts putting in his work and then . . . Boom!

Game over.

Before it ever really began.

He didn't want to go out like that, but the sexual chemistry was too strong for him. He tried to slow down, because that orgasm was coming on too fast, but the truth is there wasn't much he could do.

Unfortunately, that man isn't going to feel comfortable sharing what I just told you. There is very little chance he's going to roll off you, look you in the eye and say, "Wow. Sorry I couldn't hold out. You just felt soooooo incredible that I couldn't help myself."

More likely, he might try to play it off like everything is cool, but then find an excuse to leave right way. He'll promise to call so you guys can see each other again, but he'll probably be too embarrassed to ever do it.

If he's really insecure about what just happened, he might actually try to flip it and act like you did something wrong. He might insinuate that you don't know what you're doing in bed. Or maybe he'll try to act like he finished so fast because he wasn't into you and just wanted to get it over with, when in reality just the opposite was true.

Either way, he's going to start disengaging from you almost immediately even though he was really feeling you and probably thinks you're amazing.

I realize that sort of behavior seems counterintuitive. It sounds childish to push a woman away because of a little embarrassment, but it all comes back to what I said at the beginning of the chapter—namely, that guys often have a very distorted sense of how sex is supposed to go down, not because of anything women have told them but from all the garbage they've been fed from other *guys*.

If a man has spent his entire life hearing other men talk about how they "hit it like a champ all night long," he's going to feel like a failure for just giving it a lil' tap and then bowing out. Even if the woman doesn't say a thing about what just happened, in his mind he's still going to hear those dudes making fun of him. "You did what? You busted how fast? Aww, man, it's over for you." Hell, I was laughing just writing the words *lil' tap*. Men *love* to clown other men who come up short.

Women make a critical mistake when they chalk up this sort of performance to "selfishness" on a man's part. If a guy taps out too quickly, a woman might think, *He just wanted to get off and didn't care about my needs.*

Here's what you have to remember: while there are certainly selfish lovers out there, a lack of staying power is not necessarily a sign of being one.

Trust me, no man wants to go out like that. I've tried to stay away from making sweeping generalizations in this book, but this is one truth that applies to *all* men. *Every* man wants to create a sexual experience that leads to an orgasm for a woman. *Every man wants to be known as a guy who is able to sexually deliver and hold it down in bed.*

So if you find yourself with a man who taps out early, the best thing you can do as a woman is address what happened before he succumbs to his insecurities. Even though it might feel cruel or uncomfortable, say something about what just happened. Or more accurately, what didn't happen!

Not in a hurtful or accusatory way, but in a playful manner. Try something like, "Wow, I didn't know I was that sexy." Or laugh and say, "Don't worry, I was almost there too. That was soo intense." A little white lie or even just a laugh can go a long way toward defusing the tension and embarrassment that man is probably feeling. Then tell him that you want to do it again with him, but this time *you* promise not to move around too much. Or maybe you can do what a female friend of mine told me she did with her minute man: suggest that next time he wear two condoms so that the sensation won't feel quite so overwhelming to him.

However you choose to express it, you need to let your one-minute man know that there could be a next time. If you can make him feel comfortable before he gets defensive, you can salvage not only the evening but maybe even the entire relationship as well. Otherwise he's going to feel like a failure, and failures don't normally like to return to the scene of their flops.

Why am I suggesting you do so much work for a guy you just met? For a guy who, despite his best intentions, just put you both in an awkward situation?

— Because tapping out early is actually a sign that a man is really into you, not only physically but emotionally too. A man doesn't do that when he's just looking for a one-night fling. No: it's only when a woman's entire aura is so alluring to a man that he can't hold on any longer, when the energy is so strong that he loses all self-control.

I know Missy sang, "I don't want no minute man," but what I'm saying is, "Maybe you do."

TOO MUCH STAMINA

As frustrating or awkward as those experiences with one-minute men may be, you need to be more concerned about those guys who seem to go on forever.

Back when I was moving around a lot, if I was having sex with a woman and it was going on for more than forty-five minutes, to me it meant that there was some sort of disconnect taking place.

We might have felt a mutual attraction and were initially excited to be lying on top of each other, but if I didn't feel like I was on the verge of a climax once we reached the forty-five-minute mark, then something wasn't right.

It could have been a strictly physical issue. Maybe I was too big and the shape of her vagina simply didn't match up well. I don't mean to get too technical on you, but that can be an issue. If you find yourself in that situation, then the two of you need to have a conversation about positions and angles. Yes, that conversation might be uncomfortable at first, but can it be any worse than having unfulfilling sex with someone?

And while we're talking about physical issues, I can't dance around this one—there are some of you out there, and I've heard you ladies say this about each other, who have experienced a little too much activity. To the point where when you wonder, "How is this guy lasting that long?" Well, the answer is, "He ain't feeling nothing." He's basically pumping air. No disrespect, and not to make anyone feel insecure about their bodies, but a man should feel something. This part is supposed to make you laugh, but I'm also being serious; I have spoken with dudes who say they were having sex with a lady, but didn't feel nothing. One of my boys even told me, "Man, it felt like I was in an open window!"

Maybe it's not a physical thing. Sometimes, and I used to experience this a lot, the guy is just bored. Maybe he thought there was going to be magic when he got down to business, but after a few minutes it actually started to feel like work.

— This is why chemistry and communication are so important. When I used to experience that sense of being stuck at "work" with a woman, do you think I ever said anything? Would I slow down, take a breath and say, "Baby, something doesn't quite feel right for me here. How does it feel to you? Can we talk about this?"

Of course not. I did exactly what a lot of you ladies do in similar situations.

I faked it.

You already know the drill. When you've got some dude on top of you stroking and stroking, but he ain't doing nothin' for ya, you just want it to stop, right? So you'll start shaking your legs and hooting and hollering, whatever it takes to help him do his thing and then get up off of you!

Well, men get down like that too.

If I was forty-five minutes in and the end didn't seem

anywhere in sight, I'd start picking up the pace and grunting like I was really getting into it.

I hadn't matured enough yet to learn how to be bold in my truths with women. I was more comfortable working hard at telling a lie than being honest. Are you noticing a trend here? Thankfully, when I finally did open up with a woman about my sexual frustrations, it helped lay the foundation for the greatest relationship I've ever been in.

HAVING THE HARD CONVERSATIONS

If you're looking to get a man interested in you, great sex is the fastest way to grab hold of his attention. I know Rev isn't going to like me saying that, but it's an indisputable truth. When a man jumps into bed with a woman and the fireworks just start popping off, he's going to become very focused on finding ways to spend more time with her. Even if I wasn't looking to get into a relationship, whenever I started having great sex with a woman I'd find myself thinking, *Well, this sex is so good we're going to have to find a way to get to know each other better!*

Great sex is going to speed up a man's desire to be around you. A man who's having great sex with you is going to call back. He's going to leave you little messages on Facebook. He's going to wine and dine you in order to ensure that you wind up in his bed at the end of the night. He'll even put up with a lot of drama and arguments he normally wouldn't stick around for because he's not prepared to let go of the sex quite yet.

A lot of you ladies are the same way. You'll tolerate all kinds of garbage from a man just because he does something to you in the bedroom that other men can't. Sadly, it's what often keeps your feelings alive for a guy you should probably just forget about.

I've had female friends tell me that even after a guy has played her out, disrespected her and made her feel like crap, she still has a hard time letting go of amazing sex. Even after finally dumping the bum, she'll think, *The physical chemistry we had was so amazing that everybody else just seems like a downgrade.* She can't be with him because he was so disrespectful, but she's still with him anyway. Even if he's not physically in her life, the ghost of his sex still haunts her bedroom. And if a new man doesn't instantly measure up, that ghost is going to run him out of the bedroom for sure.

If you find yourself in such a situation, I encourage you to give the new guy a second chance. If he has all the qualities you might be looking for—funny, committed, intelligent, hardworking—but doesn't give good sex, then have faith that you can build that element of your relationship. All it takes is honest dialogue. I know it's possible, because I've been down this road before.

Years ago, I met a beautiful woman, lets call her Lisa, who worked in the television industry. She was beautiful, intelligent, successful, funny, compassionate, sassy, sensual and exotic. Plus her body was absolutely bananas; one of the first times I stepped out with her, a famous rapper—the type of guy who should have been jaded—pulled me to the side and said, "Yo, Tyrese, I ain't never seen nothin' like that!" I don't think I had either. I usually wouldn't start thinking long-term about a woman before we'd been sleeping together for a long time, but this case was different. I just knew that if I managed to get her to bed, the sex was going to be incredible. That wasn't even an issue. I was already sizing her up as potential wifey material.

When we finally did, however, there weren't any fireworks going off. Just a bunch of fizzles and duds.

To be extremely specific, Lisa's head game was just ho-hum. That might not seem like a big deal, but for me it was a major issue.

To put things in context, I'm actually pretty conservative when it comes to sex. As an R&B singer I'm expected to be doing cartwheels all across the bedroom and serving up peaches and cream, but the truth is that my sexual tastes run closer to meat and potatoes.

I like straight sex and I like head. That's it.

The lingerie, foot fetishes, toys, whips and chains—you can keep all that stuff.

When it became apparent that Lisa was not going to be able to satisfy an admittedly large part of my sexual appetite, I found myself at a crossroads.

My instinct was to head out the front door the first time she went down on me and felt like an amateur. Like she'd been practicing and I'd been a crash test dummy.

But before I ran away, I said to myself, *This woman has too many special qualities. You're in love with her. You can't just jet because the sex wasn't what you expected. You have to figure out how to improve the situation.*

The question was, how? As bold as I am, I was still not comfortable with the idea of calling up a woman I was still just getting to know and saying, "Listen, baby, I don't know how to tell you this, but the sex we're having is simply no good."

No one wants to have a conversation like that. No one wants to call up their girl and tell her that they're feeling unsatisfied sexually.

But I had to man up and have that conversation.

I won't lie, it was tough. At first Lisa claimed she had no idea that I was feeling that way. In her mind, she was putting it down between the sheets. She even told me, "My God, you're so rude. Who says something like that? There is definitely something wrong with you." She hadn't been with too many men before me, but certainly none of them had ever complained. So why was I suddenly telling her that she needed to step things up?

I had to explain that no one had ever been *honest* with her before. You see, most men are so desperate to be with a beautiful woman that they won't ever call her out on bad sex. Do you know how many men have spent months wining and dining a fine woman, putting in all sorts of work to get her in bed? And then, when the big moment finally comes ... blah. Do you know what that man is thinking after he's done having sex with that woman for the first time? "Wow ... and you made me wait for four months for this? Give me my fifteen dinners back. Because that was *horrible*."

Will most men tell her that? Or even hint at it? Of course not. Because they don't want to lose that fine woman, no matter how horrible the sex. Men are addicted to the rush of walking into a club with a dime piece on their arms and having every guy look at them and think, *How the hell did he pull that?* They're afraid that if they tell that woman they aren't satisfied sexually, she might leave them and take all that validation with her. Essentially, they're more interested in having other men sweat them (much more on this later in the chapter about validation) than having great sex with their own girlfriend or wife.

Personally, I'd walked into enough clubs with beautiful

women on my arm that I didn't crave validation anymore. I was much more concerned about a wedge developing between myself and someone I saw so much potential in.

Not surprisingly, after she got over the initial shock and indignation, Lisa finally admitted that she had been feeling awkward about our sex as well. She hadn't wanted to say anything, mainly because she'd been too embarrassed. So while she fronted at first, it was actually a relief to her when I put my concerns out there. It felt so much better to be open with our feelings than to be living a lie in the bedroom.

It took almost a year for us to be completely compatible sexually, but we got there. And one of the reasons we were able to improve is that we tried to keep the conversations light. We'd laugh and make little inside jokes to each other about our initial lack of chemistry, instead of making it feel like someone was accusing the other person of doing something wrong. Instead of putting too much pressure on the issue, we had fun with it.

And as it turns out, things didn't work out between us. But it wasn't because of bad sex. Instead, we ended up dating for well over a year and did end up having several conversations about marriage, but ultimately we both decided that we were too focused on our careers to settle down at what felt like a fairly young age. In fact, I saw Lisa not too long ago and we shared a laugh over how long it took us to get things together.

We can laugh about them today, but I can't lie: brutally honest conversations about sex can be difficult to initiate.

There are some steps, you can take to soften the sting of what you're saying. For starters, I've learned that text messages are great for conversations like this because texting keeps things ordered.

When you are in the same room together trying to talk about a difficult issue, it's inevitable that you'll start talking over each other. With text messages, one person writes what they are feeling, then the other replies. It's impossible to jump all over someone before they get to finish their thought. Additionally, texting gives you the opportunity to consider what you're going to say, even if it's only for a few seconds, before you put it into the world.

I'm at the point where if it's time for a difficult conversation and my girlfriend and I are in the same house, I'll tell her, "Look, baby, there is something difficult I want to tell you, but I don't want to do it here. So I'm going to drive up the street and send you a text about what's on my mind. I think this conversation will go better if we type out what we're thinking."

If texting seems too impersonal to you, you can take the old-school route (like I did with Chilli from TLC in the *Nothing on You* video) and pen an actual letter. You can start off by writing, "These are some of the most uncomfortable words I've had to write, but they're only being written out of love. I'm not looking to tear you down, or pressure you or make you feel bad about yourself. No, I'm only telling you this because I want our physical love to be at the same level as the rest of the love that we share. . . ."

Tell that man why you're worried about how long it takes him to climax. Or explain to him why it's not a problem that he's climaxing too fast, that you want to work with him. Or even that you need him to improve his head game. Whatever the case may be, if you feel like it's jeopardizing your relationship, don't be afraid to address it. Once that awkwardness evolves into awesome sex, you'll be so thankful that you did.

I'll never forget listening to my friend tell me that when he was stuck in a similar situation with his girlfriend, he took things to the *next* level and began editing together little highlight reels from adult movies and sending them to his girl so she could see *exactly* what he was looking for. When he first told me that I was like, "Huh?," but surprisingly he told me his girl wasn't offended. His explanation was that for her, watching the tapes was sorta like a nerd reading a comic book: she was able to gain confidence through watching someone else do something that intimidated her.

I know, I know. He sounds like a pimp. A pig. A jerk. The biggest MAN-ipulator to walk the face of the earth. However you want to label it.

But it worked for them. Probably because, to hear him tell it, those sex education tapes were delivered with love and honest affection (and lots of playful energy). Because when you love someone and don't want to lose them because the chemistry isn't right, you'll get creative real quick and come up with new ideas that re-spark a flame that might be dwindling. Personally, I never quite moved on my friend's advice, but I do give him points for creativity!

And while his approach might not be for everyone, as my friend put it, it can work for men who aren't living up to their potential between the sheets too. After all, if a woman as sleeping with a guy who was simply terrible in bed, shouldn't she encourage him to step up his game?

Wouldn't it make sense for a woman to tell herself, *Even if this doesn't work out between us, I'm doing the next girl he lands a big favor, because the way he is now is* not *the business?*

The key is just facing those issues head-on. If you love someone, or think you could love them, have that hard conversation with them.

━ I don't mean to sound fatalistic, but improving what happens in your bed might literally save your relationship. Case in point: there's a great scene in Tyler Perry's *Why Did I Get Married?* in which Malik Yoba's character breaks down what he calls the 80/20 Rule—men are going to get 80 percent of what they need in a relationship, yet when a new woman comes around offering that other 20 percent, most men will be ready to leave the good thing they have.

What's left unsaid in the scene is exactly what that other 20 percent is actually comprised of. But we know what Malik was talking about: good sex! Even if you give a man 80 percent of what he needs from a relationship—love, compassion, advice, inspiration, companionship, support and laughter—out of the corner of his eye he's still going to be sneaking a peek at that other woman who might be able to give him the other 20 percent.

On paper, what that man is doing doesn't make any sense. Would you ever trade eighty dollars for twenty dollars? Of course not. So why would you trade 80 percent of your ideal woman for one who is only 20 percent ideal?

Because that 20 percent that represents great sex takes up a disproportionate amount of a man's attention. When he kisses his lovely 80 percent good night, all he's going to see when he closes his eyes is visions of that freaky 20 percent. Even if you're consistently providing your man with that 80 percent, please take what's been discussed in this chapter to heart. As we'll discuss in the next chapter, you don't want your man looking elsewhere for that 20 percent.

THE HYPOCRISY OF HEAD

Since we were talking about oral sex, let me add one thing about men and this topic:

We're hypocrites when it comes to head.

Or at least a lot of African-American men are.

I'll admit that despite having put together highlight reels for the women I've been with, I've never been into doing too much for them in that department.

Yep, I said it.

I'll do it for my current girlfriend, but even when I was at my most promiscuous, I still looked down, ahem, on going down. The only way that oral sex could even enter the conversation was if I had an *established* physical, emotional and spiritual connection with someone.

Why? Because I was raised in a community where performing oral sex was considered a sign of weakness. Growing up in my hood, if you hooked up with some chick and went down on her right off the bat, you'd better pray your boys didn't hear about it. If they did, for the rest of your life all you would hear was, "Whoa, you just met her and you already eating the cat? You a nasty freak!" Or "You ate that after another man was in her? Man, you gay!" That's how guys think in the hood. If you were into performing oral sex, then you were soft in the eyes of the community.

As I've grown older, seen more of the world and expanded my circle of friends, I've come to learn that not all men feel this way. In particular, a lot of my white and Asian homies don't have a problem with performing oral sex on a woman. It just doesn't have the same stigma in their communities. And they tell me that often the first thing they do is go down on a woman, simply because they are more confident in their oral skill set. They know they can make a woman climax that way.

If that sounds good to you, then maybe you need to send your man a text and tell him what you're looking for. It'll be a tough sell to someone raised like me, but hey, you'd be surprised with what you can accomplish through honest sexual dialogue.

REV RUN

I'll be honest, when Tyrese first read me his part of this chapter, I felt that even though I am a grown man, I might still not be ready for his *Manology* after Dark.

While I'm not be as comfortable talking about sex as Tyrese clearly is, I do agree that men and women need to be more open about what they're experiencing in the bedroom.

However, I disagree with Tyrese on an even more fundamental point: I simply don't believe that a man and woman are even supposed to wind up in the bedroom until they're married.

That might sound very old-fashioned, but it's what I told my wife before we got married, and it's what I tell my kids as well.

No, there isn't much TwitterAfterDark happening on my time line. Instead, I'm much more likely to wake you up in the morning with a Tweet like this:

"It's hard to find true *love* if your (L)egs (O)pen (V)ery (E)asily."

I send out that Tweet because I believe that when your legs open up very easily, you are telling a man that you're not serious about getting married. You are telling him that you're just looking to have some fun instead of being serious about finding a husband.

That may not be the message you think you're relaying, but it's still the message a man's receiving.

As a woman, you might believe that by having sex right away, you are setting up a man for love. *If I give him what he wants now, he'll get into the habit of coming around,* you'll tell yourself. *Then we'll start to spend more quality time together and he'll learn what a great person I am, and* then *he'll fall in love.*

It comes back to what Tyrese said earlier about how great sex "speeds up" a man's interest. That might be true, but it's not necessarily a good thing. As they say out on the highways, too much speed can kill.

Let's keep it real here. Great sex might speed a man up, but where is he really going when your relationship is built in the bedroom? It's not impossible for a booty call to become a proposal, but it's highly unlikely that will happen. Most of the time booty calls just lead to more booty calls, which in turn lead to more disappointment, disrespect and heartbreak. Don't take it from me, just ask yourself: How many of your booty call dudes have ever evolved into serious, steady men in your life? Probably not many at all.

So stop playing hard to get and *be* hard to get!

I'm sorry, but Tyrese cannot set up a man for marriage through sex. You can set him up for booty calls, dating or even baby mamma drama but not a healthy, committed marriage.

The only formula that leads to a healthy, committed marriage includes a heavy dose of keeping your legs closed as long as possible. That's the formula written by God, and it's one that I know for a fact works.

Of course, it's easy for me to sit here and encourage women to say no. It's a lot harder to actually do it, since it seems like almost every man out there is walking around with a toolbox and a crowbar looking to pry those legs open the first chance he gets.

So how can you find the faith and confidence to stick to saying no in a world where there's so much pressure for women to say yes? I decided to put that question to my daughter Angela, who has remained celibate well into her twenties. She's not sitting at home knitting scarves while she waits for some man to come and marry her. She might be saying no to sex, but she's saying yes extremely loudly to the rest of life. She's out there going to school, launching a business, staying on the scene, and being fashion forward. Plus, she's dated rappers, football players, socialites—the types of guys who are used to legs opening up *very* easily for them. And she's still not having it.

When a woman can tell a man "I'm into you, but I'm not ready for sex," she's holding on to so much power in a relationship.

Angela is certainly a beautiful young lady, but her confidence and discipline only make her even *more* attractive to all the young players she's dated.

And let me say this: aside from her faith, Angela is confident in saying no because she understands a basic math formula that all women must master:

Being "boyless" doesn't have to equal being joyless.

NEVER FEEL LOST WITHOUT A MAN

In other words, if she meets a man and there's a connection, she's not afraid to pursue it and see where it goes. But if he doesn't step up and start acting right almost from the jump, then she *is* going to walk away. Because in her mind, as long as she's dancing, she's good. A solo is just as good as a duet.

If a man is coming correct, Angela will be a very supportive and sensitive girlfriend. But if he starts messing up, she'll harden up in a flash and kick him to the curb.

She's not afraid to do that because she knows that even without a man she won't feel lost. The second she's boyless again, she'll get into a routine that makes her happy. She'll work out. She'll go climbing in the Hollywood Hills. She'll chill at fashion week with her uncle Russell. She'll hang out with her friends. She'll hit the red carpet at a movie premiere in a hot dress.

Without skipping a beat, she can transition from being serious with a man to enjoying single life. She understands that while having a good man in her life is something she wants, she's not going to sit around and mope waiting for him to arrive.

GETTING COMPLETELY BUSY

Just to be clear, I'm not pushing anything on Angela or on you that I haven't practiced myself. As I mentioned, Justine and I did not have sex before we got married. When Tyrese first heard that, he couldn't believe it. "Hold on, you were in your thirties when you met and you two still ain't touch each other?" he asked me incredulously. "How is that even possible?"

I explained it was possible because we both believed very strongly in the word of God, which makes it pretty clear that you shouldn't have sex before you get married. And I'm not just talking about intercourse either. I'm talking everything. There's a reason "you may now kiss the bride" is the very first thing they say when you get married. It's because you're not even supposed to *kiss* before things are official.

That sounded crazy to Tyrese, and it might sound crazy to you too, but it worked wonders for us. In fact, Justine got pregnant after the very first time we had sex, and the child who resulted from that union is our son, Diggy, who today is a superstar rapper in his own right and is on course to do things bigger than his old man ever did.

So you can't tell me that there isn't value in waiting! And it's not just Diggy; in addition to all our other wonderful children, I would even humbly suggest that the entire lifestyle shown on *Run's House,* which inspired Tyrese and so many others, is a direct blessing for that obedience too. It was as if God wanted people to know that if this rapper could live by the word, then y'all can too.

While there were certainly moments before our marriage when we felt frustrated or were tempted to stray, we still stayed the course. And the great news is that course leads to a really sexy place. Because according to Scripture, once you do tie the knot, then you are free to get completely busy in the bedroom!

The Bible says that the marital bed is "undefiled," which basically means that married couples can get busy any way that they can dream up. Remember that quote about "one thousand positions" I mentioned in the last chapter? Well, when you're married, you get to run through all of them. Believe me, I'm excited to come home to my wife every night knowing that we've only run through twenty-two positions in the last few weeks and there's another nine hundred seventy-eight to go. What could be more exciting than that?

The other great thing about being obedient to God is that it will help you avoid what is probably the biggest miscommunication most couples have when it comes to sex—namely when to have it.

Corinthians states, ". . . defraud ye not one the other, except it be with consent for a time, that ye may give yourselves to fasting and prayer; and come together again, that Satan tempt you not for your incontinency."

Basically that means if the other person is in the mood, you have to be ready to go too. You are allowed to jointly decide to take a break from sex for a determined length of time, but otherwise you have to be sexually on call 24/7.

I realize on the surface that might sound like a very harsh approach to sex—after all, who wants to have sex with someone else, even a spouse, when he or she isn't "in the mood." But I've found that it's actually a very sensible way to deal with the realities of marriage.

While I didn't agree with a lot of what Tyrese said in the beginning of this chapter, he was definitely right about one thing: for men sex is more physical, for women it's more emotional.

And since men and women are coming from different places, it's unlikely that they're going to arrive at that marital bed at the same time.

I'm sure you ladies experience this all the time. It's probably very frustrating for you when there doesn't seem to be a connection between your man's emotions and his sexual desires. For instance, your husband might spend the entire day in a sullen mood, getting short with you and the kids and in general being a grouch around the house, yet at the end of the night, he's rubbing your back and looking for some lovin'. In your mind, you're probably thinking, *This man is out of his mind. He's going to be a pain all day and still think he's getting some? No way.*

But in that man's mind, there was never any connection between his energy during the day and whether or not he wanted to make love at night. They were two completely different things to him.

Conversely, you might be in the mood, but your husband could be the one who's not feeling so sexy. The kids are in bed and you've just had a glass of wine, but he's completely preoccupied by a bill he has to pay or a situation that's going on at work. You start rubbing his shoulders, giving him hugs and sending him all sorts of loving signals, but at that moment they're just annoyances to him. So he shoos you away, which of course is incredibly frustrating. *You're always looking for sex, but when I try to give you some, you act like I'm bothering you. That's the last time I try to be sexy with you!* you start to think. And presto, an emotional wall has just gone up in your home. And over the course of a marriage, it can be very easy to build up walls between you and your mate, until you two can barely see each other anymore if you're not careful.

Under God's plan, there's no room for those sorts of misunderstandings. The Bible takes all the guessing, nuances and expectations out of the equation and boils things down to a very simple formula: when your mate wants to make love, it's time to make love.

Certainly there are going to be times when one of you might not be feeling that sexy or might be preoccupied with a situation or might be just plain old tired. *Especially* when kids come into the equation.

But when you let go of those issues and give yourself over to your spouse (and to God), that intimacy you'll experience together will overshadow any little dramas or issues you were previously experiencing. As I like to say, "Whatever sort of love was missing from your life *before* you make love will be in full bloom *after* you do it."

SEXTERNSHIPS

Even though I have complete faith in The Word, I worry at times that my views on sex and marriage might feel very hard, almost militant, to those who don't share the sort of faith that my family and I do. I don't want to turn anyone completely off with my views on sex, so let me end this section by meeting some of you halfway.

If you don't see yourself being able to say no to sex before getting married, then at least make a man wait awhile before you say yes. I liken this approach to putting a man through an internship, or, if you will, a "sexternship," before you officially "hire" him.

Make it clear to him that while he's free to come by the office every day, you're not prepared to put him on staff quite yet. If he shows consistency and dedication, then maybe at the end of his term there will be a discussion about bringing him on full time.

With a sexternship, try to think of yourself as the company and sex as the salary. Put a man through a sexternship to see if he's really committed to the company or if he's just there for the free stuff. If he's truly dedicated, he's going to show up every day and put in that work without giving a thought to getting paid. If he makes that commitment, day after day, month after month, then you'll have a much better idea of whether or not he deserves to be "hired" full time.

In terms of how long that sexternship should last before you offer a man the job, that's something you'll have to decide. I'm uncomfortable putting a number on it, because again, I think you should wait until you're married to give him that job offer.

If it's just impossible for you to wait that long, at least make it several months. Make that sexternship long enough that he can't fake it; if he's only in it for the "money," his frustration will start to show and his interest will start to wane. Then you'll know that he was never really that serious about your company, and you'll save yourself all the stress and heartache of making a "bad hire."

CHAPTER 3

THE MAN-OGAMY MAN-IFESTO

TYRESE

Back in 2011 I appeared on *The Wendy Williams Show* to promote my book *How to Get Out of Your Own Way*. Wendy and I always have a great time together, so I figured it would be a lively conversation. I had no idea, however, just how lively it was going to get.

The fireworks started when Wendy asked me to break down the chapter "Why Do Men (and Some Women) Cheat."

"Most mothers raise their daughters to believe that if you cook, clean, and thoroughly take care of and go all out for your man, that's going to keep him home," I explained. "But unfortunately that's not the truth."

"Yep," concurred Wendy.

"Once my daughter grows up and starts dating, I'll tell her that if she gets cheated on, she shouldn't own the cheat," I continued. "It's like he seen something in that skirt and legs and decided to dip off. Does he see the value of what he has at home? Yes. But if he ends up dipping off . . . that home-cooked spaghetti couldn't have kept him at home."

"Right, it's not 'my fault,'" interjected Wendy, cosigning my line of thought.

Then the tide began to turn.

"So suppose you get cheated on by your next wife. Does she get a pass?" she asked.

"No," I replied honestly, adding, "no way. It's expected of men to cheat."

And with that, I had apparently crossed Wendy's line.

"OK, it is time for you to go!" she said, tossing her head back in mock outrage.

"No, let me clean it up," I shot back. "It's expected for me to cheat, even though not all men cheat . . . it's a part of our upbringing . . ."

"You know what," said Wendy. I knew I had lost her, so I turned to the women in the audience for support.

"Listen, can y'all agree or disagree that it's a horrible double standard?"

Wendy jumped in before I could get an answer. "Girls, you better not fall for a pretty face and say yes," she said to laughter.

"Listen . . . ," I pleaded.

"We've listened enough, Tyrese."

I tried again to explain how society celebrates men for having sex with multiple women, but Wendy wasn't trying to hear it.

"Look, our time is up," she said, wrapping up the interview.

"Oh, we could have been talking about this for soooo much longer," I laughed before giving Wendy a hug.

I didn't get a chance to do it that day, but in this chapter we're going to get to the bottom of this issue once and for all. Judging from how many people watched that interview online, it's a conversation a lot of you want to have too.

Having said that, I am also very clear that this is going to be an uncomfortable chapter for some people to read (as well as it was for me to write) because of just how sensitive this subject is.

That's why I will try to shed light on this topic in the most brutally honest way without making it feel like I'm trying to justify any man or woman *not* being "honorable" in their relationship.

Sometimes I feel like I'm one of the few men willing to have an honest, albeit often painful, conversation about cheating. In fact, I can't think of many topics that guys want to talk about *less* than cheating. Maybe castration or flower shows, but that's about it. Most men are hesitant to talk about cheating because they've learned that everything they say on this subject, even if they're only speaking hypothetically, will potentially be used as evidence against them one day.

Well, I'm not worried about anyone throwing this back in my face one day. No, ma'am. You might not agree with my perspectives on cheating, or my prescriptions for dealing with it, but I'm going to give you my unfiltered truths.

So let me start by reiterating one of the points I was trying to make with Wendy: I am not saying that *all* men cheat. I know it because I don't cheat—anymore.

Before meeting my current girlfriend, however, I was a chronic cheater. No woman could stop me from fooling around, no matter how hard she worked on keeping me satisfied sexually or mentally. At some point I still dipped out.

I remember one woman looking me right in the eyes after

we first met and proclaiming, "You will never cheat on me 'cause there is nothing better out there." That was an extremely sexy moment, and her confidence actually did keep me in line—until I slipped and cheated on her. So when I say I was a man who was pretty out there in the cheating world, please believe it.

The fact that I, of all people, have remained faithful in a relationship is proof that *every* man possesses the ability to be monogamous. Indeed, many men are perfectly happy committing to one woman. I don't need to look any further than my partner in this book to know that.

I've been many places with Rev and encountered all kinds of situations, but I've never seen him even *look* at another woman, let alone engage in inappropriate behavior. Rev won't even get on an elevator with a woman if he can help it. I'll be trying to rush and get in there with her, but he'll put a hand on my arm and say, "Nah, let's just wait for the next one."

When Rev comes to Los Angeles, he usually stays at my place. Both he and my girlfriend are early risers, so they used to bump into each other in the kitchen making their morning tea. After the last time Rev was here, my girlfriend actually came to me and said, "Does Rev have a problem with me? Because every time I come into the kitchen and it's just the two of us in there, he'll make some excuse about why he has to leave. It's like he doesn't want to be in the same room as me."

"Don't worry, baby," I said, laughing. "I know for a fact Rev really likes you. It's just that he's so focused on not in any way disrespecting his wife that he doesn't even want to be in the same kitchen with another woman if no one else is around. That's how far he goes to make sure his wife stays secure."

So ladies, even though the picture I'm about to paint of men and monogamy might seem to be a dark one, understand that every man has the ability to eventually move into the light. Rev went from being a wild rapper who was chugging 40s, smoking weed, and running through groupies left and right to being a family man who doesn't even want to make tea in the same room with a woman who's not his wife. Personally, I've come so far that my girlfriend even has the password to my phone, which, as we'll discuss, is ground zero for most men's infidelity. That's a serious level of trust right there.

My girl doesn't even bother to check it, though. With her last boyfriend, she used to spend hours searching through his phone for evidence of his infidelity, but she hasn't even opened mine up once.

In sharing these secrets about cheating, I'm going to violate the unwritten "man code," but I'm OK with that. I've had these kinda conversations with my older sisters, and when my daughter gets older I'm gonna give her the inside scoop too on the many games we play as men. So that hopefully she'll be able avoid some of the heartbreak that comes from dealing with men who are unfaithful.

I'm hoping to give you a bold and realistic view inside a man's mind, insights that will help you develop a realistic attitude toward cheating, an attitude that's not shaped by old-fashioned fairy tales about how life *should* be but is actually rooted firmly in reality.

And finally, not to sound too dramatic, but this is a particularly important chapter for you to pay attention to because the stakes are very high when it comes to cheating. It's not just your relationship that's going to suffer. Your cheating man might also bring home something that could change your life physically. I'll never forget when I saw an interview with a woman who just knew she was being cheated on, but felt uncomfortable asking her man to put on a condom. Sadly, she ended up catching AIDS from that man. So ladies, whether or not your man sounds like any of the men I'm going to describe in this chapter, if you have *any* suspicions, make him protect *both* of you!

BE REALISTIC

Before I get into the reasons why men cheat and then how they often get caught doing it, I want to touch on some different ways you might consider dealing with a cheating dude if that issue does creep up in your relationship. And the first piece of advice I'd give is: as hard as it may be, try to be realistic and rational, as opposed to emotional and irrational, when dealing with a man who moves around a lot.

Not long after I first started living with the woman who ended up being my ex-wife, I went on a short tour. Even though I was excited about the relationship I was building with her, I wasn't going to let that stop me from having some fun out on the road. It was a wild tour, and there were so many women coming in and out of my tour bus that I finally told my boys, "Let's just let some of them stay on board and ride to the next city with us." Let's just say it was a wild trip.

I still called home and checked in often, trying to act like everything was OK. I felt bad about what I was doing, but I was able to justify it by telling myself, "She is dating an R&B singer who, by his own admission, had a very substantial sexual appetite."

And because we talked so openly, she was also aware of how rappers and singers generally get down while they're on the road. She knew, as a rule, most of us indulge.

While I couldn't ever say that my ex was OK with my behavior, let's just say that she wasn't really aggressive about getting me to stop it either.

I'll never forget, one time after I was caught red-handed, she told me, "You're just a boy trying to figure out what it is to be a man, but you'll grow out of it one day."

She was trying to introduce me to the concept of being real with what I was doing and who I was doing it with, but like most men, I was never comfortable with the concept of telling a woman the truth. Like most cheaters, I considered how I was moving as a secret, not something they're willing to discuss. That's why they call it "cheating."

I know some of you read my ex's reaction and probably thought, *Oh, hell naw! Who stays with a man if she knows for a fact that he's cheating. That's exactly why she's an ex!* But before you start judging her, understand this: my cheating was not the sole reason we broke up. I'm not going to sit here and tell you that it didn't weaken our relationship, but it's not what broke it either. My ex was right; I did eventually grow out of that cheating stage. Unfortunately just not before we called it quits.

Ours was a very complex relationship that probably should not have gone as far as it did. I don't think either of us would claim, however, that we split because of how she reacted to me running around.

If anything, I started cheating *less* after she gave me that pass. I'm not going to lie and claim I stopped moving around completely after that incident, because as I already confessed, I didn't.

The truth is that I did start to second-guess my behavior after that day. Whereas previously I had been out there moving without a thought, after that incident I found myself walking away from situations that previously I would have dove into headfirst.

A large part of my reaction was due to the fact that by not going in on me after I got caught, she had taken much of the *fun* out of running around. You might assume that all the fun and excitement in cheating lies in the sex itself, but that's actually not the case for a lot of guys.

For many men, the sneaking around is just as exciting. The idea of tiptoeing around and coordinating all the wild activities becomes a game unto itself. And if there's one thing that unites almost all men, it's our love of games. We love the competition, the excitement, the drama, and the intrigue.

Once you take all the hiding and sneaking out of the equation, the game almost becomes boring. Realizing that I wasn't going to get in trouble and that I didn't have to sneak around as much, I lost a lot of my motivation to cheat. I almost felt like, *Well, this isn't even fun no more. You basically gave me permission to get some extra goods on the side and now I don't even want them.*

NOT EVERY CHEAT IS THE SAME

When my ex gave me a pass, I don't believe she was playing Jedi mind tricks on me and somehow knew that if she let me cheat, I'd actually cheat less. Instead, I think the reason she was able to respond the way she did was that she was raised in a different culture. Again, so much of this comes back to upbringing. My ex was born and raised in Europe, where they generally treat social situations much more pragmatically than we do in the U.S.

Take, for example, the issue of underage drinking or drugs. In the U.S. we generally believe that teenagers shouldn't do those things, so we make lots of laws to keep them from doing so. We also believe that any teenager who breaks those laws should be punished. In theory, I agree. Like I said, I don't drink or do drugs myself, and I would hate to think of my little girl chugging beer when she's a teenager and then getting in a car with someone who is drunk or high.

Theory and reality, however, are often different. In reality, some teenagers are going to want to drink, and all the laws in the world aren't going to stop them. The problem is that by holding the threat of punishment over their heads, we force our teenagers to go underground with their wildness. They feel like they can't talk about it with us, so in the absence of any communication, they tend to drink irresponsibly. The worst part is when they get offered a ride home from a party by a drunken friend and they're too afraid to call up Mom and Dad and say, "Listen, I was just at a party. I know you're going to be mad at me and I'm sorry I went, but I need a ride home because everyone here is drunk." Instead, they get in the car with that drunk teenager, a ride that ends in tragedy too many times.

A lot of Europeans, conversely, understand that teenagers are going to want to drink, so they deal with it instead of trying to sweep that reality under the rug. Many parents let their teenagers have a little wine at dinner. That way, drinking never becomes such a big deal, and when teenagers do drink, there's always an adult there to cut them off after one glass. As a result, a lot of European kids develop a much more responsible relationship with alcohol. I believe that's because it's always easier to breed maturity when you're confronting reality instead of living a lie.

Europeans have a similar attitude toward infidelity. It's said that while they view staying faithful as desirable, they also accept that fidelity is not always achievable.

Several of my close European friends have told me that as a culture, many Europeans seem to accept you can't ever really stop cheating, so rather than try to live in a fantasy land, they accept it for what it is: a less than desirable aspect of a man's nature, but one that a woman might have to tolerate if she's got an otherwise good man.

It's not just Europeans who view cheating differently than we do. Not long ago I was reading about a book called *Lust in Translation: Infidelity from Tokyo to Tennessee,* in which the author discussed international attitudes to cheating. For example, in Moscow it's not considered cheating if the affair takes place at a summer resort. Huh? In Japan, it's commonly accepted that if you pay for sex, then it's not cheating. In parts of China, it's accepted for wealthy businessmen to have "second wife villages," or apartments where they put up their mistresses.

I understand that these attitudes might seem waaaaay too loose to most American women, but it's important to remember that there's not only one set way to deal with or look at cheating. In America, all women are expected to follow the same script if they find out their man is cheating. First, they're supposed to break up with him. Or if they do decide to try to salvage the relationship, their man is expected to undergo extensive therapy (counseling that, as *Lust in Translation* points out, has become a multimillion-dollar industry) to get at the root of his cheating.

The problem is this: if you've ever been cheated on (or done the cheating), then you know that not every situation is the same. There are countless different factors, reasons, and contexts behind every cheat. Even though they might seem the same on the surface, if you dig to the root of an infidelity, you will see that like snowflakes, no two are identical. So why then are there only two acceptable responses to cheating?

Listen, maybe those two choices sound like the only appropriate responses to you. Or, like my ex, maybe you might take a different approach. All I'm saying is that as a woman, you shouldn't feel like you have only a single script to follow when it comes to cheating.

CHEATING DOESN'T HAVE TO DEFINE YOUR RELATIONSHIP

Far from making her weak, not sticking to the American script actually provided my ex with a lot of strength when it came to dealing with me. Because the one thing she didn't do, which is what trips up so many American women, was *own* my cheating. She accepted that she was holding down her end of the relationship and that if I was still running around on her, it was a negative reflection on me. Not on her. Just because I still needed mentorship and guidance didn't mean that she needed new direction too.

In America, we force women to own the cheat. We throw it in their laps and say, "Here, no backsies." Break up with your man or you're a fool. A sucka. We don't afford women the dignity to simply say, "I'm disappointed in my man, but I still love him. So please don't judge me while I try to make this thing work."

But the truth is, a lot of successful, strong-willed, and confident women *do* make that choice. This is not a tell-all book so I'm not going to say any names, but you can take it on me that a lot of your favorite actors and singers, especially African-American ones, have been caught cheating not once, not twice, not three times, but multiple times, and they are still married. And yes, their wives are African-American too. The wives weren't happy about what happened, and there was hell to pay for those husbands, but the wives also understood that nobody's perfect. Even these dynamic leaders and charismatic artists who you look up to can screw up. It's tough, but there are worse things to deal with in life.

That's all I'm really saying here. Cheating is certainly not what you dream about when you walk down the aisle, but I would figure it's much worse to have to nurse your spouse through a serious sickness. Or through a freak accident that leaves him paralyzed. Or worst of all, to actually lose a child that the two of you brought into the world. So yes, cheating sucks. And it wasn't my mission to justify it on any level, more so to shed light on the factors that lead to infidelity. Just don't let him moving around be the action that defines you or your relationship.

Which is why this is the fundamental lesson I hope women take away from this chapter: Don't beat yourself up over the cheat. Understand that a man's inability to keep it in his pants has much more to do with how he sees himself than how he sees *you*. It means he's stuck in that boyish mentality that I've been alluding to throughout the book. It means that no matter how old he is, validation from other men is still his first priority, a mind state that we're going to explore in greater detail shortly.

And finally, whatever you do, don't let him "reverse the cheat" on you. Most women who have dealt with a cheating man know what I'm talking about: after getting caught redhanded, a guilty man will try to MAN-ipulate you into thinking that you are the reason he dipped out. I've played that immature game myself.

Maybe after y'all had kids you were so consumed with taking care of them that you never got back that Coke-bottle shape he married you with. Or because of what you are not doing in the bedroom, he gets the urge to go out and get it elsewhere.

He will try to put those things on you. He will belittle you and have you crying, believing that it's all your fault. But you have to tell him, "No way, no how." Do not let him reverse that cheat on you.

BEING TAUGHT TO CHEAT

As a woman, you're never going to be able to fully understand your man until you accept this basic fact: he was raised in a culture of cheating.

I don't care if he came up on the streets of Watts, a mansion in Bel Air, or a shack in Shreveport. No matter his background, he was raised in an environment in which a certain capacity told him that his value as a man was directly tied into the number of women he had sex with. Not, as Rev likes to promote, how many times he had sex with *one* woman. No, he's been told that his value is based on the *total* amount of women he had sex with. Might sound crazy, but it's true. (What's sad is that these same boys grow up to be men who become heartbroken if they find out a woman cheated on *them*).

This is true across the board, but it's especially prevalent in the African-American community. Growing up, I can tell you what sort of dude got the most respect on the street. It wasn't the guy with the steady girlfriend, no matter how hot she was. It was the guy with the beautiful girlfriend *and* multiple side pieces. That's who got all the love from the homies on the block.

It wasn't like we were receiving a different message at home either. The majority of us didn't have fathers who lived under the same roof as us, let alone remained faithful to our mothers. It wasn't like we were so young that we were oblivious to the fact that our father or stepfathers were dipping out on our mothers. Remember, our houses were small and we heard every one of those arguments.

We certainly didn't have a married MAN-tor to point us in the right direction. No, most of our pops had chosen promiscuity and sexual freedom over monogamy and commitment—a choice that weighed heavy on our minds every single day.

You might think that growing up yearning for a father would have made us value monogamy even more, but the opposite was true. The absence of male role models at home left us even more susceptible to street values. In one ear we had the streets loudly telling us, "Run through as many women as you can, young pimp," while in the other ear, where our father's voices should have been, all we heard was . . . silence.

I think all of America judges young ladies especially hard. It's considered unacceptable for a woman to have sex with half the dudes on the football team. The other dudes on campus are going to say, "She's a hood rat, she's wild, all the homies smashed." But the other women on campus will go in even harder. "That whore," they'll call her. "She ain't nothing but a rat." Instead of singing her praises, they're going to trash her reputation. Most of the fights

71

she'll get in in high school and college will be with other women who see the way she's moving and call her out on it.

This is because most women have been brought up to believe that their value lies in their ability to secure a relationship with one man. From grade school to high school all the way up through college, the women who get the most props are the ones with a steady boyfriend.

This is not to say that women don't cheat, because obviously they do. What I'm suggesting, however, is that for women, cheating is usually a last resort. From my many talks with women, it seems like when women cheat, they often feel like their hand was forced. As if they had no other way to react to the lack of attention, affection, and mental stimulation in their relationship. I believe as a rule, a woman is not going to go to the intersection of deception and infidelity on her own. No, her man is going to have to practically put the keys in the car, turn on the ignition, and drop his woman off at that intersection.

The other major difference between men and women when it comes to cheating is that y'all are much better at covering your tracks than we are. When you do cheat, you don't tell anybody what you're up to. A female friend told me that when she was a girl, her mother told her that the key to a woman cheating was being discreet. "You can be the biggest whore in Harlem. But if you don't run your mouth, no one will ever know." Men don't like to know it, but it seems like a lot of you ladies had similar conversations with your mothers back in the day!

JUSTIFIABLE INFIDELITY

If most women have to be driven to infidelity, the majority of men are looking for any excuse to get up out of the house and take a stroll over there. Like, right now.

I say *excuse* because another major difference between the sexes is just how easily men can justify their cheating. Women like to believe that men cheat primarily because they can't control themselves sexually or because they're selfish, but it's not that simple.

Unfaithfulness comes so easily to many men because they actually feel justified in cheating. Despite what women think, very few men walk around saying to themselves, *I'm going to cheat on this woman and I don't care how she feels about it.* In reality, we actually care a great deal, as twisted as that might sound.

It's just that for men, there isn't the same emotional attachment to sex as there is for women. For us, it's as easy as taking off our shoes.

So, what's the number one reason compelling most men to feel so sorry for themselves that they can justify cheating?

That's easy: a lack of sex at home. If a hungry man is not getting his big appetite for sex met at home, he is going to feel justified looking to another woman for it. It's really that simple.

It could be an issue of quality. It always used to surprise me when a woman wouldn't want me running around on her yet the sex she was giving me was lackluster. Don't get me wrong, I'd still take that lackluster sex from her for a while, but I'd also be thinking, *It's time to go out there and find some of the good sex that I'm used to. I have experienced something better than this and I couldn't erase those memories even if I tried.*

Or maybe it's an issue of quantity, not quality. Perhaps a man is getting good sex, just not enough of it. One time I asked a friend why he was always stepping out on his girl and he told me, "She knows how often I need my 'medicine,' but she won't give it to me. What am I supposed to do, just stay here? No, I gotta do what I gotta do, period." For my friend, sex was the fix he claimed he "needed."

That sense of entitlement even extends beyond physical sex. I once was hanging with this girl whose line of work had her traveling a lot. I tried my best to stay faithful, but she was what I considered to be a horrible "distant lover." She pretty much wouldn't budge on phone sex, sexy text messages, virtual sex, nothing. For instance, I wanted to have some sexy Skype sessions. I would try to make a joke out of it and using my Chris Rock voice say, "Can I just get a titty? Half a titty?" But I guess it just wasn't her thing. It began to make me feel like she wasn't willing to do anything to help keep me focused on her sex when she wasn't around. So after a few more of her trips (they say too much downtime for a man becomes the devil's playground), of course I started sniffing around for something to keep me occupied while she was gone. And, well, it didn't take long to find what I was looking for.

It's not an exaggeration to say that a man deprived of sex will feel so justified in cheating that when he finally does get caught, he'll tell himself it wasn't the cheating itself that hurt his woman. It was only the getting caught.

After all, how could she expect him to do anything else *but* step out? She isn't going down on him anymore. She also isn't keeping sexy sexy in the bedroom anymore. In his mind, she isn't taking care of her body anymore, or putting any effort into appearing sexy to him anymore. He interprets her attitude as a tacit invitation for him to start moving around and cheating.

How could she claim to be hurt by his cheating? That's like someone who doesn't take their dog out for a walk claiming they're disappointed when Spike eventually pees on the rug. That's what dogs do when they don't get outside, right? So how could you be offended by that? You might be offended by the indignity of having to clean the pee up, or smell it every time you walk into the room, but how could you be offended by the actual *act* of your dog peeing in your house? You left that dog with no choice. Well, a man deprived of sex will feel like he didn't have a choice either.

A lack of sex might be men's most common justification for cheating, but it's far from the only one. A man might cheat because he feels worn down by the responsibilities of his life. As if the weight of earning a living, putting a roof over his family, being an example for his children and planning for their future are slowly crushing him. A weight that his wife seems inexorably linked to.

He might love his wife, but he also wants to experience an intimacy that isn't connected to all the issues that seemingly take up so much of domestic life. He doesn't want his post-sex buzz ruined by someone asking him, "By the way, who's taking the kids to soccer practice tomorrow?" or "Hey, I forgot to ask you earlier if you paid that car note yet."

If he can just get a little bit of sex that's disconnected from domesticity, he feels like it will make shouldering those duties a lot easier for him. So yes, he's cheating, but in his twisted rationale, it's only so that he can better handle his duties as the head of the family.

Another classic justification is when you've already been caught cheating before and your lady tells you she's "forgotten" about it. Yet whenever you're having sex, it feels like her mind is still caught up on the fact that you were doing the same thing to another women. So as a dude, even though you're the one who created that dynamic, it's still a turn-off to you. And then you start looking around again.

I'm also going to share another justification that a lot of ladies aren't up on, which is a man being a late bloomer sexually. Or, as one of my female friends put it to me even more plainly, "Some of these dudes cheat cuz they started getting [laid] late in life."

In other words, a man might have a beautiful woman on his side today, but growing up, maybe he was a nerd who was the last guy on campus the girls would ever look at. Or maybe he flat-out didn't get *any* play from the ladies. I know a very high-powered attorney who fits this profile. Throughout high school and even college, he was, by his own admission, always on the outside looking in when it came to women. He told me that he spent all his time at college studying and literally never got laid.

As he got older, however, that nerdiness started to pay off for him. His good grades got him into Harvard Law School, and after getting high marks there as well, he was soon practicing at a top firm. He also started growing into his looks, and by the time he was in his late twenties he definitely had the ladies fighting over him. He ended up marrying a beautiful, intelligent woman who was also an attorney. To the world, he had it all: a stunning wife, great job, beautiful home, and bright future.

In the back of his mind, however, he is still that nerdy, horny kid who couldn't ever get laid. So instead of being satisfied with his beautiful wife, he's haunted by the thought of all the chicks he never had growing up, obsessed by the memories of all the women who shot him down or that he didn't even have the courage to approach in the first place.

So he cheats, not because he's in any way dissatisfied with his wife—he'll be the first to tell you she's incredible—but because he still feels like he has to make up for all those good times he never experienced as a young man. His wife, of course, isn't even aware of his issues. He'll sometimes make jokes about what a nerd he was, but all she's ever known is the finished product, the successful, confident attorney who all the ladies considered a catch. It would never even cross her mind that he's still wrapped up in his issues from fifteen years ago.

It's very real to him, though. He feels bad about creepin', but until he feels like he's gotten enough out of his system, even if it means jeopardizing his relationship, he's going to do whatever he wants to out there to make up for the years of lost time.

So I would say to some of you ladies, keep a close eye on guys who are "late." They won't exactly announce their status when they meet you, but pay attention when they talk about being a nerd back in the day. Don't assume that they're just being humble—they might be trying to tip you off to their propensity to prowl.

BREAKING THE MAN CODE

OK, I've said my piece on cheating. So, as promised, I'm going to break the "man code" and share some stories different guys (and their ladies) have told me about how they got caught. I'm sorry if it sounds like I'm snitchin', fellas. But as much as it hurts me to break the code, I can't stray from my mission in this book, which is revealing hard, uncomfortable truths.

Before I teach you ladies how to find a cheater, however, let me offer this warning: be careful, because chances are you just might find what you're looking for!

OK, so here we go. If you think your man is cheating, one of the first signs to look for is a break in his routine. We like to believe that we're James Bond, but most of us are a lot closer to Homer Simpson. In other words, we ain't slick. We ain't smooth. We ain't dashing. We're much more likely to be sitting on the couch watching a game with a hand down their pants then being out in the world doing something exciting.

We men like to do the same simple things, day in and day out. We like to take the same routes home from work, go out to eat at the same restaurants, watch the same games, hang out with the same friends, click on the same websites, etc., etc.

One of my boys definitely got caught by switching up his routine out of the blue. His lady couldn't help but notice he was going out to different spots after work, eating at different restaurants, or hanging out with a different crew. It put her antennae up just a little bit higher, and sure enough she found something.

So while I'm not saying he's definitely stepping out on you if you notice a break in your man's routine, but chances are something is up. Very few things can knock a man out of his routine. And sex with a new woman is usually at the top of that short list.

Something else that should always set off your internal alarms is when a man says, "Oh, she's like a sister to me." One of my boys *always* used to use that line. He'd even throw in a little tinge of outrage in his voice, as if he was saying, "How could you even suggest that I'd want to have sex with *her*?" When of course that was exactly what he was doing. Believe me, I used it too. "My backup dancer? Please, she's like a sister to me." Or, "That publicist who keeps calling? She's just doing her job. Besides, she's like my little sister." Well, let me tell you something: you know who's like a sister to a man? His sister. That's it. Period. So if the woman in question did not come out of the same vagina as your man did, feel free to call him on his BS. Sorry to give that one away, fellas, but you've got to come better than that.

Also, a lot of my boys like to tell their woman that they're "too busy" to cheat, but don't go for that one either. This is one of our favorite cards to play, especially when we're the ones bringing home most of the bacon. A woman might have suspicions, but she'll be extra cautious about questioning the breadwinner's responsibilities at work. We know this, so we'll try to play up how busy we are. It was certainly one of my favorite smoke screens. "Man, they've got me working from sunup to sundown. I can't believe how packed they've got my schedule," I would sigh when a woman would ask me how a tour was going. Or even if she didn't ask, I'd still be quick to volunteer how insanely busy I was going to be. "I don't think I'm even going to get fifteen minutes to just chill out and read a magazine or something," I'd say with fake annoyance, implying that she shouldn't even bother bringing up the possibility of me being unfaithful.

Yeah, right. The second I put down that phone, I'd be off looking to get into some trouble. Believe me, no job is so demanding, no schedule is so booked, no boss is so unfair that a man isn't going to find the time and run off and get some new sex if *that's* what's on his agenda.

For a cheating man, new sex is like water. If a man's thirsty, he's going to find a way to quench that thirst. No. Matter. What.

If he can keep it simple and just pull into a 7-Eleven for a bottle of water, then that's what he'll do. If no stores are open but he finds a water bottle in his backseat that's hot from the sun and starting to look a little stale, he'll still take a sip from that. And if he can't find a store and there's no water bottle in his backseat, then he'll pull over and jump somebody's fence so he can steal a drink from their sprinkler. If he's thirsty, he is going to find a way to quench that thirst. Period.

Whether you check his sleeve when he gets home to see if it's wet from where he wiped his mouth, or you look to see if some water splashed on his Timbs, hey, that's on you. But never believe that he's going to be too busy to get that proverbial drink.

I've also had plenty of my boys tell me that they've run into trouble when a woman has checked their cellphone or the websites they go on. Even though by now men know that it's very easy to get caught electronically, guys are still incredibly lazy when it comes to covering their tracks online. A lot of dudes will use the same password for different websites even though some of those sites are where they like to do their dirt. So if your man makes a big deal of giving you his Facebook password, saying he's got nothing to hide, try plugging that password into some of the other sites that show up on his browser. Or if it doesn't work, just try adding a 1 or 2 at the end of it, since even when men do try to switch things up, they'll *still* be lazy. He might be keeping things clean on Facebook and Twitter, but there are still plenty of other sites for him to be doing his dirt on.

I know some of you women will take it a step further and actually create fake Facebook or Twitter accounts just so you can contact your man under an alias and see how he reacts. You'll post a picture of yourself with a fat butt or big boobs, then send him a flirtatious DM just to see if he flirts back. Guys should know better, but so many of us still fall for that one. Fat butts and big boobs are like traps to men. We know we're not supposed to go near them, but we just can't help ourselves.

I have to admit, that while many guys make it easy, a lot of women are very impressive with their online snooping. Monitoring activity, concocting fake identities, and even hacking into websites—I swear the government needs to hire some of you for Homeland Security. Forget about catching your man cheating, y'all need to be protecting this country!

For example, I know of one woman who grew suspicious after her man claimed he had to work late for several weeks in a row. There was something about the way he spoke about one of his female coworkers that just didn't sit right with her. So she went online, figured out where the coworker lived, and then cased out her apartment. She staked it out all night and didn't see anything, but something told her not to give up. After noticing a convenience store right across from the coworker's building, she came back the next day and convinced the owner to let her watch all the footage from his security camera. Sure enough, several hours after she'd gone home, there was footage of her husband with his coworker at the counter buying a pack of condoms. Busted! It was impressive work, but just imagine all the good work she could be doing if she was tracking down bank robbers instead of cheating boyfriends.

Sometimes a woman doesn't need to do all that work, because the other woman is doing it for her. I once heard this story of a married man who was cheating on his wife in their house while she was out at work. He eventually got caught because it turned out his mistress would spray his bed with her perfume when he wasn't looking. She'd also purposely leave strands of her hair on the bathroom sink, or one time even went as far as leaving her drawers on his dresser. She was so determined to steal that man that she left a trail of deceit that of course the wife couldn't help but notice and eventually led to their divorce.

Oftentimes, though, woman don't need the evidence planted in front of them to figure out what's going on. They can just use their own insight. Some call it "feminine intuition"; others even say they are told through their dreams that their man is moving around.

Let's look at that word *intuition,* which so many woman credit for knowing that their man is up to something. *Intuition* actually derives from the Latin word *intuērī,* meaning "to gaze at." In other words, intuition is less about what you feel in your gut and more about what you are seeing with your eyes.

When a woman says she's responding to "intuition," she's really just responding to *evidence.* She's seen the change in routine, the suspicious conversations online, the endless emails from a coworker, even the way her man ever so slightly shields his cellphone away from her before he answers certain calls. She's observed all of that, and she knows what it means. Whether or not she chooses to dig deeper and find that indisputable proof or actually catch him in the act—again, that's a personal choice.

Just please remember this one thing: your first responsibility and commitment in life is to rest well at night. If nothing else, you deserve that for yourself.

So let's say you've confronted your man about another woman, but he's sworn up, down, and sideways that nothing's going on. You don't have any hard evidence against him, just that intuition I spoke of. So you feel you have no choice but to let it go.

But when you get in bed at night and pick up a book, after

five minutes you find your mind drifting. You think to yourself, "I'm reading this book, but I'm not comprehending the words that I'm reading." When you finally turn out the light and shut your eyes, you might fall asleep, but it's not good sleep. When you wake up nine hours later, you're still tired because your mind has been wrestling with something all night. Then you go to work, but you find yourself unable to focus.

When you find yourself in this state, unable to get that good rest that every person deserves, then it's probably time to start trusting your intuition. No matter what your man has told you, it's time to use some of the tactics and techniques that I just described. Even if you end up finding out that everything your man told you is lies, at least one day down the road you'll be able to get a proper night's rest again. You owe that, at the very least, to yourself.

REV RUN

It's funny, the very first conversation I ever had with Tyrese was about his view on cheating. Here we are so many conversations (and an incredible friendship) later, but I still can't cosign his views!

Don't get me wrong, I agree that cheating is a real issue for a lot of men—which is why if you ladies start breaking into your man's Facebook accounts, checking his phones, and even watching surveillance tapes, some of you unfortunately will probably find what you are looking for.

What I think is wrong, however, is the assertion that men are bred to cheat.

I don't think men are bred to cheat. I think most men *decide* to cheat.

Which is why women need to remind men that cheating is a *choice.* And like every choice we make in life, it has repercussions.

For example, I accept that if I make the choice to eat a slice of red velvet cake after dinner, my diet won't work. That doesn't mean, as Tyrese suggested, that I won't be able to come up with some good justifications for eating the cake. I might tell myself, "My wife doesn't really mind my belly. She thinks it's cute." Or I might say, "Well, Rick Ross has made big guys sexy again, so I should enjoy this cake and not worry about the weight thing too much."

I can tell myself those justifications, but I know that my wife would be happy if my belly went away and that while Rick Ross is doing his thing, *I* still need to drop thirty pounds. So even though I make the *choice* to keep eating cake, I haven't lost sight of the fact that I've *chosen* to do so and that the repercussions for that choice will be felt the next time I step on a scale.

You've got to keep a man firmly rooted in the same zone when it comes to cheating. He can't ever start to believe that if he cheats, it's in an environment where cheating was celebrated. Or because his wife hasn't been giving him enough nookie. Or because they've been arguing a lot lately. Or because he's getting stressed out over paying his mortgage.

If he cheats, it's because he and he alone made that decision. You have to hold him accountable for that action. What sort of repercussion you want to dole out is something you'll have to decide based on your individual circumstances. In every case, however, there must be a repercussion.

I don't agree that sometimes it's OK to just let a man off the hook. At the very, very least you put him on that hook and let him squirm. Make him think he's going to get thrown to the sharks. Whether you end up throwing him in or letting him go is up to you.

When we talk about being "realistic" or having a "European attitude" toward cheating, I think that's code for relieving men from having any responsibility for their actions. But a relationship is only going to work, however, when both people take on *more* responsibility for their actions. Not less.

I believe that being unfaithful is for the weak, sneaky, and undisciplined. And for example, I know that Tyrese isn't *any* of those things. He's so much better than that. Which is why I used to get so frustrated when he would act like cheating was somehow out of his control.

Weak? Please, I don't know anyone stronger than Tyrese. He's a guy who was able to overcome an abusive, dysfunctional upbringing and turn himself into a star. Nobody gave him anything. He pulled himself up. You have to be strong like Samson to do that.

Sneaky? If you haven't figured it out by now, Tyrese is *unbelievably* honest. He's the last guy to talk behind your back or make a move without telling you. If he's got an issue with you or something you did, he's going to tell you directly.

Undisciplined? Tyrese is one of the most disciplined people I've ever met—a man who can say no to every drink and drug he's offered in Hollywood, who goes to the gym and works out every day, who always eats the right food. (When we go out to eat I try to get what he has—he has *amazing* self-control with food. It's a real inspiration to me, in fact.) Yet this guy who works out, eats right, doesn't get high, doesn't have a bunch of random kids running around beyond his daughter, and is incredibly focused on his career somehow wasn't disciplined enough to refrain from cheating for all those years? How could that be?

I believe part of the problem was that back then Tyrese, like other men in his position, had waaaay too many choices when it came to women. To use our diets as an analogy, when someone is really disciplined with what they eat, when they walk into a restaurant they're not even *looking* at all the fried and greasy foods on the menu. It's almost like they only see the fish and baked chicken. Me, I'm checking all that greasy, fattening stuff out. And as a result, I usually end up ordering some of it.

When it comes to women, we're just the opposite. I've never even looked at the menu since I've been married, but most guys only want to know about all the specials, how the steak was cooked, what sort of ice cream they served for dessert, where they got their cakes from, and all of that. Most men are curious about every little thing on the menu. As a result, they end up ordering a lot of dishes, even though he often had a better meal waiting for him back at home.

It's like Chris Rock's famous quote, "A man is as faithful as his options." Well, most guys give themselves too many options. They won't be able to control their sexual appetite until they limited their options.

That might have seemed like a Herculean task for someone constantly surrounded by beautiful, available women, but I always tried to stress to Tyrese, my brother Russell, or many of my other friends that no man (or woman, for that matter) is a slave to their situation in life.

If that were the case, it would mean that someone like Tyrese would have no choice *but* to cheat because of his unlimited options, while a fat guy driving a delivery truck could *never* cheat, because his options were limited.

That isn't how the world works, though. There are plenty of fat delivery truck drivers who cheat, while there are also plenty of good-looking, rich celebrities who don't.

Take yours truly, for example. I'm not suggesting that I'm a sex symbol like Tyrese (though hopefully to my wife I am), but I am a living, breathing testament to the fact that you certainly can be a celebrity and still choose not to put yourself into compromising situations.

I *choose* not to go out to dinner with women unless there's another person present. I *choose* not to go to parties. I *choose* not to drink or take drugs. I *choose* not to watch pornography, or even just surf the Internet looking for sexy girls. And I *choose* not to spend too much time around people who *do* choose to do those things.

➤ By making all those *choices,* I've limited my *options.*

Frankly, those choices have probably offended some people. If you're a good-looking woman and you approach me to say hi or even just ask for a photo, I'm going to seem weird around you. I'm probably going to keep the conversation very brief, or constantly try to steer it back toward my wife and my marriage. Not because I think you're trying to flirt with me but simply because I don't even want to let a whiff of drama into my life. The prettier the woman who tries to speak with me, the faster I'm ending the conversation and running away.

If my wife even suspected that I was flirting with another woman, let alone cheating with her, it would bring so much pain and insecurity to my relationship. Living with that sort of energy in my house would feel like being trapped in one of the lowest levels of Hell. So I'll do everything within my power, even if it means appearing antisocial or rude, to avoid going there.

If I seem stronger and more disciplined than other men, it's not because I'm immune to temptation. If I'm strong, it's because I'm ➤ aware of just how vulnerable I am, which is why I limit my options accordingly. My strength is knowing that as man, I'm not going to do great with a lot of choices.

Which is why you don't want to look for a guy who on the surface appears all powerful, like Superman. If that man believes his own hype, eventually he will encounter kryptonite. Instead, look for a man who is sensitive and honest enough to admit that he has weakness but who is also willing to take the steps necessary to limit his exposure to temptation. That's the kind of strong man you really want.

I WON'T CHEAT ON GOD

I sense that Tyrese sometimes thinks my choice *not* to cheat stems entirely out of me being scared of my wife. He's right about the scared part, but he's wrong about who I'm scared of.

I don't avoid cheating because I'm scared of my wife (though I admit she's got me a little shook).

No, I don't cheat because I'm scared of *God*.

I don't ever want to have a conversation with God where I have to explain why I messed up this wonderful situation he's blessed me with. Obviously I don't want to hurt Justine, but if I'm going to keep it real, I'd have to admit that staying on God's good side is actually my biggest concern. If having my wife suspect me of cheating would make me feel like I was trapped in one of the levels of Hell, then having God know that I cheated would be like being stuck in the nastiest, darkest, absolutely rock bottom of Hell.

I don't think there's anything wrong about saying that. If my wife was my highest motivation, then there might still be a chance that I'd slip up. Men are pretty good at being able to justify their cheating, even when they're scared of their wives. Maybe I would be able to talk myself into believing that my wife "forced" me to mess around by picking a fight with me, or that I needed some "relief" when I was feeling particularly stressed about supporting our family. Or, after so many years of being faithful, maybe I'd start to believe that I "deserved" to be with other women. I don't even like typing those words, but maybe, under different circumstances, I could sell those justifications to myself.

There ain't any circumstances, however, where I would try to sell those justifications to God.

Ever.

Personally, no matter how stressed I feel, no matter what situations I find myself in, or no matter how long I've been "good," I'm never going to even *consider* having a conversation with God where I try to justify disobeying his laws.

God is crystal clear on how he feels about cheating. The seventh of the Ten Commandments states, "Though shall not commit adultery." Pretty straightforward, huh?

And in case someone just happened to miss catching the Ten Commandments, later on in Proverbs it states, "A man who commits adultery lacks judgment. Whoever does so destroys themselves. He will get wounds and dishonor and his disgrace will not be wiped away."

So why does God look down so harshly on adultery? I believe it's not because he's an unreasonable taskmaster, or trying to stop us from having fun down here on earth, but because he's actually a loving God. He wants to help us avoid a lot of needless suffering. Remember, the Bible isn't here to trip us up. It's here to help us get our steps in order.

God knows that no matter what culture you come from, or how progressive your views are, cheating is going to cause a lot of pain and insecurity in a relationship. I don't care if a woman is English, Ethiopian or Eskimo; if she opens up her man's bag and a bunch of condoms roll out, she is going to be seriously hurt, probably even devastated.

At the very least she is going to feel extremely insecure about her relationship. Personally, I never want my wife to feel insecure about *anything* in our home. The second I even catch a whiff of insecurity sneaking into my home, I start acting like Outkast in the "Ms. Jackson" video, running around fixing leaks and sealing up every crack. I won't tolerate any holes that might be letting hurt and insecurity into Run's house.

I'm not only talking about cheating. I won't let *anything* through my door that might make my wife feel insecure or start to question our relationship.

I'm also not making any phone calls or sending texts to any woman who might make my wife feel uncomfortable. It's true, a lot of guys will never let their phones out of their sight, but not me. I'll leave mine on the kitchen counter or in our bedroom and never think twice about it. I've got nothing to hide.

In fact, if my ex-wife calls to discuss our kids, I put the call on speaker just so my wife is comfortable knowing that I'm not discussing anything that could in any way make her feel uncomfortable. Everything is on the surface and transparent between us.

Having said that, the heck with my wife! How would I hide those phone calls from God? Do I think God isn't going to see those text messages? Or that God won't know what's being said on my Facebook account? Or that God wouldn't know if I was trying to reignite some old coals with my ex?

I might sound old-fashioned or simpleminded, but there is no way I am going to diss God on this topic. None. I've seen what happens when you follow God's instructions about family, and I'm not prepared to risk one iota of that happiness and contentment for some foolishness.

PICK ONE!

I believe the shift in Tyrese's thinking on commitment and fidelity started one night when he called me to complain about his girlfriend at the time. I listened to him go on for a while about how she wasn't stimulating him intellectually. About how he also wasn't satisfied with what was happening between the sheets. About how he loved her, but he needed to be with other women if he was going to stay with her. After a few minutes of hearing him complain and make excuses, I'd had enough.

"Shut up! *Pick one!*"

"Come on, Rev," he started to say, but I wasn't done.

"Man, stop messing around and just *pick one* woman and be happy with her. Stop acting like you have to be a playboy for the rest of your life. That part of your life is over. It's a wrap. Just like this phone call." And with that, I hung up on him.

I didn't mean to snap on him, but he needed to know just how frustrated I'd become with his behavior. He later told me that I really messed him up that night, but it was exactly what he needed to hear.

When I snapped on him, he finally understood why he needed to change. He recognized that if I was that frustrated with how he was living, he really must have been out of control.

Why was I so upset? Because I felt like his attitude toward relationships had become a joke. Was I expected to believe that Tyrese Gibson, who'd had women screaming his name since that Coke commercial, couldn't find a single woman who satisfied him sexually? While also stimulating him intellectually? Not one of all those women had the whole package? They all could provide him with 80 percent of what he needed but not that other 20 percent? Sorry, I didn't believe that. Not one of those women had the combination of the big butt, brains and freakiness that he claimed to need so badly? Sorry, not true.

The thing that was hard for Tyrese to accept (though he gets it today), and is hard for a lot of men to accept, is that one day it has to be over. By *it* I'm referring to the games. The running around, cheating, partying, eight girls waiting for you in a hot tub games. Listen, I'm sure Michael Jordan would've liked to play basketball until he was sixty-five. Just as I'm sure that Peyton Manning would like to still be throwing touchdowns when he's ninety. But it doesn't work like that in life. At some point, you have to say "Game over," and pick up a new hobby.

Chris Rock, as he has a habit of doing, said it best. Men have two choices: be married and bored, or single and lonely. To me, that's an easy choice. Are there moments of boredom in married life? Sure. But there's a lot of excitement and a whole lot of love too. The loneliness that comes with single life, on the other hand, can be extremely dark and depressing.

It's not just Tyrese; there are a lot of men I know whose lifestyles get me so frustrated. I feel like everywhere I look in my life, I see men who are still clinging to the games. I have a friend named Scott, who suffers from the same inability to pick one. He's a handsome guy, makes a ton of money, has a great sense of humor and is a lot of fun to be around. Yet somehow he can never seem to find one woman with the right combination of looks, smarts and sexiness. Scott hangs out with my brother Russell and gets to meet tons of beautiful, attractive and supersuccessful women, but somehow none of them seem to have "it all." Sure, Scott, whatever you say. It's like a joke to me.

I'm even starting to see the same attitude develop in my sons. It seems like all they can see is the flaws in the women who are interested in them. All they can see is reasons why they can't settle down. I don't want to sound like I'm bashing males, but as a man who understands the power of picking one woman and sticking with her, it can become frustrating to see all this hesitation, indecision and lack of commitment.

I'm going to return to this directive again throughout the book, but I want to clarify one point right now: when I say, "Pick One," I'm not suggesting that a man should go out and slap a ring on the finger of the first woman he dances with tomorrow night at the club.

What I am saying is that, at some point a man will find himself in a relationship with a good woman. A woman who makes him happy, who stands by him when times get tough, who makes him laugh and has a kind heart. A woman who he just knows will make a great mother too.

A guy's friends can see those qualities in his woman, his parents can see them, everyone in his life can see them except, it seems, for him. It's not that he's blind. No, his eyes work just fine. It's just that instead of focusing on and appreciating what's in front of him, he's always straining to see what's around the next corner. He's always thinking that someone a little sexier, a little smarter, a little more exciting is waiting for him just around the next bend.

MALE PATTERN BLINDNESS

You've heard of male pattern baldness? Well, this condition should be called "Male Pattern Blindness," or the inability to see the good thing that's right in front of his face. A lot of my friends, my sons are showing signs of developing it, and I'm sure you've dealt with men who've got a bad case of it too.

MANOLOGY

As a woman, your challenge is to help your man take his eyes off that nameless prize and realize that he's already got a winner in you. I honestly wish I could call up every playboy and bachelor in America, say, "Hello, this is Rev Run," and then *scream,* "Pick One!" But I can't. You're going to have to tell your man yourself.

CHAPTER 4

COMMUNICATING WITH YOUR MAN

REV RUN

When it comes to building a healthy, stable relationship, one of the biggest obstacles women must overcome is a man's inability—or perhaps unwillingness—to communicate his feelings. A man might tell you what he wants for dinner, what sort of movie he wants to see and definitely when he's in the mood for sex, but when it comes to his emotions, he's often reluctant to share what's on his mind. *Especially* when it comes to relationships.

I'm a pretty normal dude on most issues, but I'll confess I'm actually a little abnormal when it comes to expressing what I'm feeling. Unlike most men, I happen to be extremely comfortable with verbal communication. I'm not going to let any issue go unaddressed or unexplored in my house. Whether it's Justine feeling like I've been ignoring her, or Russy starting to act like I've been too hard on him, or even

MANOLOGY

Miley getting mad at me for not letting her watch any more TV, I am going to talk about every and any issue that starts to bubble up under my roof before it can *ever* reach a boil.

Tyrese is cut from the exact same cloth. You might not always agree with what he says, but you're always going to know where he stands, whether it's regarding relationships, business, philosophy or whatever. He's never going to hold back his emotions. Which probably is one of the reasons our friendship works so well. We're both entertainers who get paid to run our mouths in public and have no problem keeping that motor running when we get home. We both love to talk, express, emote and share.

Most men, you might have noticed, aren't quite like that. So, given that communication comes a little easier to us, we decided to open the floor on Twitter to some of our female followers and hear about what trips them up when it comes to communicating with their men. Not surprisingly, a lot of their email responses had to do with men's unwillingness to share their emotions:

The most annoying thing is when they don't say exactly what is on their mind. You can see and tell they want to say something but don't. And when you ask, they say nothing. But let us (women) do that, they get agitated and now it's a big fight.

One thing that pisses me off is when I'm having a conversation with my man and all his responses are short, e.g., "yes," "why," "OK," "maybe." Those answers make me wonder if he's listening to me.

The one aspect of a man's character that just annoys the hell out of me is that they mask their emotions. I've written letters, screamed to the top of my lungs, sent emails, text messages expressing how I feel and what issue I was having at the moment and all he could say was "OK" or "I got you." It's like men are scared to open up or show some type of emotion other than happiness when they're getting the goodies.

Well, ladies, the good news is that even if your man might act like he hasn't, Tyrese and I *have* heard you. And we have a lot to say about the issues that tend to clog up communication between men and women. It's essential that we have this conversation, because no matter what advice or prescriptions we offer in this book, none of them are going to take unless you and your man can communicate. Aside from sex, there probably isn't a single issue that causes more dissention within a relationship. Thankfully, it's one of the easiest issues to not only address but also to fix. Once you get to the roots of his silence, you'll be able to come at conversation in a way that will open him up rather than shut him down.

It's something you really have to be diligent about, because if communication dies, then the relationship is eventually going to die too. It's really that simple. Communicating is the number one answer to keeping a relationship going. At the end of the day, that's all this book is—an exercise in communication. Sometimes what we say might be funny, other times it might seem a little out there, and hopefully some of it will be insightful and inspiring too. But no matter what, we're not letting the conversation die in these pages. You must approach your relationship the same way if you want it to work.

THE ARGUMENT

Let me start off by getting right to the heart of why so many men are tight-lipped with their emotions: they simply don't like to argue with women. At first glance, that might not seem like a credible reason to be uncommunicative. After all, men don't seem afraid to argue in other aspects of their lives. Have you ever watched a bunch of guys play basketball? They spend about 50 percent of the time playing and the rest of the time arguing with dudes on the other team. "You fouled me." "That ball was out." "Stop cheating, you know you traveled." Instead of trying to avoid arguing, most guys actually seem to gravitate toward those little quarrels. Sometimes you'd swear they showed up at the gym just to argue.

To take it a step further, men don't seem to have any reluctance about arguing when it comes to politics, right? Whether it's disagreeing about an issue with the guy in the next chair over at the barbershop, screaming at a rival group of protesters across the street, or debating the other party's presidential nominee, men will gladly jump into a political fight, to the point that they will go to war and try to kill each other over a disagreement.

When it comes to dealing with women, however, it's a whole different story. From the weekend warrior on the basketball court to the military warrior threatening to invade another country, men who show no fear in the rest of their lives will put their tails between their legs and run from having a difficult conversation with their women!

Why is that? What turns all these loudmouthed, boisterous, opinionated men into mutes when it's time to address a tough part of their relationship?

They clam up because they don't think they can "win" those arguments.

Remember, the concept of winning is paramount to all men. The ballplayer only plays to *win*. The politician only runs for office to *win*. The general only goes to war to *win*. It's what men strive to do in every aspect of their lives, including their relationships. And no matter what games they play, what political party they belong to, or what country they live in, 99 percent of men share this common belief:

It is impossible to "win" an argument with a woman.

Ladies, you might be saying "Hmphh" or "Whatever," but until you accept this basic premise, you're *never* going to be able to understand where your man is coming from.

Warranted or not, the vast majority of men believe that when an argument with a woman seems unavoidable, their best bet is to simply shut up and play possum. They know if they try to debate or argue a point with a woman the way they would with a man, they are just going to end up even more frustrated than they were at the start of the conversation.

Why is there such a disconnect between the sexes when it comes to arguing? I believe it's because men and women approach arguments from different perspectives and armed with different agendas. Many times women will argue just because they want to be *heard*. They're arguing not to prove a specific point but to express how they're feeling in general. Sure, they'll start off talking about something in particular, but ultimately their agenda is about finally airing out some of the frustrations or insecurities they might be feeling in the relationship.

Men, on the other hand, don't care about getting something off their chest or addressing a festering issue as much as they care about actually winning the argument at hand. To use an analogy, women argue like poets—they want to express their emotions. Men argue like lawyers—they want to prove the facts.

For example, let's say a woman always gets the hamburger with onions when she orders from the takeout place near her home. One night her husband comes back with a salad and salmon steak instead of a burger and says, "I wasn't sure what you'd want, so I got the fish because I figured it'd be good for your diet." Of course she's going to get pissed and want to talk about it.

In her husband's mind, she doesn't have a legitimate argument. He told her he was going to be stopping by the restaurant after work, and since she didn't specifically say what she wanted, he got the fish. In his eyes, those are the facts, and that's what the argument should center around.

For the woman, the argument isn't about semantics or the facts of who ordered what. It's about how her husband has a tendency to not really pay attention to the things that *she* likes. Plus, she's tired of him always breathing down her neck about what she eats. She is grown and doesn't need him trying to make decisions for her, especially when he should be more worried about keeping his own gut tight.

Here's the thing: after a few minutes of arguing about the food, the wife will actually start to feel better. Why? Because she might not have gotten her burger, but she finally got a chance to vent the frustration that had been building up in her. She got to tell her husband that she's tired of his paternalistic and controlling attitude. He might not even concede the point, but after their argument, she's actually going to feel better about their relationship. Because she knows that at least she addressed a nagging issue for her.

The husband, however, leaves that argument feeling even worse. In the small picture, he can't figure out why his wife is so upset about the burger when she never gave him explicit instructions. In the big picture, he's frustrated because no matter how many valid points he raises and how much evidence he presents, he can't seem to win *any* argument with his wife. He always leaves those conversations feeling like he lost. And that's a very dangerous feeling for a man to have.

Let me keep it really funky here: deep down, the man *does* know what he and his wife are *really* arguing about. He might like to tell himself that his wife "don't make no sense when she's mad," but he knows she's upset about his attitude in general, not specifically that he brought home the fish.

The problem is that he won't want to address the larger issue unless his wife explicitly forces him to do so. He'd like to put off that talk for as long as possible. *If I address this part of our relationship that's fundamentally flawed, it will mean a lot of tears and soul searching,* is what he'll be thinking. *If I can keep the conversation limited to burgers and fish, it will be a lot less painful.*

Adding to the disconnect is the fact that the woman might not spell out what's really bothering her. This is because a woman wants her man to recognize the larger issues on his own. That's what proves he's paying attention and is sensitive to her emotions.

I can understand why women feel this way. If a man tells a woman "sorry for being too controlling" after she had to explain how controlling he was being, then the woman is still going to wonder whether or not he truly gets it. A woman will always feel much better about an apology when it's unsolicited. So if that man calls his wife up out of the blue during the middle of the day and says, "Hey, baby, just wanted to say sorry about the other night with the burger. I got no business being on your case like that . . ." the call will put that issue to rest. Unfortunately, a lot of you ladies will be waiting a very, very long time for a call like that, which is why you always end up in arguments.

In my house, we address the big issues right away. If I get on my wife for breaking her diet and she lets me know she's not in the mood to be lectured, then I back off right away. I won't try to debate what I said; no, I'm jumping back in my car and going out to get her that burger with onions. Maybe I'll even pick her up some cheesecake for dessert, because my wife's happiness is always more important to me than proving any point.

THE RIGHT TIME TO TALK

Even though most men would rather shy away from or completely avoid difficult conversations with a woman, it's impossible to put them off forever. So the question becomes, when is the optimum time to approach your man with a problem?

Before I give my answer, let me start by breaking down the *worst* time to approach your man: when he's about to go to sleep.

Whatever you do, don't bring any drama or stress to your man late at night. That might seem like the most opportune time to talk, but for a man it's actually the worst. Personally, nothing makes me grouchier than when Justine tries to slide something on to my plate when I'm getting ready for bed. She might tell me, "I'm sorry to be bothering you with this right now, but you just seemed so busy during the day that I didn't want to bring it up then," but I'm still trying not to hear it.

I'm thinking, *I've already tackled eighteen things today—dealing with the accountant, talking to the lawyers, straightening out our flights, negotiating with the dude who's going to fix the roof and talking to Russy about his schoolwork. I'm puckered out. It's 11:30 and the only thing I'm trying to think about is hitting this bed.*

Those conversations are bad, but the worst happen when I've already closed my eyes and started to count sheep, but Justine comes over and gives me a little nudge.

"Joey, Joey, wake up for a second. We never decided what time Russy's tutor should come tomorrow."

"Huh? I'm sleeping."

"I know, but I need to send him a text. You were so crazy today, it's the only time I could talk to you about this."

"Noooo. I'm not having this discussion right now."

Trust me, nothing is more annoying to a man than being woken up to talk about household issues. In fact, once a man's started snoring, you should never wake him up to talk about *anything* other than the house being on fire, the fact that there's a burglar downstairs, or you want to have sex. To a man, *everything* else can wait.

Till when, you ask?

Until first thing in the morning. That's the *best* time to talk to a man about things he'd rather avoid.

I realize that might seem to defy logic. After all, he just woke up. Why hit him over the head with drama first thing in the morning? You certainly wouldn't like that if he did it to you.

Well, he probably won't like it either. He might even bite your head off a little bit and say something like, "So I'm getting a headache for breakfast today? What ever happened to French toast?" He might be a little grouchy, and you're going to have to deal with his morning breath and eye sleep, but first thing in the a.m. is *still* the best time for *both* of you.

If Justine wants to talk at 9:00 a.m., then I'm normally ready to get into it. I wake up ready to take on the world, not just about household issues but about larger topics too. I'm ready to talk about the dreams I had last night, the breakthrough I finally had on an idea or about a conversation I had with God.

For men, it's critical to start the morning off strong. Personally, if I don't get a running start to the day, I feel like a punk. So yes, I want to talk about Russy's tutor, plus whatever other loose end Justine needs tied up. Then I want to make sure I give myself a close shave without missing any spots, check that all my cars are washed and vacuumed, that I've got clean clothes on and that there are groceries in the fridge, plus money in all the right accounts. Basically, I want to check off everything on my list before I step out into the world so that I can hit the streets feeling like the flyest negro on earth!

I'll be honest, some of that is due to the sense of competition that men feel with each other. One of the reasons I'm so gung ho in the morning is that in my mind, there's another dude out there who's off to an even *faster* start.

Remember, when it comes to pinning down your man and making him have the discussions he's been putting off, the nighttime is *never* the right time. In the afternoon, you're going to have too many competitors for his attention. You always want to make your move first thing in the morning.

UNARTICULATED EXPECTATIONS

One area where communication almost always breaks down between men and women is sex. Or more specifically, when to have it. The problem in many relationships is that while a man will expect sex on certain occasions, he'll never *tell* you exactly what they are. Even worse, he'll hold it against you if you don't meet those unarticulated expectations.

Because Justine and I follow the Bible instructions on sex, which I mentioned earlier, this is a little less of an issue in our house than it is in most. I'd be lying to you if I claimed that my expectations for sex still don't get Justine frustrated on a lot of nights. If there's one level of communication in my house that always needs fine-tuning and adjusting, it's my expectations for sex.

The most common unarticulated expectation most men have is that there's only a certain amount of time that they're expected to go without sex. For some, it could be a few days. For others, it could be a week or ten days. Some guys out there might even be able to last a month without any action going on between the sheets. Every man has his own tolerance level.

As a woman, it's in your best interest to know what his level is. Because even though a husband might never say, "Baby, you know I can't last more than a week without having sex," in his mind it's an *obvious* fact. It might as well be written in neon lights across his forehead. That means when he gets to four or five days since your last session and there doesn't seem to be any sex in sight, he'll start to get antsy. You might notice that his tone with you becomes sharper, that his mood gets edgier. Then, if he goes to sleep on the sixth night without having gotten any, his mind-set becomes, "OK, fine. No sex tonight. But that means that I'm *definitely* getting some tomorrow night."

His wife, of course, might not be aware of any of this. All she's probably aware of is that he's getting ruder and crabbier around the house, which is not exactly the type of behavior that makes her want to jump into bed with him.

So when the seventh night comes and goes without any sex, in the man's mind a major violation has occurred. I know this sounds silly—after all, he hasn't told his woman he's expecting sex.

In his mind, however, he's like a piece of meat at the supermarket. He's got a "sell by" date, and once that date passes, it's a problem. In the last chapter Tyrese spoke about a man's justifications for cheating, and I would definitely add this one to that list. It might be immature and selfish of him, but if a certain kind of man gets too far past his "due date," he's going to start to feel like he's justified in looking for sex somewhere else.

Birthday sex is another unarticulated expectation almost all men have. Some men will come out of their face and say, "Remember, baby, it's my birthday, and you know what I want tonight," but a lot more will just *assume* that something is going to go down. In fact, I was just talking with a buddy who was complaining about how his wife hadn't had sex with him on his birthday. He told me, "On my birthday, people were texting me, saying come on out and party, but I stayed home because I just *knew* we were going to get something poppin'. But when I came into our room, her head was under the covers and she was asleep." It had been a couple of months since his birthday, but he was still steamed. Even though he was upset, he's a good man and wouldn't consider that a justification for cheating. I know a lot of lesser men who probably would, however.

Men will also expect sex on their anniversaries (as long as they remember them). I say that only half jokingly, because when a woman makes a big deal about her husband's needing to remember their anniversary, she has unwittingly promised him sex that night. By a man's reckoning, if he does what he's "supposed" to do on his anniversary and comes through with flowers, a nice dinner and a sentimental card, then he is *definitely* expecting sex at the end of the night.

So try to get your man's unarticulated expectations out in the open. Don't bring it up during a tense moment when you can tell he's expecting sex but rather when sex isn't on the table. Maybe when you two are out for dinner, just come out and ask him, "Baby, what are your expectations for when we are going to have sex? Your birthday? After you've cleaned up the house? Gone to a movie that I wanted to see? Bought me flowers? After we've had some drinks?" You'll be surprised by how many of those he'll say yes to. In fact, he might add a few more to the list, like, "After I brought home a big paycheck . . . After I spend some time with your family . . . After I ran some errands for you . . . and some chores for me . . . After I watched the kids so you could go out with your friends." The list might end up seeming a little overwhelming to you, but at least you'll know what's being expected of you, which is much better than getting into bed blind to the fact that the man next to you is ready and waiting for sex.

What you're teaching him is how to start communicating more and expecting less. It's not necessarily going to change his expectations, but it will make them easier for you to deal with. To use an analogy, I have a friend from way back in kindergarten who only visits when he needs money. If I see his car pull up, I know why he's here. In the past, he wouldn't even try to hide what he was after. He'd walk in the door, and the first words out of his mouth would be, "My man, I got a situation on my hands and I need you to hit me off." Not an attitude that exactly put me in a giving mood. Yes, I'm his man from way back and I want to be there for him, but I didn't enjoy feeling like I was being taken for granted. I'd ultimately give him the money, but only after giving him a hard time first. "Wait, what happened to the last roll I gave you?" I'd say. Or "Hold up, before we get to that, where are things with that job I tried to set you up with? Tell me how that's going first. . . ."

To his credit, my friend picked up on how I was feeling and has learned to butter me up a bit before putting out his hand. Now when he comes over he'll say, "Hey, what's up with the fam? How's Miley doing?" Or even just "Did you catch that Knicks game last night?" It's the corniest routine ever, but it works. Even though I know what he's doing, it puts me at ease. It doesn't make me feel like I'm being used, or disrespected, so he ends up getting his money without too much of a headache.

I've had to learn to take the same approach with Justine when it comes to sex. Even though we both know what I'm after, and even though we've promised not to deny each other, I have to remember to butter her up a bit. Maybe I'll ask her about her day or tell her something funny I noticed one of the kids do at dinner. Or just rub her back for a while. She even told me once, "Don't worry. I probably already know where you're going, but I'll be much happier if you touch my hair for a while before you go trying to touch my butt."

I always try to remind men that no matter who they're sleeping with (and again, hopefully married to), their women feel the same way. Some guys like to fantasize about having a stripper or a porn star for a wife because they think someone with that background will be down for sex every night. I doubt it, though. I'm sure that when a porn star gets home, she doesn't want her man having any unarticulated expectations about sex. She probably just wants to change into some sweatpants, eat some ice cream, watch a little TV, read her magazines and then go to bed. She's not any more comfortable with having her man just expect sex than a preacher's wife is. This is why a man has to stop just expecting sex and learn how to tell his lady what he's feeling. And then put in the work—even if it's corny or a little bit forced—to help her feel that way too.

TYRESE

I want to start by taking issue with something Rev said earlier, which is that he and I are "comfortable" with communicating. I don't know about Rev, but I consider myself an *amazing* communicator. To me, being "comfortable" only makes you above average. As I said at the start of the book, I would put myself in the top 5 percent of men when it comes to communication.

Yes, I'm capable of saying exactly what I want and how I'm thinking at all times in a relationship. There's no need to be clued in or have to interpret subliminals when you're dealing with me. I am going to give it to you straight and to the point.

I'm going to share my emotions with my woman *and* with the world. A lot of men are uncomfortable with public displays of affection, but I don't change my lovey-dovey energy when other people are around, even my homies. They might call me "soft" or "whipped," but I don't sweat it. I will rub my woman's feet, massage her shoulders and tell her how much I love her in front of my entire crew.

I wasn't always moving that way. As I shared earlier, for many years my modus operandi was to create smoke screens instead of being transparent. That approach started to change, however, after my divorce, which was a very painful and humbling experience for me.

After all the court battles were waged and the legal papers were signed, I made a vow to myself: from that point forward, I would be completely up front with the woman in my life. I would lay my truth out on the table in front of her, and she could either choose to sit down and eat with me or stand up and keep it moving. I would respect either decision, but I didn't want any woman to be with me under false pretenses.

At that time, my truth was that I wasn't ready to get back into a serious relationship. I wanted to converse with women, go out to dinner and enjoy their company, but I didn't want to feel like I was tied down to them. As anyone who's been through a divorce can tell you, the process leaves you feeling very skittish toward the concept of commitment. If I was being honest with myself, then I knew that it was going to be a while before I could start to think long term with any woman.

It was time to let go of the MAN-ipulator and MAN-gician personas that used to fit me so well and just be honest on *all* counts. That meant the moment things started to progress with a woman, I told her exactly what was going through my mind: that I enjoyed being with her, but I wasn't planning on settling down anytime soon. If she was comfortable with that, if she could accept being with me while I was with other women, then we could continue the relationship and see where things went. If she felt uncomfortable with that arrangement, I would understand completely and respect her not wanting to see me anymore.

To keep it real, some women took it personally and resented my honesty, but some of them actually appreciated it because at least they knew exactly where they stood with me. It might not have been the type of footing that they preferred, but at least they weren't operating under any illusions. Believe me: when a man tells you that you stand one place with him when in truth you're standing somewhere else, that's when you end up blindly walking off emotional cliffs.

In fact, it's because of my honesty that I'm still good friends with several of the women I met during that period. They've since told me that if I had pulled my old MAN-gician routine on them, they would have eventually figured me out, broken things off and stopped speaking to me. Because I was so up-front and honest with them, they were fine moving forward with me as friends.

MAKE HIM COMFORTABLE SHARING HIS TRUTH

It took going through the fires of a divorce to burn away my connection to MAN-ipulation and deceit (as well as a lot of MAN-torship, which I'll describe shortly). As a woman, your goal should be to guide your man to a similar state without having to go through all that drama first.

And the easiest way to turn a MAN-ipulator into a truth teller is simply demonstrating that you can *handle* his truth.

When a man tells you the truth and your immediate reaction is to fly off the handle, to get loud and emotional, then he's going to retreat back into his lies. Don't get me wrong—he might have told you something that truly deserved to be met with screams, tears and insults. Still, if you react to his honesty with hysterics, it might be the last time you ever hear the truth out of his mouth. At least *willingly.*

Sure, you might be able to *pry* the truth out of him later on, or catch him red-handed in a lie, but those are Pyrrhic victories. When you're living your life trying to pull the truth out of a man or catch him in a lie, you're not really living. You deserve so much better than that.

As hard as it may be at times, stay focused on making a man feel comfortable telling you the truth. Discipline yourself to present a controlled, composed façade when you are presented with what he's done. Even if you can feel the fires of hurt and resentment burning out of control inside you, don't let him see that heat. Only let him see that cool and controlled exterior.

Just to be clear, I am in no way implying that the hurt and resentment you might feel aren't justified or don't need to be

111

addressed. No, they definitely need to be addressed, but at the *right time,* after things cool off a bit.

Instead, I'm trying to give you some perspective into a man's relationship with the truth so that you can get real facts out of him instead of those same old lies. The facts on where he sees the relationship going. The facts on what he wants to do with his life. The facts on whether or not he wants kids. The facts on whether he's really stopped drinking. The facts on whether he's really over his old girlfriend. The facts on whether or not he's stepping out on you. What you do with those facts is up to you, but you need to have them in order to empower yourself and make the right decisions in your relationship.

The first step in getting the facts is easy: simply let your man know that you're ready for them. "Baby, I'm sure you've heard this before, but I need you to be honest with me," you can tell him. "And I promise that whatever you end up telling me, I might not be happy about it, but I am not going to lose it. We will discuss it like adults."

The second step is a bit harder. The very next time he comes to you with the truth, you've got to absorb it. Even if the information he just shared makes you feel like your entire world is about to crumble, don't let him see you shaking. Pull yourself together and stand as strong and firm as you can. Take that information and process it *before* you react to it.

Here's a crucial point: whatever you do, don't start off strong and *then* fall apart if the conversation gets too hard. Often women will start off a conversation in control, but then switch into what a man perceives to be the "damsel in distress" mode. Those tears might stem from real pain over what's been revealed, but a man's not going to see it like that. He's going to think, *Aw, she just felt*

like she was losin' this argument so she turned on the waterworks.
That's going to make him feel like *he's* being manipulated and that
sharing the truth was a mistake. This is why if you feel like a conversation is going to make you break down, please do it at the very
beginning, instead of switching gears halfway through it.

Why is it so important to a man that you don't respond emotionally to hard truths? you might ask. It's difficult to say, but there
are a lot of factors that go into it. As men, we're programmed to
always try to help and comfort a crying female. Even little girls
too. I know that if my daughter and I are going back and forth
about what dress she's going to wear to the zoo or what she's getting for dessert and she begins to cry, she's going to get what she
wants. Quickly. I'm no pushover, but I'd rather have her dressed
too lightly, or let her get ice cream for the second time that day,
than deal with her tears for another moment. Her mother might
see the same tears and say, "Whatever, it's too cold out there. Put
on that sweater." But I'll do anything to make those tears go away.
Yes, a man will do anything to avoid seeing a woman cry. Including hiding the truth from her as long as possible. It's pretty much
an instinctive reaction when we see tears.

Another reason a man often can't handle watching a woman
become emotional is that he really does care about her. He really
doesn't want to see her going through any pain. That might sound
like the height of hypocrisy—I wronged you, but because I love
you, I don't want you to get upset about it—but that is *exactly* how
a lot of men feel.

In *Baby Boy,* my character, Jody, tells his girlfriend, Yvette,
played by the incomparable Taraji P. Henson, "I'm out here on
these streets every day telling these hoes the truth. I lie to you
because I care about your feelings." That line might elicit groans

from a lot of women, but again, it truly reflects a dominant male mind-set. Men often conceal their truths not because they're heartless but because they consider their women to be such a big part of their hearts. And the idea of seeing them in pain and tears feels like too much to bear.

My point is that you shouldn't provide a man with that excuse—no matter how weak it might be—to lie. Show him time and time again that you can handle his truth, from a little mole-hill like whether or not he smoked some weed while he was over at his man's house all the way up to the mountain that towers over most women's lives, which is whether or not he cheated.

Remember, men can handle *cool.* What they can't handle is heat. So if you can keep it cool no matter what gets thrown in your face, eventually the lies are going to slow down to a trickle and you'll start to get a steady stream of the truth instead.

You might not like those truths, but again, you're going to know exactly where you stand. And that's the position you want to hold in *every* relationship.

SHOW HIM YOU'RE INTERESTED

One of the realities of the male-female dynamic is that while women are usually considered much better communicators, the truth is that a lot of ladies have room for improvement in this area too. It's not entirely your fault—after years of dealing with men who don't seem like they care about what you think, it's only natural that you might begin to shut down your lines of communication a bit.

Even though men have essentially set it themselves, please don't fall into that trap. For all the detached and disinterested energy we give off, we are actually *extremely* needy creatures. We crave women's attention, interest and, most of all, approval. Nothing can fill up our sails like a woman's admiration, just as nothing can suck the wind out of them like a woman's indifference.

To give you an example, in 2011 I released an album called *Open Invitation* on my Voltron Records label. Releasing an album independently, as opposed to putting it out on a major record label, as I had always done in the past, was a nerve-wracking process. Instead of getting a budget from a label, I paid for all the elements that went into making the album—renting the studio and instruments, hiring musicians, producers, engineers, marketers and publicists—directly out of my own pocket. If the record ended up doing well, I would keep most of the profits. If it tanked, I would lose almost all of my investment. Thankfully, going independent turned out to be a fantastic decision—the album earned great reviews, revitalized my singing career, and, as I'm writing this, has sold over three hundred thousand copies—making me a verrrrry nice return on my investment.

Prior to *Open Invitation*'s release, however, I was very nervous about the record. I had heard that a prominent African-American record executive had told people that the album wouldn't sell very well because "only black people would buy a Tyrese record." Determined to prove him wrong, I spent the weeks leading up to the release tinkering with the album, trying to make it as captivating and heartfelt as possible.

Even after we had finished the final track listing, I felt the album still needed something extra. Then one night, I was struck by a vision of how much my life had changed for the better since I'd met my girlfriend. In a matter of minutes I composed a heartfelt ballad about her called "What Took You So Long." I stayed up all night working on, and then recording, it, finally putting the song to bed just as the sun came up.

The next day was a busy one at my house; the director Matt Alonzo had come over to help me edit the video for my single with Ludacris called "Too Easy," and my staff was running around trying to wrap up countless loose ends before the album's release.

That afternoon my girlfriend came over with a friend of hers named Theresa. When I saw them, I excitedly pulled them into my studio so I could play my girl the song that was written in her honor.

With my girl sitting on my lap I pressed play, confident that we were about to experience a magical moment together. "It's been taking forever/don't know where you are," my voice sang through the speakers. "You had it before I even had my heart . . ."

I was amped up, but my girl listened to the song impassively. When it was over, she simply said, "That was nice, I liked it. Hey, could I go show Theresa the 'Too Easy' video now?"

No happy tears. No huge hugs. No blushing. No hands on her heart. Not even, "That was beautiful. Thank you, baby."

Just "I liked it."

I'm going to be real—I was fuming. I couldn't believe that I had played her a song (written in her honor, no less) looking for some sort of feedback or energy but hadn't gotten anything in return. It was such a deflating moment for me.

Later, when my girlfriend sensed how I was feeling, she started making excuses. She claimed she had so many favorites on the album that it was hard for her to get excited about yet another one. She claimed she didn't realize the song was for the album but thought it was just something I was messing around with. She even claimed she felt a little shy opening up with her friend there.

There might have been some truth to those reasons, especially the last one, but the bottom line was that at the very moment when I needed aggressive support and encouragement, the energy I received was tepid at best.

I'll admit that I didn't respond in the most mature way. "You know what, this song is no longer dedicated to you," I told her in my coldest voice. "Don't worry, I'll find someone else to dedicate it to, someone who will give me the response, as a lover and an artist, that I need." She started to protest, saying, "No, it wasn't that," but I wasn't done. "I don't give a crap if you didn't think this song was as good as some of the other ones on my album. As my girlfriend, you should be trying to make me feel good, amazing even, for writing a song like that for you."

Perhaps I could have expressed my disappointment better, but I really felt abandoned in that situation. Despite all the times I'd told her how stressful it was to make an album, especially one I was putting out myself, she still didn't appreciate my need for feedback and encouragement.

We eventually got past it, but that was a moment in our relationship.

HE NEEDS CONSTRUCTIVE CRITICISM

That story is an example of why it's so important to be completely tuned in to your man when he tries to bounce ideas off you. Remember, a man has a different relationship to the truth in his professional career than he does in his romantic relationships. As I stated, a man often needs to be coaxed toward the truth in his romantic relationships, but when it comes to his ideas and visions, he's almost always ready to jump right in.

It's certainly how men deal with each other. If a man isn't feeling something that another man is working on, he's going to tell him right away. At least if he's a straight-up dude (which is the only kind of man you want in your life anyway). I know that if someone reads me a script that doesn't feel right, or sings me a hook that doesn't seem to fit, I'm going to say so. "Naw, son, that's not it. Let's try again." And I'm going to sit there with that man and work on it again and again until we finally get it right.

This is why when a man is sharing his ideas with you, you have to try to break out of that shell. If you think the idea is great, then tell him. If you think it needs fine-tuning, then tell him that too. If you think it'll never work and he's wasting his time, then definitely tell him that. Make him keep coming back to you with ideas until you're convinced. Whatever you do, give him a real answer.

Trust me, a man will not only appreciate your feedback but he will come to rely on it too. I'm extremely sensitive about my work, but I still want the people I'm close to—especially my woman—to be honest with me when I'm seeking feedback. If my girlfriend had said, "I kinda like the melody, but the lyrics feel corny" or "It's got a nice melody, but I feel the tempo is waay too slow," I might have been a little disappointed, but it would have been with myself as *an artist,* not with her as *a girlfriend.* I would have considered what she'd suggested, and if it had seemed like there had been merit to her opinion, I would have gone back and made the necessary changes. Or maybe I would have said, "Shoot, I swore you were going to love this, baby. But I'm still really feelin' it, so I think I'll keep it the way it is."

As an artist, and as a man, I can handle a difference of opinion. What I can't handle is no opinion. That's why one of the worst ways you can mess up is by saying *nothing* or acting indifferent when a man communicates an idea to you.

So even if you aren't feeling his idea, or you have some thoughts on how it could be improved, you've got to tell him anyway. Never keep your perceptions inside. Otherwise he will shut down on you.

As a girlfriend or wife, you want to be the FIRST person a man wants to turn to when he has an idea he's really excited about. You never want to surrender that position to anyone else, *especially* another woman. It could be one of his coworkers, someone at your church, even someone he met on Facebook. If your man starts going to her for the feedback and support that he's not getting from you, then it's only a matter of time before he's getting something else from her too.

You also don't want your man relying on other men for that feedback. For instance, there have been times when I've texted or called Rev with some great news about my career and he will seem more genuinely excited and happy for me than my girl does. He doesn't have to do that—he's a legend with plenty of things on his own plate to deal with—but he makes sure that I feel great every single time I share with him.

I appreciate his support so much, but I never want to be relying solely on Rev or another person *outside* my home to make me feel good about something. The support I get from the world should be in *addition* to what I'm getting at home. To be real, I don't always feel that way, unfortunately. In fact, I have told my girl on more than one occasion, "I don't really know or believe that you're really happy for me . . . because of the way you react to my blessing."

That's not a question you want floating around in your man's mind. You want your man to be excited about sharing good news with you instead of wondering whether or not you're truly happy for him.

Having said that, I understand that there are some men for whom it might be harder to show that support. I'm talking about the kind of man who is always plotting ways to make more money but never wants to put in the work to get any of those ideas off the ground—the type of guy who is like Fred Flintstone, where every day seems to bring a new get-rich-quick scheme.

If your man is one of those guys, then yes, I understand why after a while you'd stop giving him feedback. If you've heard it all before and have never seen any follow-through, then it's reasonable that you don't want to invest any more energy in his ideas.

Most men, however, aren't like that. I believe that most men are not only willing but also eager to put in the work necessary to improve their situations.

CHAPTER 5

MALE VALIDATION IS HIS REAL MOTIVATION

TYRESE

I've been speaking to the ladies so far, but I want to switch gears and address the fellas directly for a second.

I've hesitated to do so up until now because I've been told it's a waste of time to try to speak to men through a book like this. That men simply aren't interested in hearing another man's advice on how to improve their relationships. Will they seek out another man's insights on how to improve their bank accounts or their career paths? Sure. But anything having to do with relationships? No way.

I refuse to believe that. I know that when individuals like Rev and myself open up, other men won't just tune us out. That's because over the years we've both established ourselves as the men that other guys can relate to and trust. Maybe it's an unspoken street code or just real men doing real things. Either way, real men have always supported us in everything we do and have done.

So ladies, it's critical that the man in your life hears the message that I am about to share. Not the entire book, just part of this one chapter right here. So go get him and tell him that you've got something for him to read.

And here's what I want to tell him: Fellas, it's time that we're honest with ourselves. It's time to admit that despite what we might tell ourselves, whether we're actually conscious of it or not, the people we're working so hard to impress aren't actually all the ladies out there.

Nope. You think more about getting props from other *men*.

Yep! I can hear y'all now. "You trying to say I'm out here sweatin' other dudes? You really on one, man!" But before you drop the book and run back to your game, hold on. This is going somewhere!

You wasn't expecting that, I know, but relax. Stay with me.

If we are being honest with ourselves then I'ma flat out say we do dumb things seeking validation from other men.

Don't get me wrong—you probably desire those women— of course we do! You probably missed it, but I even wrote earlier that women's sex is like water to us. Either they take care of us and quench that thirst or we die. That's how serious it is to us. Still, our addiction to a woman's sex is mainly a physical addiction.

Emotionally, what we're actually unconsciously addicted to is validation from other *men*.

Sadly, we're not even aware of it most of the time, but it's true.

From the time we're young boys often up until the day we die, many of us live our lives secretly (and in some cases openly) consumed with our perceived standing in the eyes of other men.

That longing for approval is what steers so many of our decisions and actions.

Don't believe me? Then let's consider some of our favorite activities.

We can start with cars. Most men spend a lot of time and money on their rides. I know I have. There have been times when I've dropped a small fortune at a showroom just because I craved that new-car smell so much. A smell that to me is synonymous with success and having "made it."

Who was I really trying to impress with that ride, though? Women? When it comes to cars, all most women really care about is that their man has a nice, clean car. The 36-inch rims, candy-color painted exteriors, racing stripes, and tinted windows; let's be real: most women don't care about that stuff. Those extras are really to impress other dudes. Hey, I'll admit that outside of impressing chicks, part of my motivation for getting a white Maserati was knowing dudes would look at me and say, "Look at Tyrese smashing in that Gran Turismo. He out there doing it! ..."

It's a similar dynamic with working out at the gym. Or being on a football or basketball court. Don't get me wrong, there's no doubt that women like a fit man with nice muscles. But most of that heavy lifting in the gym is really about making a scene and competing with other dudes. Do you really think women care about how much you can bench? Of course not. As long as a man is lean and a little cut, most women are good. All the other stuff, if we're being truthful, is to impress other dudes so that when they see you they're going to think, "He's ripped. I need to get back in the gym myself," or "That dude could probably take me out. Let me watch how I act around him."

123

For another example, let's consider our obsession with sexy models. Yup, models are beautiful, and we are undoubtedly drawn to that beauty. But outside of a beautiful face, let's be real: most models don't have the types of bodies that men really desire. Small boobs and flat butts are kinda old school. Some dudes still like it, but we crave that Pow Wow. We like to drive on curves, not straightaways! Or as my friend's grandfather once told him, "Remember, a man doesn't go to the butcher for bones."

If we are to believe the fashion magazines and the media, however, the most "desirable" women are usually superskinny. Is that what we really want as men, or is that what we've come to believe other men respect the most? Do we want a girl who's short but also nice and thick? Or do we want the validation that comes from walking into a club with a six-foot stunner that has all the right assets in place? If we're being real, we're going to say that stunner. Because as I mentioned earlier, there's nothing better to a man than walking into a club with a bunch of bad chicks on his arm, the kinda chicks that will steal the whole show, and soaking up the envy from all the other dudes. I'm talking about getting a private table with them and ordering fifteen bottles just so the club can light up with fireworks as they walk the champagne over to your table; let me tell you, that's a pure man ego trip right there.

After experiencing it just one time, you want to experience that high again and again. It becomes like a drug, which is why you see so many famous men with new models on their arms practically every night. Those models could be—and trust me, often are—terrible in bed. They couldn't do half the tricks that a thick shorty from around the way loves to throw down. Yet it doesn't matter to those men because they're more addicted to validation from other men than they are to great sex.

THE SILENT KILLER

It's not only rich guys ballin' out with models and bottles, though. The need for validation affects men on every level of society. And nowhere is that more evident than on the streets, in the hood.

Being born and raised in Watts, I've witnessed so many brothers pay a hard price for their validation issues. Brothas who've been taken out by what I call the "silent killer." When you're in on the streets, it's very easy to get sucked into hood stuff like who's feared and who has the most respect. You want to prove that you're the hardest gangsta, that you're going to be the first one to pull the trigger, that no one else has a heart as cold as yours. That might go over some of y'all heads, but you real cats from the block know exactly what I'm speaking on.

But let me also say this to the real men reading this: no matter how much work you put in on your block, no matter how big a legend you're tryin' to be in your hood, no matter how much money you're getting in the streets, do you know what it's all worth in the end?

Nothing.

That's because when your dope hustle inevitably lands you in jail, or your trigger game gets you locked up, do all those dudes whose validation you craved so badly hold you down?

Hell, no.

None of those dudes you've been going out of your way to impress will ever be there. I repeat: *never!* Not even remotely.

It's not until you get sent away that you realize who was really holding you down. And it wasn't the block.

It wasn't the gangs whose colors you wore so proudly. It wasn't those homies whose validation you needed so badly. It was the *women* in your life. It was the wife, the fiancée, the girlfriend, the mother, the auntie or grandmother you ignored all those years when they begged you to leave the streets and the hood dudes alone. It was the girlfriend you disrespected because your need to be seen with a steady stream of new women was more important to you than her steady love. It was the baby momma who never got enough for new furniture, or a nicer apartment, because all your money went toward gear, jewelry, and whips.

Sadly, we often treat those powerful women in our lives like mosquitos, trying to swat them away when they keep popping up and annoying the crap out of us. Yet they're the only ones keeping it real with us, telling us to get off the block, stop running with gangs, and overall "stop being dumb."

Yet despite your having treated them so poorly, *they* are going to be the ones who always put money on your books. *They* are the ones who will write you long letters to keep you encouraged, the ones who will not only accept your collect calls but will be waiting by the phone for them. *They* are the ones who will take seven-hour bus rides to visit you every month just so you can see your kids and get a fresh reminder of why it's so important that you stay sane.

And that, my friend, is if you're lucky.

If you're lucky, you're sitting in a cell waiting for a woman to write or visit you. Man, who really wants to spend each and every day surrounded by other dudes, constantly worrying about being attacked or raped. To spend your nights jerking off with mayonnaise and butter. If you're lucky, you get to look forward to fifteen more years of taking orders from other men. Men who look at you as if you're an animal.

Who would embrace a lifestyle where what I just described is the best-case scenario? I don't know what you on, but not me!

I can remember watching an episode of *Locked Up* and seeing this OG who was only about forty but had already done twenty years behind bars. He was explaining that Grandma had raised him and always shown him love after his drugged-out-mother left him for dead, but she had recently passed away. All he wanted to do was say good-bye to his grandmother, the woman who had raised him when no one else cared, but they wouldn't let him out of jail, even for just one day, for her funeral.

After he finished telling that story, he just looked at the camera so sadly and said, "Man, if I knew then what I know now I would not be up in this place." And when he said that, it was like he jumped through my TV set and shook me by the shoulders. It's not even like I was living a lifestyle that would have put me at risk of going to jail, but the helplessness in that man's face made me realize that I had to be extra careful not to ever wind up behind bars.

Again, what's it all worth in the end? Being a depressed OG *only* if you're lucky? If you're unlucky, then your final street validation comes in the form of being shot dead. So that your family can sit there in the front row at your funeral, hoping that it's all a nightmare and you're going to get up out of that coffin.

Or a car ride with your "friends" that you never come back from. Maybe you'll get that final level of "hood stripes," or hood validation, ending up with your face on a mural next to "RIP" and the homies pouring out a little liquor in your honor before they take a sip. At least they haven't forgotten about you, right?

Don't you think you're worth so much more than that? Then act like it. Stop worrying about impressing these dudes so much and start focusing on finding that validation in the love and respect of the people who really care about you.

I call male validation the silent killer because even though it strikes every day, it's rarely spoken of.

Until now.

So if no one has ever told you this before, I'm telling you now that your life and what God has in mind for you is greater than your circumstances. God didn't create any of us to be average. So if you've made it this far in this chapter, you wont be able to say you didn't know any better. From this point on you need to decide you love yourself enough to do things differently.

WHO ARE YOU WORKING FOR?

It was five years ago that I finally quit seeking the validation of other men.

Now I seek a woman's validation. Or, to be more accurate, a five-year-old girl's. That's right, my daughter Shayla. I like to say that she's "my employer," because I truly work for her.

Everything I do is to ensure that she has a better childhood that I did, that she has all the advantages and opportunities that I never experienced. Sometimes she doesn't get to see her daddy on weekends because I'm out here grinding so hard. I can't lie; that hurts. But it's only for her. Not for anyone else.

In fact, my motto is that I won't leave my house unless I know that what I'm doing and where I'm going is going to benefit my daughter.

Now that I'm working for my daughter, it means I can't worry that much about the dudes I came up with on the streets, or even some members of my own family. That might sound like a very harsh thing to say, but as I've grown older, I've come to realize that it's not my job to pay everybody's bills. That it's not my job to put clothes on their backs and cars in their driveways.

I used to think it was. I used to give things away till I was down to my last dollar, not because I was such a good guy but because I was so afraid of people saying I "changed" or that I was "acting Hollywood." I was seeking validation. From the block. From my family. From people who weren't even happy for me but instead were secretly jealous of my blessings.

Thankfully, I don't need their validation anymore. I don't feel compelled to be around people who make me feel bad about being blessed. Because I realized a lot of my family and friends would manipulate me and make me feel bad about being so blessed.

I've come to terms with the realities of the dysfunction I grew up in and find that I don't really want to be around some people in my family too much because they bring me pain. After all, it's called "Merry Christmas," not "Horrible Christmas." We have to remember that in life we have more control over the outcome of our minutes, our hours, our days, weeks, months, and years that we believe we do. It's OK, like I did, to decide that you no longer want to be a victim in your own house and be on the receiving end of other people's dysfunction.

I'm not suggesting that you cut off your entire crew. I still hang out with some of my boys who have been there from day one. But only the ones who have their own—their own jobs, their own families and, most importantly, their own dreams. The ones who honestly want to see me do well but aren't *depending* on me to do well. Which means that if I do happen to come through in a new Benz, or show up to their house with a beautiful woman, they're not intimidated or resentful. They're happy to see my blessings instead of scheming on ways to block them.

My attitude toward my old homies or my family members might sound selfish or egotistical, but I'm not saying any of this out of spite. I've truly got a lot of love for all the street dudes out there. I want y'all to reach the same heights I've reached. Which is why I'm speaking so candidly on this dynamic.

Trust me, in order to reach your full potential, you have to be prepared to leave those streets behind. You have to decide that you love yourself too much to keep giving your power away to jealous, dysfunctional, and unnecessary people, even if once upon a time they "held you down" or "had your back."

Trust me, they weren't holding you "down." They were holding you "back."

Don't let them do that anymore. I promise you, once you break free from the grip of the streets, you'll be amazed at just how high you can soar personally and professionally.

That was the end of my rap directly to you fellas, but I promise that if you stick around or, even better, start from the *beginning* of the book, you'll find there's a lot of information here that will help you evolve as a man and sharpen your skills as a husband.

And a final message to all you fathers out there. It might be a little off topic, but it still needs to be said.

Just as I only work for my daughter now, you're only working for your kids too. Whether you know it or not.

The question is, are you working to improve their chances in life, or are you working to add another member to what I call the "lost generation?"

The sad truth is we are among the lost generation of fatherless sons and daughter. Children with deep-rooted anger, abandonment, and validation issues because a father, maybe like you, let the wars you had with your baby momma or ex come in between your relationship with your innocent kids.

I know that relationship might not be your fault, but I also want you to know that it's only the kids that are suffering because of your act. Now please understand that you're not under attack here, I'm in this with you. I know all too well that it's hard for most of us to be what were never raised by: a great father.

But I want you to sit still and just ask yourself why are you so OK with your child potentially being raised by wolves? Why aren't you fighting against that fate for you child? Because if your daughter doesn't have your guidance, trust me, she's gonna seek it elsewhere. And if your son in the course of trying to figure out what it really is to be a man, ends up looking up to the wrong type of man for direction, are you really OK with that? Remember, kids fall in love with the people they get used to. So make sure they're falling in love with you, not someone you don't even know. When you stop fighting for that love, you *are*, my brother, contributing to the lost generation.

That's why I want you at this very moment to take on the mission that by any means necessary, you will have a relationship with your child. You will regain that access and re-spark that relationship with your child.

You will get resistance but stay in it and stay at it. Please man up and do whatever it takes to be a father to your child no matter what she might say about you or how many insults she hurls your way.

And ladies, if that baby daddy or ex that you can't stand does start fighting to get back into his child's life, don't try to shut that door. Think about what having a healthy, loving relationship with their father will mean to your child, and then push all your issues aside and clear a path in your heart to allow that man to have access. The devil wants nothing more than to break up our families, marriages, and relationships with our kids. Don't make the devil happy. Stay in it and at it, no matter how much drama you're dealing with. And trust, me I'm saying this to myself as I'm saying it to you.

Thank you for hearing me out on that. But I also know the ladies are getting impatient for more information, so let me get back to them.

MALE GROUPIES

Ladies, I want to touch on another type of man whose need for validation might not be as obvious, but who still lets it seriously erode his relationships with women: the type of dude I call a "male groupie."

Ladies, y'all know the type of guy I'm talking about. This guy will do pretty much anything to court you. Because you're sexy, as soon as he meets you, he's offering you shopping sprees, jewelry, paying your rent, flying you places—you know, all the stuff you didn't earn from someone you just met. Basically all the tricks that MAN-gicians will use.

What makes a male groupie very difficult to uncover, however, is that on the surface he seems to be a very safe and reasonable man to get involved with. He certainly ain't a thug—he'll tell you how much he loves you, he'll go out of his way to make you feel appreciated, as well as happily go out to dinner with your parents or meet up with your coworkers for a drink. A male groupie will be more than happy to do everything a street dude won't do for you.

Except tell the truth.

Not even because he's necessarily a bad guy at heart but because he's terrified of losing a beautiful woman like you. I've already touched on this, but I need to reemphasize just how much validation a man receives from other men when he's got a beautiful woman on his side.

As a man, you can be validated by money. Validated by athletic achievement. Validated by intellectual respect. Validated by critical acclaim. A beautiful woman on your arm, however, trumps *all* of them.

In many ways it's similar to what happens to male athletes. As soon as a boy shows he's a gifted athlete and becomes the star of his team, grown men start treating him differently. They let him act up during practice and slide with his schoolwork. They buy him sneakers and sweatsuits even though he doesn't even say thank you. When he's failing in school, instead of sitting him down and saying, "Hey, fool, get your grades up or else," they convince his teachers to let him pass. Which means that talented young athletes grow up never hearing no from most of the men in their lives. So why do you think so many athletes cheat on their wives, get into trouble with the law and can't seem to keep their finances straight when they're older? Because no one ever kept it real with them.

So many beautiful women end up falling into the same trap. For years and years male groupies cater to them, never challenging or pushing them to be anything other than beautiful. After all, what does a male groupie care about helping a woman develop her intellect and expanding her horizons?

The problem is that as these women get older, they don't know how to deal with men who do keep it real with them and are willing to challenge them. They only know how to be the star in a relationship, instead of having equal billing with a man. And let me tell you from experiences how groupies treat stars: they lie to you. They do and say whatever they think you want to hear because they're afraid of being cut off. Period. This is why so many beautiful women are in terrible relationships.

I see this happen all the time in the entertainment industry. I see gorgeous, intelligent and dynamic women end up in relationships with men who seem more like butlers or servants than their equals. These women are so used to being the star that they're more comfortable dating a backup dancer than the other headliner on their tour. They'd rather be with one of the carpenters on their movie set than with a male costar. The headliner or male lead might actually keep it real with them, but they know that the backup dancer or carpenter ain't going to do nothin' that might mess up their meal ticket.

That's why I really believe that as a beautiful woman, you must challenge yourself to look past the male groupies that are always surrounding you. I'm talking not only to Hollywood actresses and R&B singers and models, but also to beautiful, attractive women from any walk of life. You might have never left your hometown and are happy there teaching kindergarten, but your beauty and body are still going to attract plenty of male groupies.

Instead of dating yet another groupie, challenge yourself with a man who's been around a lot of beautiful women before. Find a man who isn't terrified of losing you. It's not that he doesn't value you; he's simply secure enough in himself as a man that he doesn't need your beauty as validation of his manliness.

I was definitely still a male groupie even after I first got famous. As I mentioned earlier, when I first started pulling beautiful women, I was literally in disbelief that they were interested in me. Even though I was acting cocky and cool, the whole time in my mind I was thinking, *How the hell did I pull this off?*

The problem was, our relationships were completely superficial. I didn't really care what those beautiful women said or even felt; I just wanted to know that I could sleep with them. Period. And then once I'd proven that I could, it was on to the next one.

After a while, however, I stopped being so starstruck. While I was still extremely attracted to beautiful women, I didn't feel like I'd just won the lottery every time I slept with one. As a result, I was able to keep it real with them, instead of feeling compelled to tell them only what I thought they wanted to hear. My relationships became stronger and more rewarding for both of us. They were far from perfect, but they were certainly better than when I had been behaving like a groupie. At least I was challenging and engaging the women in my life, instead of just being content to have them on my arm and in my bed.

I won't lie: choosing a confident man who's experienced with beautiful women can present its own set of dangers. A man who's been with a lot of voluptuous, beautiful women probably has some combination of the gift of gab, good looks and money, if not all three. Undoubtedly, there are going to be a lot of other women looking to edge you out of the picture.

With that being said, what are you doing to do, continue

to settle for male groupies who still end up breaking your heart anyway?

Yes, that same man whose whole world seemed to revolve around you and who claimed he couldn't live without you when you two were courting will often start singing a different tune once he's "had" you. When you're finally "his girl" and it's just the two of you sitting at home on a Saturday night and feeling bored, you're going to realize that he actually isn't that into you at all. Don't get me wrong, when the two of you are out at a party or hanging out in the club he probably turns it on and starts flaunting you again, but after a while, when it's just the two of you at the house, none of that spark is there anymore. It's all just fizzle.

He acts bored, or even worse, resentful of you. Everything he says is short, and he seems irritated. You wonder, *What the hell happened? This guy seemed soooo in love with me just a few months ago.*

Well, here's what happened: he was *never* that into you. He was into the validation. He was into the props. He was into the envy *and* the respect he felt from other men. But he wasn't that into *you*. Women already understand that a man is willing and able to fake emotions in order to get sex. Y'all underestimate, however, just how much we'll fake for *validation*.

Hell, we'll get ourselves killed for it out on the streets. So you don't think we'll lie to a woman about how we feel for some validation? We basically put ourselves in jail for it. So you don't think we'll put ourselves in a dysfunctional relationship for some too? Of course we will.

The male groupie might come with a very different energy from the street thugs, but ladies, please be careful, because he's just as likely to let you down in the long run.

WOMEN SEEK VALIDATION TOO

Ladies, I hope reading this has helped you better appreciate the depth of men's desire for validation from other men. It's a dynamic that shouldn't be completely unfamiliar to you either, because certainly a lot of y'all seek validation from other women too.

It's probably most evident in your relationship with clothes and makeup. Just as men will spend hours obsessing over cars that women will barely pay attention to, women will worry about fashions and styles that men will certainly never notice. A woman will spend forever trying to figure out which eyeliner goes best with her new dress, even though her man is never going to notice no matter what decision she makes. A man doesn't care about makeup or dresses. He cares about how fat your butt is. The name of whoever designed the fabric that's covering that butt is irrelevant to him.

Don't get me wrong, I appreciate the value in staying stylish and looking good. The truth is, however, that no conversation between two men (or at least two straight men) has ever started with, "Yo, you should have seen this Berkin bag this chick had in the club last night. And her red bottom game was serious, my god! The red and white patterns were crazy." Nah, more likely they were talking about how later that night they wanted to see those red bottoms up!

So while they might not be talking about women's shoe game, almost every second of every day, however, somewhere in the world a man is telling his friend, "Man, you should have seen the ass on this girl I just saw walking down the street. And her legs was like kawpow! It was crazy!" The conversation might be taking place in English, Turkish, or Japanese, but somewhere right now those thoughts are being conveyed.

I'm not saying that you necessarily even want it, but if male attention is what you are after, then let me give you a tip: instead of wasting your money on a bag or a new dress, you'd be much better off spending it on a personal trainer twice a week who'd help you get your butt tight and your stomach nice and flat.

Trust me, if you walk down the street in some shorts that show off a flat tummy and nice calves, you could be holding your phone and wallet in a greasy paper bag and dudes are still going to try to holla.

Men simply don't sweat all the superficial details of clothing and style that women do. To share an example, I have a friend, a successful screenwriter, who's currently dating a woman from Asia. When he first met her, she was still a little rough around the edges. It wasn't her fault—she'd literally come from one of those villages where they still wear those cone-shaped hats and use water buffalo to work the rice paddies.

Not surprisingly, though they met in the States, her fashion game wasn't exactly on point yet. She was wearing outfits that most of y'all would be embarrassed to wear around the house, let alone out on the street.

None of that bothered my friend. Behind all her fashion struggles and messed-up hair, he saw a complete package. In other words, a sharp brain, good heart and great body. He could teach her style and sexiness down the road, but she was already in possession of the most important qualities. So he stuck with her, and today he has a serious keeper on his hands.

That is not to say that you should stop getting your hair done, or that it's OK to walk around in sweatpants and a T-shirt all the time as long as your legs look good. No, I'm just trying to help you understand that like men, you ladies can very often fall into the trap of seeking validation from other women.

Never forget that men really don't get hung up on the things that other women would have you believe we do. If we approach you at a bar, it isn't because you have a skirt on versus a dress, or wear black instead of a bright color, just as we don't holla at you in the streets because you are wearing a designer we like or because your hat matches your shirt. Sorry, but books that try to sell you on those sorts of theories aren't giving it to you straight. They're selling you a dream. For better or worse, Rev and I are giving you reality.

TELL HIM HOW GREAT HE IS

By addressing men's validation issues, I'm not suggesting you automatically give them a pass for making the wrong decisions in life. Or that you should reward them for listening to the streets over the people who truly love them.

Instead, I'm simply trying to help you be aware of all the different forces that shape and influence a man—forces you might not see when you look at him but are often still affecting him. Helping you better recognize a man's motivations is one of the fundamental goals of this book.

If it's a little depressing to think about just how much of a hold those forces have on many men, the good news is that if they can get more validation at home, they won't be so desperate for it out in the streets. If a man feels great and appreciated when he's with his woman and his family, he won't feel as compelled to go hurtling down so many dangerous, dead-end paths when he's back out in the world.

That's probably an annoying message for some of you to hear. You might think, *He needs more validation? Well, I'm tired. I've been taking care of the kids and holding down a job. I want somebody to tell me I look pretty, that I'm beautiful, that I'm appreciated. What about my validation?*

If that's what is going through your mind, it's an understandable frustration. All I can tell you is that without validation, a man isn't going to make it. Not at home and not in the streets. A woman, however, just might. For better or for worse, women have proven themselves adept at surviving without validation. Y'all are like camels in the desert. If validation is like water, women have figured out how to go a long time without a swig. Men are closer to horses. If we don't constantly stay hydrated, we're not going to last long.

That doesn't mean I'm suggesting you go around telling an irresponsible and inconsiderate dude that he's the best thing that ever happened to you. No, all I'm asking is that if you do have a man that you love, a man who hasn't stepped out on you and who is, all in all, a fundamentally good person, then tell him.

Let him know.

DON'T DENY HIM VALIDATION

Women have a bad habit of letting everyone BUT their man know how much they love him. Just how greatly they appreciate him. It's a condition not unlike the lack of creative feedback I just spoke about.

You'll tell your momma how great your man is. You'll tell

your girlfriends how much you value him. You might even tell his friends when he's not around. But when it's just the two of you at home, when there's no one to feel uptight in front of, you get tight lipped instead of giving him that validation.

Please try to think of validation as a kind of encouragement that a man really needs. In my previous book, *How to Get Out of Your Own Way*, I spoke about making sure that when your man does something right, you let him know that you notice. I know it might seem otherwise, but a man wants nothing more than to know that you're pleased with what he's done.

I'm constantly having this issue with my girlfriend. One time, despite being incredibly busy on a movie project, I shut everything down so I could fly back to L.A. and surprise her with a romantic weekend. We had a great time going out to eat, walking on the beach, catching a movie—the works. I didn't expect her to send me a thank-you card or make a huge deal about it, but I did expect her to at least let me know that she appreciated the gesture. But she never did.

So once I got back on set, I sent her a text to let her know I was really frustrated with her inability to verbalize how she feels about me. "Let me tell you what's messed up: right now your friends know much more about how much you appreciate me stepping up as a man than I do," I wrote. "I think your reasoning is that if you give me too many compliments or openly show me how much I do mean to you, then my good behavior is going to stop. But it's not true. Just the opposite. I'm going to be encouraged to keep going in that direction because I really do want that positive feedback from you."

My girlfriend called me back right away and insisted that I was overreacting.

"Something's wrong with you," she said, annoyed. "Everything always has to turn into an ego-feeding frenzy with you. Why is it never enough to just do something nice? After you do it, you always need to know that people are sitting around saying nice things about you and giving you compliments." She also claimed I was wrong about her motives. "It's not about worrying that the compliments are going to stop," she told me. "It just that I don't feel the need to just sit here and tell you how amazing you are. Look, I loved that you dropped everything and surprised me. If I happen to mention how great it was with my friends, that's fine. But I don't want to feel pressured to tell *you* all the time how amazing I think you are. You should already know that's how I feel."

She had a point. Like most men, I do have an ego that constantly needs to be fed. Maybe even more so than most men. The way to deal with such an ego, however, is not to starve it, because if you deny validation to a man who needs it, he will seek it elsewhere.

I never want to feel like I'm searching for approval, whether it's on the streets or at home. So, being the communicator that I am, I texted her my needs so there would be no confusion moving forward. I very clearly stated, "Validating me isn't something extra u can do in the relationship every once and a while. Being a steady source of validation is an actual *responsibility* of yours."

Some women might not be comfortable with the idea of being "responsible" for keeping their man validated, but there's really no other way to put it. Giving a good man validation isn't an option or a luxury or a reward. No, it's a responsibility. Just like a dog owner has a responsibility to walk the dog when he needs it, as a woman you have a responsibility to validate a good man. We know what happens when dogs don't get walked, and the results are often just as distasteful for a man who doesn't get validated.

Again, I am not asking you to validate a man who doesn't deserve it. I'm just saying that if you tell your friends how good the sex is, then make sure you tell him too. If you tell your mother how great he is with the kids, then tell him too. If you tell your coworkers how much you appreciated the little gift he brought you back from his last trip, then make sure you tell him too. It's really impossible to overstate how important validation is to a man. So before you give it to anyone else, make sure he gets it first.

REV RUN

I had originally planned on starting this with a speech about how Tyrese was going a bit overboard again with this whole validation rap. Because for me there is only one man whose validation *I* seek, and that's the Lord's.

But then a funny thing happened. While I was working on that intro, I found out that RUN DMC had been asked to play the Made In America festival in Philadelphia, a concert being put together by Jay-Z. It would represent our first performance since the death of Jam Master Jay over ten years ago. It was a very big deal, and I knew it was only a matter of time before my phone started blowing up with congratulatory calls from my friends. So I sat back and waited. And waited. And waited. But the calls and texts and emails I expected never came.

Finally, the next day, I was talking to a friend about an unrelated topic when the subject of the concert came up. "I can't wait," he told me. "It's going to be incredible."

"You really think so?" I asked.

"Of course," he replied. "How could any real hip-hop fan not be excited for that?"

"Well, it's just that when the story broke, I figured you would call or send me a text to say congrats or can't wait. But you didn't, and truthfully, no one really did. So I was beginning to wonder if people were really that excited."

"Naw, it wasn't that at all," my friend replied. "I was excited—both as a fan and for you as a friend—when I saw the story, but I figured, 'He's Rev Run. He doesn't need me calling him up every time something good happens. If he's going to take congratulatory calls, he probably wants them to be from Jay-Z, Will Smith or someone like that.' "

"I get it," I sighed.

"Man, you are so sensitive," my friend laughed. "You're Run from RUN DMC. You could never lift another finger for the rest of your life and people like me in their thirties or forties are still going to love you for what you've already given us. So it's not going to even occur to us that you need that reaffirmation or validation. But I see that maybe you do. So I'll text next time."

We laughed about it some more, but when I was thinking about the conversation later on that night, it occurred to me that my friend was right. I really am very sensitive. It's not that my original opening was false—ultimately, as much as I'd like to hear that people are excited about a RUN DMC concert, I'm much more concerned about my standing in God's eyes.

But if I'm being truthful, then I have to admit that I am pretty sensitive. Even though a rapper isn't ever supposed to say this, I guess I really do need to know that other people appreciate me and are excited about what I do. Hey, I'm human.

And if I'm being honest with myself, then I'll also admit that much of what Tyrese says about cars is true; one of the reasons I like to keep a Rolls parked in my driveway at all times is that it gives me a certain sense of validation. That's also why I like to fly in private planes or stay in fancy hotels. Even though I'm focused on earning God's approval, I still have little moments seeking a bit too much in validation from other men.

BE THAT SECURITY BLANKET

Thankfully, my hunger for male validation isn't nearly as powerful as it used to be when I was "on top of the world" with RUN DMC. In retrospect, it seemed like everything I did back then was to win the approval and acceptance of other men.

Our music certainly reflected that. Other MCs at the time were wearing eyeliner and rockin' Jheri curls so that they would look cute to the ladies, but we didn't want to have *anything* to do with being sex symbols. We didn't sing love ballads. We rapped hard rhymes over big beats that were designed to get other men hyped up. We wanted to make the music that other men would scream and fight to; music that would be the theme music for whoever wanted to prove he was the baddest dude on the block. We were positive, but we toed the line too. In fact, one of the things that came out while we were working on this book and absolutely blew Tyrese's mind was that Tupac was on his way to see RUN DMC in Las Vegas when he was murdered. It's true, we were this close to signing with Suge Knight and Death Row Records and were planning on hooking up the very night that tragedy occurred. So while we were not thugs, we did have some of that energy.

You might have thought that selling millions of records, landing on the cover of magazines and having our videos played on MTV, as well as having the respect of a rapper like Tupac, would have sated that hunger for validation. You would think that if anyone from that era wouldn't have had male validation issues, it would have been Run from RUN DMC. Just the opposite, however, was true.

Rather than feeling secure in my standing with other men, it was as if each accolade I got only made me crave validation even more. No matter how many penthouse suites, bags of weed, groupies and limos I stuffed into the void, nothing seemed to fill up the empty space I had inside of me. I was a fiend for validation and approval, but there wasn't any drug strong enough to give me the fix I needed. Believe me, Tyrese was not exaggerating just how powerful a man's need for validation from other men can be.

Thankfully, once God came into my life that constant yearning for validation faded away. Like I said, I still have moments. But God has poured so much love into those formerly empty spaces that they don't define me anymore.

God blessed me with the ultimate deliverance from neediness, but I have to give a lot of credit to my wife as well. She's helped me get past any insecurities I still struggle with by sharing her strength with me. In fact, she was the inspiration for a Tweet I sent out just the other day: "Ladies: stop saying your partner is insecure. When someone you love is feeling insecure, secure them up. Be their security." Justine spends so much time securing me up, and I love her for that.

Where I disagree with Tyrese, however, is over the premise that women can somehow deal with a lack of validation better than men can. I believe that women actually need validation just as much as, if not *more* than, men. Which is why I tell men all the time that they should never let their women feel insecure. It is their *job* to be their security.

Tyrese called it a "responsibility" earlier, but I think it's actually even more than that. When you're committed to another person's happiness, it becomes your *job* to make them feel great. That goes for men *and* women. In our house, both my wife and I keep a "security blanket" on call at all times. That means the *second* one of us starts to even feel the slightest chill of self-doubt, the other one is ready to wrap them up in that security blanket and make them feel loved again. We've both accepted that if our relationship is going to work, we have to have zero tolerance for any behavior that leads to insecurity.

A couple of years ago I started going to Los Angeles every few weeks to hang out with Will Smith. Will's an old friend (we used to tour together back in the day when he was the Fresh Prince), and he was kind enough to show me the ropes after I decided I wanted to learn more about the whole Hollywood scene.

The first few times I went out to L.A., it was just a given that Justine was coming with me. I couldn't have even imagined taking on this new world without her strength and support. We didn't even have a conversation about whether or not she was coming; whenever Will was ready for me, I would just tell Justine, "Come on, honey, pack your bags. We're going back to Cali."

After a few trips, however, I started getting a little *too* secure. The Hollywood scene didn't seem so alien to me anymore, and I didn't feel the need to hug that security blanket Justine represented quite as tightly. Don't get it twisted—I wasn't even remotely getting into any bad behavior out there. I just wasn't as needy as I had been. So when it was time for the next trip, I said, "Hey, Justine, I'm going to L.A. next week. Do you want to come too?"

"Did you really just ask me that?" she asked after a long pause. "You ain't never once asked me before, 'Do you want to come?' It was always just 'Pack your bags.' It's pretty clear to me that you *don't* want me coming along. So I'll just stay here, thank you very much."

The moment she snapped on me, I knew I'd messed up. Simply by presenting the idea of her coming along as a question, I'd invited some insecurity into our relationship.

I don't want to make it sound like I'd only invited Justine along initially for the security she provided me. Justine is more than my wife—she's my best friend, and there's nothing in this world that I'd rather do *without* her than *with* her. Yet it is true that once I felt more secure out in L.A., I didn't feel the need to hold her hand quite as tightly anymore. Which of course made *her* feel insecure.

Now here's the key—a lot of women might not have said anything at first, but Justine knew to check me on my nonsense, no matter how subtle it was, right away. She fixed me before I could say, or do, anything else stupid.

One of the main reasons I believe our relationship has worked so well is that Justine knows how to strike the right balance between supporting me and demanding her own validation. Off being melty like butter one moment and no-nonsense the next. It's a challenging equilibrium to maintain, one that requires constant attention and adjustments, but Justine has always found a way to do it.

It's a particularly difficult balance for African-American women to strike because they've had such a harsh history in this country. Going all the way back to being abused by their slave masters and having their families ripped away from them, African-American women have experienced so much negativity, disappointment and tragedy. Then, compounding all that trauma, African-American men have beaten, both emotionally and physically, on our women so badly over the years that many of them have been forced to develop these incredibly rough exteriors just to survive.

I don't think it's in a woman's basic nature to think *that man ain't nothin'* and then build a wall around herself. I believe that women are actually way more compassionate and understanding by nature than men are. But if for years and years you mess up women's minds like we men have done to African-American women, it's almost inevitable that "he ain't nothin' " might become your default setting.

African-American women might not be carrying around the same burdens they once carried, but I can still feel a lot of them moving through life with the same hard, inflexible mentality toward men that their mothers and grandmothers were forced to develop. Women are in a much better place today than their ancestors, but the second their man slips up, they will still automatically say, "He ain't nothin'," instead of trying to get under his arm and supporting him.

BEING SOFT DOESN'T MAKE YOU A SUCKA

One of the primary reasons our relationship works is that Justine is able to put her ego and tougher instincts aside and be content propping me up. That doesn't mean that she has to spend her entire life under my arm, but rather that she doesn't hesitate to rush there the second she senses I need some support.

When *Run's House* first came on the air, I could tell that other women felt Justine was actually too soft. I won't lie, sometimes I would visit chat rooms to see what people were saying, and the vibe from other African-American women seemed to be that Justine was *too* supportive of me, too calm and too complacent as a wife. Then, around the third or fourth episode, there was a scene where I did something stupid and pissed Justine off. All of a sudden, that calmness disappeared and she just screamed at me, "Jooeeeeeeey!!!!! I am *not* playin'." As soon as she did that, the tide turned in her favor. Once other women could see that she tempered the support with sternness, that she wasn't willing to let me get away with stupid stuff, they could relate to her. I was happy that so many women were able to connect with Justine through *Run's House,* but the truth is a lot of women still have a very difficult time embracing the idea of getting up under a man's arm and supporting him. It's like instead of feeling good about being his support system, all they can smell is his funky underarm odor. They just want to get out from under there.

No matter what man you're dealing with, trust me, he needs that support. Look at me: for many years, I was the epitome of cockiness. I was the king of New York City before I was even out of my teens, and I let the whole world know it. I stood onstage at Madison Square Garden and screamed, "Whose house? Run's house!"

That was the confidence I presented to the world, but the truth was I couldn't do it alone. I learned the hard way that I couldn't make it without God and a good woman by my side, and under my arm, if need be. I love *Run's House* today, but I also know that it would crumble down to the ground in a second without Justine's support. It's not that she ever lost the tough, rugged instinct that African-American women have been forced to rely on all these years, but rather that she's learned when to use it and when to tuck it away.

In my marriage, I work extremely hard to keep Justine feeling special and supported at all times. In fact, I don't even like to say I always try to put Justine "up on a pedestal," because in my mind she's never come off that pedestal since the day I met her.

I am not asking you to give that support to a man who takes your love for granted, or who is always looking for ways to keep you underneath him. But if you do have a man that keeps you up on that pedestal and works hard every day to be sensitive to your moods and needs, then give him that support. Because no matter how macho or tough a man might try to come off, we all need to know that when it's time to lean on our woman, she's going to be as strong as an oak. I'm not saying that you shouldn't take a switch off that oak and use it to whip his behind when he deserves it, but you should always strive for a balance between support and that switch.

CHAPTER 6

YOU CAN ONLY CHANGE A MAN WHEN HE'S A BABY

TYRESE

I know you want us to change.

Certainly a lot of women have tried to change me. In particular, my ex's need to change me was one of the main reasons our marriage crashed before it ever really got off the ground.

You might be experiencing a similar desire to change your man, but here's the hard truth:

The best time for a woman to change a man is when he's a baby.

If you try to change a man once he's grown, he's not going to like it. He's going to kick and scream. He's going to throw a tantrum just like a little toddler.

That doesn't mean, however, that he can't change. It just

means that you have to let go of the expectation that *you* can be the one to bring that change about.

Or that you will even be able to predict when that change will happen.

That's probably not the message you were hoping to hear. After all, changing a man constitutes many women's top priority. I can understand why—a lot of men could seriously use some change for the better.

Every day, women watch men make the same mistakes, leave the same messes, miss the same turns, tell the same stories, make the same excuses, forget to turn out the same lights, cause the same arguments, tell the same lame jokes, forget to put down the same toilet seat, make the same inappropriate comments—the list goes on and on. It must be maddening.

How could you *not* want to change us?

I'm a real pain to be in a relationship with. I'm not blind to that reality. There are many things about me that my girlfriend would like—no, make that *love*—to change about me.

If I represent the highest standard and my girlfriend is still going through it, then I know a lot of you ladies must really be fed up with your man's ways, especially the mothers out there. Y'all must feel like you're raising a child *and* a man. It's not enough that your kids make messes, don't put away their clothes, forget to close the refrigerator door, leave the top off the toothpaste, and drink milk right out of the carton, but your *man* does all those things too. At times it must feel like your entire life is spent taking care of and cleaning up after other people. Why wouldn't you like that to change?

The really sad thing is that dealing with those sorts of annoying habits actually represent the *best-case* scenario for a lot of women. That's because if your man is driving you crazy by leaving the toilet seat up or doing a lousy job washing the dishes, it means that he's around. That at least he's part of your life.

For many women, a man's inability to evolve into a mature, responsible partner is more than just annoying. Getting tangled up with a man who can't seem to mature can be downright destructive to a woman's life.

Too many women have looked at a man and thought, *I know he's wild, but he has to be ready to settle down. If I work hard enough with him, and love him enough, eventually he'll change.* They bet the house on their ability to change that man, yet somehow they always seem to be dealt a crappy hand to play. Bets have led too many of them to emotional bankruptcy.

Maybe you have been one of those women, or are going through something similar right now. If so, I want you to read this chapter very carefully to ensure that you don't make that mistake again.

The good news is that at some point, every man *will* change. At some point every man will get tired of acting like a boy. Whether it's at thirty-five, forty-five or even fifty-five, a man *will* find himself sitting in a club surrounded by people half his age and suddenly think, *You know what? I'm tired of talking to young girls who look great but don't share a mature connection with me. And why should they? They were born in the year I graduated from high school.*

Then he'll look around and think, *No doubt I love sitting here watching these girls shake their butts, but this entire scene feels too young to me . . . I want out. I want out. I want to get married and have a child of my own.*

Trust me, every man will have that moment. For a woman,

the question then becomes, how can you predict when a man will have that moment? When he's ready to transition from MAN-ipulator to family man?

And if it seems like that change isn't going to happen on its own, how can you jump-start it?

It's a complicated answer, one that Rev and I have different views on. But one thing we both agree on is this: never assume that because a man is a certain age, he's ready to make that move. As Rev himself says, "Assumptions are the termites of relation-ships."

AGE AIN'T NOTHIN' BUT A NUMBER

When a man has that kind of "aha!" moment in a club, it signifies that he's entering into what I call his "grown man season." Unfor-tunately, when that season will actually come about in a man's life is often difficult to predict.

Charting when seasons will change in nature is easy—you can use a calendar, like a farmer who consults his almanac to know when the time is right to plant his crops.

The problem is that a lot of women *are* relying on a calendar when it comes to men, a calendar that follows this commonly ac-cepted schedule:

When a man is in his early and midtwenties, he'll wild out. In his late twenties, he'll begin to slow down a bit and think about a steady relationship. By his midthirties he should be actively look-ing for a wife, and certainly by his forties he should be fully into that grown man season—the season of his life where marriage, a family and domesticity fit him like a glove.

I believe the concept of men adhering to a calendar is very

appealing to women simply because they can relate to it. No matter what race, religion or creed, women all follow the same schedule (or, as you like to call them, "clocks"). The ticking of that biological clock begins to get loud as early as your twenties, and by the time you're in your thirties, it's so noisy some of y'all can barely hear yourselves think. If you haven't had a kid by your late thirties, many of y'all are ready to settle down with any man if it means getting pregnant. That's how it goes for the vast majority of women.

There are exceptions, of course. I've met incredibly driven women in their late thirties, particularly in the entertainment world, who are too focused on their careers to slow down for children. Even so, that doesn't mean they don't hear the ticking; they're just ignoring it.

Men, however, don't share that sort of communal calendar. One man might be ready to settle down at twenty-one, while another could be in his fifties and still feel the need to sow his wild oats. All his peers might have wives and kids, but he's not even entertaining thoughts of marriage and a family.

Or while all his boys are wildin' out, there could be a young man who's yearning to settle down. Look at Rev, who has essentially been a family man since his early twenties. Yes, he went through his rock star stage, but as he's told you, he hated it. He thought that was how he was supposed to be living, but it wasn't the right lifestyle for him. It not only ended his first marriage but it almost ended his life too. Looking back, all he's ever really wanted to be was a family man, even when he was barely out of his teens. In his case, his grown man season arrived very early.

You simply can't assume that because a man has reached a certain age, he'll have automatically reached grown man season as well. Have you ever heard that saying "Age ain't nothin' but a number"? It's usually employed by older men to justify the maturity of a younger woman. It suggests that while a woman might be young in years, she's already mature in her mind-set.

Well, for our purposes I want you to flip it and use it as a reminder that being older in years doesn't necessarily make a man mature or ready to settle down.

I've seen too many women fall into the trap of thinking, *Well, he's thirty-five, so he must be ready to leave all this partying behind and settle down* or *He's forty-one for cryin' out loud. I know we're not moving as fast as I'd like, but there's no way he'd keep sleeping with me if deep down he didn't want something more.*

Sorry, ladies, but you can get burned very badly making those assumptions. A man might appear to be ready to slow down because of his age, but if you go check his phone or his email, you'll see he ain't doing anything different than most twenty-one-year-olds. Though if it's any consolation, I should add a quick aside: When a man loses a woman because she had already reached her season but he was still immature, it's often very painful for him. Though he might not realize what he lost when they broke up, as he moves from relationship to relationship and none of them feel like quite the right fit, it will begin to dawn on him that he messed up. He'll begin to reminisce more and more about that mature woman he lost.

But when does run into her and wants to do nothing more than convey that he's mature and ready to settle down, he won't be able to convince her. Because when she looks into his eyes, all she's going to see is that immature dude that she broke up with. She's not going to forgot who he used to be. And that will be like a stab in the heart to him.

If a man doesn't grow more mature with age, he will definitely get better at covering the tracks of his immaturity. When a man is in his twenties, he's sloppy with his MAN-ipulation. You don't need to be much of a detective to figure out what he's up to—there's usually a trail leading you right to his BS.

But a man in his thirties, forties or fifties is capable of "pimpin' without a trace," as I like to call it. He's not going to leave any evidence of all the women he's running around with on the side. Why? Firstly, he's much tighter with his game than a younger man. If a young cat is sloppy, an older man is as precise as a master sushi chef. Every move he makes is efficient and has a purpose.

Secondly (and this is something you ladies need to admit about yourselves), older men have an advantage because they're usually running around with *older women*. A young hood rat simply can't keep her mouth shut; sooner or later she's going to let you know that she's creeping with your man.

But an older woman? Especially a woman who thinks she's got something to lose herself? She's going to keep her mouth clamped shut. You could go to the same church, have kids at the same school, or live on the same block for years and years, and you'll never know that she's got something going on with your man. An older woman will sit on that secret for the *rest of her life.*

That's not to suggest that all older men can't be trusted, or somehow can't make good husband material. I know a lot of people who have found *great* men who were in their forties, fifties and even sixties—men who, for whatever reason, took longer to get to that grown man season.

And as a society, it's becoming normal for men to stay single longer. Look at Jay-Z, who just got married for the first time in his early forties. Jay is probably the biggest trendsetter in America, so if he sets the example that the early forties are a good time to settle down, then I bet you'll start to see a lot of brothas waiting until their early forties to get married too.

Finally, let me say this: if a man doesn't seem ready or able to change at what you consider to be an appropriate time, don't interpret that resistance as an indictment of your worth. Just as you should never own a cheat, you should never own a man's reluctance to change or settle down within your timing.

Men, as you might have noticed, are generally stubborn by nature. God can place an incredible, once-in-a-lifetime woman directly in a man's path, yet instead of slowing down for her, he'll somehow still try to steam full speed ahead.

For instance, not long after my girlfriend and I started getting serious, she received several calls from a guy she used to date. Basically he was telling her, "Hey, I can see now that you were the best thing that ever happened to me. I should have told you then, but the timing was just wrong. And now that I'm in the right season and ready to settle down, I'm stuck with a woman I don't even like half as much as you. I just wish the timing had been better for us."

Instead, she had the confidence and sense of self to keep living her life and looking for love despite having wasted so much time with a man who was in the wrong season. That's why you should never, ever let a man's lack of maturity trick you into thinking that there's something wrong with *you*. No, a man's inability to move into his grown man season is a reflection of his immaturity, not your attractiveness or worthiness.

MEN COMMIT TO A *MOMENT*

When it comes to changing a man, it's critical that a woman establish up front what her comfort zone is in a relationship. One of the biggest mistakes women make is letting things slide at the onset of a relationship. Rather than tell a man what makes her uncomfortable, she assumes that there is an unspoken expectation that he will change his ways over time. And we've already established where unspoken expectations will always get you in a relationship. . . .

I've seen that happen so many times. At the onset of a relationship, a woman will appear incredibly open-minded about what her man does and who he does it with. If her man wants to hit a strip club with his boys on a Saturday night, she'll tell him, "Go ahead, boo, I'm good." Or if he likes to smoke a little weed while he watches the game, she'll say, "Hey, go enjoy yourself." If he wants to stop by a bar to meet some friends and an ex-girlfriend is going to be there, she won't act pressed to go just to keep an eye on him.

And he'll proceed in the relationship believing that his woman doesn't have a problem with him hitting a strip club from time to time, or rolling a blunt with his boys.

But once that woman transitions to live-in girlfriend, then fiancée and finally wife, she'll gain a little more confidence about articulating her comfort zone. Then once she feels like she has him completely locked in, she'll spring that 'ish on him.

"Why do your boys always have to come over *here* to watch the game?" she'll complain. "I'm tired of them sitting with their feet on our coffee table eating our food, never bringing nothin' over. Tell 'em to watch it at their own houses."

Or she'll start getting on his case about smoking weed. "You need to cut that out. This place always smells like stale smoke," she'll say. "I don't understand why you need to smoke all the time. It's nasty."

At first, a man will try to work within the confines of the new comfort zone that's been presented to him. He'll tell his boys, "Y'all need to find somewhere else to watch the game," even though he's got the best setup. Since he doesn't want drama every time he feels like puffing, he'll start going out to his car to smoke, or sneak down to the basement.

He'll try to make things work, but those compromises will come at the expense of his manhood. Instead of feeling like the man of the house, he'll start to feel like he's a teenager again, having to move within his mother's comfort zone. He might go along with the program, but he'll also deeply resent doing so.

Then eventually he'll snap.

"When we met, you never told me you didn't like me smoking, so don't start jumping all over me now," he'll say. "I don't need this. You know who you're with. You know how I get down. Don't you dare drop that on me now."

In many ways his aggravation will be unwarranted. After all, it's true his boys never bring anything over and he really shouldn't be filling up the house with nasty smoke. But a man still isn't going to see it like that. Instead, he's going to feel like he's been tricked or sold a false bill of goods.

You must understand that when a man decides to get serious with a woman, he's making that decision based on where their relationship is at that *very moment*. It's almost as if he takes a mental snapshot of what he can and can't do at the moment he commits. That list of "dos and don'ts" becomes his internal rule book going forward.

A man mentally understands that evolution and change are inevitable in a relationship. He accepts that he won't be—and truthfully, shouldn't be—the same man at thirty-five that he was at twenty-five. He knows that it's not unrealistic for his woman to expect him to change how he acts with his friends, or what his responsibilities, both financially and emotionally, will become as he grows older.

Yet even though he understands those concepts intellectually, in practice he's still going to cling to that snapshot in his mind. He's still going to insist that how he moved when he settled down should still be how he's expected to move today. His woman might say, "Well, he needs to get over that" or "He needs to stop acting like a baby," and she'd probably be right. But it's still how most men think.

WHAT'S HIS BOTTOM LINE?

The attitude I just described is why it's critical that you and your man both acknowledge at the onset of the relationship what I call his "bottom line." I'm referring to the aspects of a man's lifestyle that he simply can't live without—activities or habits that might not seem like a big deal to you but are ones that he counts on to help him get through life. So when the two of you make a commitment to each other, you're going to be crystal clear about how he expects to get down, not only now, but ten years from now as well.

A man might say, "To stay in my comfort zone, my bottom

line is that I need to be able to smoke weed and drink in the house, when I want to, without any drama."

Or he might say, "I need to feel like my friends are welcome whenever I invite them over and you'll always try to be a gracious host. Even if they're not always gracious guests."

The key is getting bottom-line items out in the open as soon as possible, which is why I never try to obscure what my bottom line is in a relationship. Admittedly, I'm a quirky dude, so the items on my bottom line are probably a little different than most men's.

For instance, while a lot of men like to smoke weed, I can't stand it. I never smoke, and I don't want the smell of weed in my home or on my clothes. So any woman who gets involved with me knows that not only do I not want her to smoke around me but her friends can't come over and light up anywhere in my home either. I don't care if it's her best friend or her sister visiting from out of town—anyone smoking weed in my home is getting tossed. Sorry, but that's my bottom line.

Now here's the twist—even though I like a clean-smelling and -looking home, I also tend to be a complete slob. That's right, even though I want things to be neat, I don't want to clean them myself. When I come home at night, I like to just throw my dirty clothes on the floor. When I wake up in the morning, I don't want to be bothered with making my bed. I don't want to even think twice about that kind of stuff.

I do, however, get on *my woman* when I catch her leaving stuff lying around. In fact, I expect my ol' lady to help keep the house immaculate, no matter how big of a slob I am.

Yes, I know I'm being hypocritical. As my girlfriend has told me many, many times, "Well, for someone who wants a clean house, you sure don't put in any effort into being clean."

Hey, I know my attitude is annoying. I know that I'm a nasty person to live with. I know that I can be a real pain.

That's who I am, however, and wanting a clean house is still my bottom line.

The reason my relationship with my girlfriend has worked is that there's never been any ambiguity about who I am. My bottom line has been written in bold ink since day one. It's not as if I was picking up my clothes and making the bed when we were dating, then I flipped it on her once she moved in. No, I broadcast all my weird and crazy behavior from the outset so that she could make an informed decision on what she was getting herself into. She was able to look at my situation and say, "It's obvious this guy is a control freak and is going to be a pain in the butt to put up with from time to time, but I love so many other aspects about him that I'm prepared to deal with it."

And she's still dealing with that behavior today. Maybe one day I'll wake up and say, "I can't keep on being such a slob. I need to get it together." But I need to decide that on my own. She would be completely justified if she woke up tomorrow and said, "You know what, Tyrese, I'm tired of picking up after you. If a clean house is so important to you, then put your clothes away yourself." Yet my reaction would still be, "Houston, we have a problem."

Even though it might represent the height of hypocrisy, the right to be a slob was undeniably on my bottom line when we got serious. As a man, I'm going to be extremely resistant to changing that bottom line at someone else's insistence.

To be clear, not every man is going to have bottom lines that are as selfish or annoying as some of mine are. No matter who you're dealing with, however, that man *will* have a bottom line. Every man is going to have certain quirks and habits that he will resist changing. He might not be as candid about his expectations as I am, but trust me, he will still have them. By going forward in your relationship, he's assumed that you've not only acknowledged them but signed off on them as well. So if you do have a problem with his bottom line, never keep that to yourself.

MEN TODAY ARE EVEN *HARDER* TO CHANGE

I'm not trying to scare you, but it also needs to be said that men today are even *harder* to change than they were in your momma's or grandmama's day. In the twenty-first century, you're really asking for it if you go into a relationship assuming that a man's idiosyncrasies will go away over time, or that he'll even be open to changing them. That's because these days, men are clinging even tighter to their old habits.

Back in the day, when most guys were settled down by their midtwenties, it wasn't quite as hard to move them off their bottom lines. They were out of their momma's house for only a few years before moving to a new woman's house. The rhythms and habits of bachelorhood never really had a chance to take root before a woman could establish her own set of rules.

Today, it's so different. For instance, suppose you start seeing a handsome, successful, thirty-eight-year-old attorney without any kids. You'd probably start thinking, *I just hit the jackpot!* In many ways maybe you might have. But also keep this in mind: it's probably been almost twenty years since that man left his mother's house and started living on his own. That means twenty years of leaving his clothes where he wanted to. Twenty years of smoking when and where he wanted to. Twenty years of eating dinner while watching TV if he wanted to. Twenty years of playing basketball on Saturday mornings if he wanted to. Twenty years of going out when he wanted to and waking up when he wanted to. And at least fifteen years of being able to drop everything and go meet his boys in Vegas for the weekend if he wanted to.

By the time you two meet, he'll be extremely set in his ways. If you think that after a few months, or even years, of living together you'll be able to just bend over and pull that lifestyle out by its roots, then you just aren't seeing things for how they really are.

In most ways, your path is much easier than the one traveled by previous generations of women. Changing a man, however, is the exception to that rule. Your mother probably never had to deal with breaking in a man with twenty years of the bachelor life under his belt. Just as your aunt or grandma most likely didn't have to contend with a man who had gotten used to having lots of money and very little responsibilities for twenty years. Yet for many ladies today, that's your reality.

This is why instead of believing fairy tales that were written during a different time, you must be realistic about the kind of man you're dealing with *today*. Twenty years of bachelorhood is more than a season, it's practically half a forty-year-old man's life. So be pragmatic instead of naïve about what you're going to be able to change.

SHOW HIM HOW TO LOVE YOU!

Perhaps the most important thing for you to remember about your man, however, is that he might not know how to change. He might truly want to love you better but just doesn't know how to do it.

He might truly be loving you the best way that he knows how. If he was raised in a household where he didn't see his father loving his mother day in and day out, or even his grandfather loving his grandmother, you cannot assume that he knows how to give you what you need. You have to become that role model in his life. If your parents loved each other and taught you what it means to be in a real relationship, then you're going to teach him too.

Or even worse, his parents might have taught him the *wrong* way to love. So before you can teach him the right way, you're going to have to help him *unlearn* all that dysfunction that he was exposed to as a boy.

Trust me, no real man wakes up every day trying to figure out a new way to hurt you. So if it seems like that's what keeps happening, ask yourself, *How can I show him how to love me better?* instead of being disappointed with this man for not loving you right.

WHAT'S ON YOUR MAN-U?

Almost all men require a little fine-tuning and tutoring, but if you constantly find yourself having to teach the man in your life how to love you better, perhaps what you really need to change is the type of man you're ordering from life.

In my last book, I wrote about the concept of life being like a menu: whoever and whatever you order is what's going to be delivered to your table. That means if you consistently order fried and fatty foods, you can't get mad the next time you step on the scale and you're fifteen pounds overweight. It's not the restaurant's fault—they've got a low-cal section on the menu, but *you're* the one who ordered that cheesecake instead of the fruit salad.

With that in mind, now I want to take that concept and narrow it down to what you're ordering from your MAN-u. In other words, what sort of men are you ordering from life? It might not always feels like it, but you do control what sort of men are gravitating toward your life. Your problem might be that you're just not ordering the right ones.

Let's consider a very basic scenario: you and your girls hit the club. You've got on your best "Freakum" dress, and you're dancing and singing along with the songs. Every guy in the place is giving you energy. Some get right up in your face, some just smile and others stare at you from across the room, but you can feel all of their eyes on you. Even if you're normally a bit shy or insecure, on this night you know that you can talk and flirt with any of them.

Basically, all those dudes are like a MAN-u. You can order whichever one you like. So who do you end up picking?

Did you order the guy who didn't have on the flyest gear or carry himself with the most swag but who seemed like a good-hearted dude? Or were you actually a little aloof and stuffy with him?

Did you order the short guy who was a little chubby but had good energy and made you laugh when he offered to buy you a drink? Or did you decline his offer and walk away?

Did you end up ordering the handsome, aggressive and flashy guy who was hanging out by the bar and buying everyone drinks? The one that deep down you could sense was probably no good but you felt yourself being pulled toward anyway?

You probably ordered the last dude, didn't you? And didn't he end up just stringing you along and playing you out after he smashed? Didn't you wake up one morning several months later wondering, *I can't believe I let myself get into this situation again. Why can't I find any good men?*

Well, now you know the answer. You're ordering the wrong ones.

To be clear, I don't want to generalize and claim that all flashy dudes or bad-boy types aren't the right choice, because as a women you might just wanna order something "right quick" for your night. But keep in mind that that's all you can count on most bad boys for. When you are realistic with what you "order" for your life in a man, you're not going to be surprised by what you end up experiencing.

The question is, If you want a good guy, why do you keep ordering a bad boy? And the reason is that when ordering off your MAN-u, you're subconsciously looking for something that feels familiar. A recognizable energy that you keep returning to. And it is most likely your father's.

Unfortunately, too often that energy wasn't a positive one. Yes you had a daddy, but unfortunately he was a lot better at creating drama than at parenting. Your memories of him aren't of him taking you on walks or giving you rides to your dance lessons, but of him coming home, having a few drinks and getting loud with your momma. Or worse.

You hated it when your daddy got like that, but when you go

into a club as an adult, you still feel yourself being drawn toward that loud, aggressive dude with that familiar energy. You know he's bad news, but you flirt with him anyway because maybe you believe that in fixing that loud, aggressive man who reminds you of Daddy, you'll be fixing your broken childhood.

Or if your daddy wasn't around at all, you'll find yourself being draw to the energy you always *wanted* to feel as a little girl. That incredible sense of security and happiness that daughters feel when their father surprises them with a little treat when he comes home from work, takes them shopping for a new bike or even just tucks them into bed with an "I love you" at night.

Because you didn't have a father showering you with that attention as a child, now as an adult you feel yourself being drawn to those MAN-ipulators who are willing to trick out on clothes and expensive dinners. Now you find yourself ordering men who are willing to shower you with that attention you never received from a father growing up.

No matter how hard we work to create our own identities, so much of who we are as adults is a *direct* reflection of our childhood. Which is why before you order from that MAN-u, take a deep breath and ask yourself, *Is this* really *what I want? Or is it just a reaction to my past?* It's not different from going out and ordering at a restaurant when you're on a diet. Yes, that sirloin steak with mashed potatoes and gravy seems to be calling your name, but aren't you sick of being overweight? Aren't you tired of not being able to fit into your jeans and getting down on yourself when you look in the mirror? So as good as that steak would taste, what you really want to do is order the salad instead.

It's no different ordering off your MAN-u. Even though you think you might want that loud, aggressive thug, he's no good for your "diet." The little bit of excitement and pleasure he's going to bring into your life isn't going to outweigh the negativity a bad boy will create in the long run.

BAD BOYS

Let's also examine why many women, despite being burned by them over and over again, keep going back to bad boys and thugs.

Aside from the fact that bad boys remind women of their fathers, one of the main reasons, in my opinion, is that women want to feel protected. Bad boys make them feel like no one is ever going to be able to hurt them.

This is especially true of women who were raised by a single mom. If that was your situation, you probably always felt a little vulnerable without a man—or at least a steady one—in the house. Your mother would have given her life for you (and in many ways she did), but she could only physically protect you up to a certain point. When it comes to problems on the block, even in the suburbs, nobody can rattle cages like a daddy can. That's why all children, both boys and girls, love being able to shout, "Oh, I'm gonna go get my daddy, and he's going to kick your butt!"

A man that projects that sense of strength is going to be very attractive to you. You're going to be drawn to that prominent male figure who makes you feel protected and who can fill that void. A man who makes you feel that no matter what goes down, he's going to be able to handle it, whether you're going to a club or just driving in his car.

Just remember that security and protection come with a price. Even though that bad boy has swag and confidence and the respect of other men, he can also be incredibly frustrating.

In most cases, faithfulness is usually not high on his priority list. Commitment is not usually something he's looking for. Nor is he usually too interested in making a good impression when he meets your parents or goes out for drinks with your coworkers. He probably isn't going to hold doors open for you, or buy you roses or tell you how beautiful you are. He might not even be too pressed about going out and finding a job to help pay his half of the rent.

If those things are important to you, then please think twice before you order another bad boy. You can't keep ordering the same thing expecting them to bring something different from the kitchen. If a bad boy is what you order, then a bad boy is ultimately what you're going to get.

Rev Run

CHILDISH WAYS

I agree with Tyrese when he says a man has to be in the right season in order for him to settle down and start doing the right thing. But that's really where our agreement ends. I think it is much easier to forecast a man's seasons than he is making it out to be.

I know for a fact that there *is* an ordered course that every man is supposed to follow, it's just that a lot of men don't want to stay on track.

I know this because in Corinthians 13:11 it's stated, "When I was a child, I talked like a child, I thought like a child, I reasoned like a child. When I became a man, I put childish ways behind me."

Bam, there you have it.

The two seasons of a man.

In the first season a man gets to do childish things like getting high, running around with his boys and messin' with all sorts of different women.

When he gets older, it's time he puts away those childish toys and becomes a man.

This concept shouldn't be too hard to understand, but unfortunately a lot of guys are, quite frankly, idiots. The formula for happiness and contentment has been laid out right in front of them, but they still try to stretch out that first season waaaay further than it was ever intended to last. They might be thirty-five or forty years old, but they still want to play with children's toys. It's not that they don't know when their season has changed, it's just they refuse to change with it. They *know* that summer has turned into fall, and even winter, but they still insist on going outside in shorts and no jacket.

Just like a child.

Many men would have you believe that they are often clueless about when it's time for them to change, that it could take years of sitting in a club before they suddenly have an epiphany in which they realize the way they're living is no longer appropriate.

Sorry, but I don't buy that.

I believe men know darn well when they're supposed to put down their childish toys. You don't think a forty-year-old man feels like a fool the *first* time he sits down in a club surrounded by people almost half his age? You don't think a thirty-five-year-old guy knows he looks pathetic walking around with his pants hanging off his butt? You don't think a forty-five-year-old dude knows he's not supposed to be sending flirty messages on Facebook like he's still in high school? Those guys all know perfectly well that they're not following the plan that's been laid out for them. They don't need an "Aha" moment to figure that out. It's just that they're too stubborn to change.

FINDING A MAN-TOR

For a woman, the real question becomes, if a man is too stubborn to change on his own, how can I help jump-start that evolution?

The answer is, you should leave that job to another *man*.

I know that might sound like an incredibly sexist or dismissive reply, but I promise it's not. Please hear me out.

I wish it weren't the case, but I know through both firsthand experience and observation that it's *extremely* difficult for a woman to teach a man how to be a man. Unfortunately, only another man can give a guy who's clinging to his childish ways the proper kick in the butt and tell him it's time to put down those toys once and for all.

To be fair, there are some men who know how to make that change on their own. The vast majority, however, need that kick.

And the perfect person to deliver it is what I like to call a MAN-tor. That's right, not just a "mentor," but a "MAN-tor." Another man who's been there, done that and isn't willing to take any of the nonsense a childish man is going to pull when it's time for him to change.

Whenever people ask me about my own evolution, I like to say, "I'm not quite what I ought to be, not yet what I hope to be, but thank God I'm not what I used to be!"

I'm certainly proud that I'm seen as a good husband and a dedicated family man today. That acknowledgment is worth more to me than any gold plaques on my wall, magazine covers or even being inducted into the Rock and Roll Hall of Fame.

But if we're going to talk about how men can change their lives, then it needs to be said that *I* haven't always been the man I am today.

Tyrese is right when he says I was ready to be a family man from a very early age, certainly earlier than most men I know. Yet rather than stay on the path that God had laid out for me, I decided to run amok. Instead of embracing being Joey Simmons, someone who knew he was happiest surrounded by loved ones, my mind got twisted into thinking that I really was "Run." I started believing that my validation (there's that word again) as a man lay in how many records I sold, how many checks I could cash, how much weed I could smoke or how many women I could sleep with. I stopped making time for my brothers, my parents, even my children and my first wife. If it wasn't about my own "pleasure," then I didn't care.

I need to stress how far I drifted away from God's plan for me because it's important that as a woman you realize that *every* man is capable of transforming his life for the better. Have confidence that it's impossible for a man to wander so far off the path that he can't find his way back. I don't think a man could veer further off his intended path than I did, but I still made it back. So no matter what your man is dealing with, never doubt that he can get back on track too.

For that to happen, however, a man must accept that he's probably not going to find the way back on his own.

I certainly didn't. And even though they all tried, it wasn't my wife, my brothers or even my parents who eventually got me back on track.

Only my MAN-tor was able to do that.

The MAN-tor who directed me back to God's path was Bishop Jordan, the head of Zoe Ministries in New Jersey. After bottoming out in that hot tub, I knew that I desperately needed God in my life. But even with that knowledge, I didn't know how to find Him on my own.

Thankfully, God ordered my footsteps to Bishop Jordan's church. All those years of trying to be "Run" had left me feeling deflated, almost dead. Yet by looking at Bishop Jordan and witnessing the type of relationship he had with both God and his family, I saw a glimmer of hope for myself.

Thankfully, my pride and ego (which I like to say stands for "Edging God Out") had left me and I was ready to soak up all of Bishop Jordan's instructions. So after hanging around his church for several weeks, finally one day I went up to him and said, "Bishop Jordan, I'm here to serve. Please put me to work."

At first he was skeptical—after all, how many celebrities are *really* looking to serve? But he offered me a job as an usher, and after he saw me embrace that role, he "promoted" me to a walking deacon (it was really just another name for an usher, but hey, what did I know?), and over time I grew more and more involved with his church. Soon my entire family was serving at Bishop Jordan's church; I'd be an usher, my wife would help out in the church kitchen, while the kids would fold flyers and videotape services.

All the while, I intently watched how Bishop Jordan conducted himself, not only in word and deed, but in soul and spirit as well. I saw his unwavering commitments to his wife and children. I saw how he refused to stray from the word of God. And I saw the incredible blessings his devotion to God had created for him.

Serving under Bishop Jordan was like getting a PhD in being a man of God and a family man. I had entered his church feeling extremely shaky about who I was as a husband and a father, but thanks to the power of Bishop Jordan's MAN-torship, I was able to develop a rock-solid belief in my ability to lead my family. After watching Bishop Jordan, I didn't just drift toward his way of life, I absolutely *threw* myself into it. That was the effect his MAN-torship had on me.

I want to stress the word *watch,* because the power of observation is really the key to a strong MAN-torship. As a rule, men respond much better to living examples than they do to words. For instance, I could have gone to Bishop Jordan's church and heard him preach about the importance of family every Sunday, but if I hadn't actually *seen* him leading that sort of life himself, his message wouldn't have had the same impact on me.

Most men need to see their MAN-tor setting a positive example, day in and day out, before they are motivated to make a change themselves. You can talk to a man about the importance of doing the right thing until you're blue in the face, but unless he sees that it's possible, it's just not going to stick.

This dynamic is the primary reason why I say it's so hard for a woman to teach a man how to be a man. It's not that I think the message a woman is going to give him isn't all that different from what a MAN-tor will tell him. She'll tell him to be more responsible, to stop being so selfish, to put his family first and to work on developing a closer relationship with God—all the same things that Bishop Jordan told me. Yet I know if I had only heard those messages from a woman when I was looking to change, I'd probably still be stuck in my old ways today. Or even more likely, I'd probably be dead.

If Tyrese hadn't *seen* all the love and commitment I poured into my family on *Run's House,* he would never have been open to the idea of receiving MAN-torship from me. Once we did build that relationship, it worked only because he *saw* that I was consistent in that commitment.

If he and I went out to dinner, he *saw* that rather than go to a party afterward, I headed back home to my wife and kid. He *saw* that if a pretty woman tried to flirt with me, I not only didn't return that energy but always removed myself from the situation. He *saw* that whenever my wife or kids called, I was never too busy to pick up on the first ring. If he hadn't been able to watch me make God and family my top priority, then I wouldn't have been able to move him even one inch off where he was when I met him.

Seeing my example has given Tyrese so much confidence that he can be a family man, that he can make a marriage work. Every time I speak with him, I can see his vision getting a little sharper, a little stronger. He's coming closer and closer to the standard I've set for him every day. I catch him thinking about dates to have a wedding, of a life in which he's settled down and happy. His vision might still be a year or two away, but now he's actively carving and creating it. And he's only gained the confidence to take these steps because of my MAN-torship. We were recently working on the book, and he even told me, "Rev, I haven't told my girl this, but if it wasn't for you keeping me on course, I would have walked away a long time ago. It's not even a reflection on her; I just don't know if I would have had the confidence in my ability to be a good boyfriend without you telling me I could."

I can remember P. Diddy sitting down with me one day and saying, "Rev, I don't even *understand* the basic idea behind marriage. It confuses me. I get lost just trying to think about it." He wasn't trying to be cute or funny, he just didn't *get* it. Puffy's father was killed when he was very young, and he simply wasn't blessed with having a marriage role modeled in front of him on a daily basis. I'm not for a second suggesting that he's not a good dad—our kids are friends, and I've spent enough time around his family to know that he's an *amazing* father. But when it comes to marriage, that's just something he's never been able to believe in on his own.

Which is why Puffy was talking to me. Which is why Tyrese talks to me as well. They need that MAN-tor in me to prove that it *is* possible. Just like I needed the MAN-torship of Bishop Jordan. Just like your man might need someone similar in his own life.

And the beautiful thing about MAN-torships is that they are often a two-way street. Earlier I mentioned reuniting with DMC for the Made In America festival; there's no way that would have happened without

178

Tyrese convincing *me* that I could do it. After taking a ten-year break for various professional and personal reasons, I wasn't sure me and D could rock a stage to our standards anymore. Tyrese was the first person outside of the group to make me believe the reunion would work. Just like I gave him the confidence to keep his relationship with his girlfriend going, he gave me the confidence to revive my relationship with D.

MAN-TORS ARE OUT THERE

As a woman, you might be reading this and thinking, *Rev, I agree with you one hundred percent. My guy could definitely use a MAN-tor. But not everyone has someone like you in their life. MAN-tors are great, but there just ain't that many of them out there.*

I know it might feel that way, but trust me, there *are* a bunch of us out here.

No matter how it might seem.

And the beautiful thing is that if your man is ready, that MAN-tor will come to him. I firmly believe that when the student is ready, the teacher will show up, just as Bishop Jordan showed up in my life and I showed up in Tyrese's life. And if your man is ready, God will help him connect with a MAN-tor too.

Now if you don't want to wait for that MAN-tor to come into your man's life, it's fine to encourage him to go out and seek that relationship. Personally, I believe the best place to look would be in a church, synagogue, mosque or any other spiritual setting. That's because whether it's a preacher or a rabbi or an imam, the very essence of that person's job is to provide MAN-torship. Any religious leader who doesn't instantly embrace a man looking for guidance needs to find a new calling—pronto. So while a man could look elsewhere for

MAN-torship, why even mess around with anyone else, since God's plan is so ordered and precise?

Run's House helped men get over their insecurities about being husbands and fathers. You see, as a society we accept that women are often apprehensive about motherhood. From books to magazine articles to movies, there's a whole industry built upon women's insecurities about their maternal abilities and their need to seek guidance in that regard. Well, guess what? Most men are just as insecure, if not more so, about their ability to be a family man.

This is especially true, as Tyrese pointed out, now that men are waiting longer and longer to get married. If a man has been single for fifteen years, it's not just a matter of him not *wanting* to change; he begins to believe he doesn't know *how* to change even if he wanted to. The idea of being responsible for maintaining a marriage and raising children can leave a longtime bachelor feeling paralyzed with fear. *I've become so used to eating what I want, watching what I want, going where I want and sleeping as long as I want that there's no way I could inject a wife and kids into this equation,* a man will tell himself. "I wouldn't know how to deal with them. I've been so focused on doing me that I can't even conceive of helping other people move through life."

Run's House showed men that it's perfectly normal for the head of a family to struggle with issues and situations. Whether it was something as trivial as Russy not liking the color his room was painted to the absolute devastation of losing our daughter Victoria Anne at birth, I showed men that they could deal with whatever family life threw at them. From the good times to the tough times to the tragic times, I taught other men, "Don't worry, you might bump your head a few times, but you can handle this responsibility."

He's never admitted it to me, but I think Tyrese still feels that insecurity from time to time. There's no doubt in his or anyone else's mind that he's a fantastic father to his daughter, but sometimes I think he wonders if he'll ever be able to wrap it all up in the same package—namely, enjoying a healthy relationship with a woman to go along with his great relationship with his child. But I know he can do it. He just needs more MAN-toring.

Which is why I keep screaming, "Pick one!" He's getting closer, but I believe he can't truly enter his grown man season once and for all until he's married and raising a family under one roof.

Tyrese has largely stopped playing with his childish toys, but I think he still worries that once he finally puts them away, or gives them to the Salvation Army, he's going to miss them very badly.

My job is to keep telling him and other men like him that he won't. I need to keep telling them that not only will they not miss those toys but it's actually a tremendous relief to leave that childish life behind. I can't speak for Jay-Z, but when I look at pictures of him walking around with his daughter, Blue Ivy, I don't see a guy who's worried about what party he isn't at, or what basketball game he's missing or what models he could be sippin' champagne with.

Instead, I see a guy who looks content. Whose body language says, "That old season is over and I'm not even mad. Because this new one feels *extremely* comfortable."

All I'm saying is that it's true that things are going to be tough when you settle down, but the love and support that you'll get from your family is going to make that whippin' soooooo worth it. To a woman that might not sound like a very romantic view of marriage and raising a family, but it's the message men need to hear.

BE A WIFE FIRST!

In stressing the importance of a MAN-torship I've probably been preaching to the choir a bit, but it needed to be put out there. Having said it, however, I don't want to give the impression that you ladies are supposed to sit around all day twiddling your thumbs while you wait for your man to build that relationship or, perhaps even more importantly, while you wait for a grown man to finally come into your life.

Even though I don't believe that a woman can teach a man to be a better man, there are steps that a single woman in particular can take to ensure that a good man *will* come into her life.

And the most important step is embracing this simple concept: become a wife *before* you get married.

I realize that might sound counterintuitive. After all, you've spent most of your life being told that a man is never going to buy the cow as long as he can get the milk for free. Heck, a few chapters ago I told you that you should resist having sex with a man until he "puts a ring on it."

So when I say you should become a wife before you get married, I'm not saying that you should be making a man dinner, mending his socks or having sex with him before the two of you walk down the aisle.

Instead, what I'm suggesting is that if you don't demonstrate the attributes and energy of a wife when a good man does enter your life, then he's not going to see you as "wifey material."

This is why in Proverbs 18:22 it's written, "He who finds a wife finds what is good and receives favor from the Lord."

That's pretty easy to understand, right? If a man finds a good wife, God is going to be happy, and as a result, that couple will lead blessed lives.

Now notice what that passage *didn't* say.

It didn't say, "He who finds a jump off." Just like it didn't say, "He who finds a girlfriend." Or even, "He who finds a woman."

No, it specifically says he who finds a "wife." Which means that if you want the Lord to favor your relationship, you have to act like, and see yourself as, a wife *before* you meet Mr. Right.

How, then, does a single woman learn how to act like a wife without actually being married?

It's simple.

She starts hanging out with married women.

If you're in your twenties or early thirties, what I'm suggesting might not sound very appealing at first. You might be thinking, *I'm not trying to be around a bunch of married women. All they want to talk about is their kids or their husbands or redoing their kitchens. I wanna hang with my girls, hit the clubs and have some fun.*

I get that, which is why I'm not saying you need to drop all your single friends and completely change your lifestyle. Instead, I'm simply encouraging you to find just one or two married women you respect—maybe they're members of your church, work at your job or belong to your gym—and simply start having lunch with them every couple of weeks. Or join their book club. Or volunteer for a charity they're involved with.

Just find a way to spend a few hours a month with these women so that you can observe where they put their priorities, how they interact with their husbands and maintain their relationships. If you spend even just a tiny amount of time with them each month, their attributes as wives will start to rub off on you.

Men and women alike need to understand that there is *zero* shame in being thirsty for that mentor who can show you the relationship ropes. Because when you know the ropes, you aren't going to get tied up!

That's why if a strong, contented and happily married woman comes into your life, you should embrace her. And if she doesn't show up when you think you might need her, then go find her.

The irony is that when you put yourself under the tutelage of a married woman, a lot of your single female friends are going to hate. "Why are you always hanging out with those old ladies?" they'll say. "What, you don't want to have fun anymore?" Don't listen to them. That's just their insecurity shouting out.

If you feel like you have nowhere else to turn to find that mentor, look to the first lady, Michelle Obama. Her example can help you. Just like watching Justine's example on *Run's House* can help you too. You will get what you need from them, whether it's someone you see every day on the block or someone you only watch on TV, as long as you sit yourself under their example and learn.

CHAPTER 7

STAY OR GO?

Tyrese

After reading the last chapter you should have a little more confidence in your ability to transform your man into a better boyfriend or husband. While you know that transformation probably won't happen overnight, at least now you have a road map for that journey.

Or perhaps after reading the last chapter your outlook isn't as positive. Even though the idea of helping your man find that MAN-tor makes a lot of sense, in your heart you don't think he's ever going to reach that grown man season.

Which is why you must now address the question so many women are forced to confront at some point in their relationships.

Should I stay with this man?

Or is it time to go?

It's a decision every woman must make based on her own particular situation. But in this chapter, Rev and I still want to share some basic insights that can at least help you feel more confident about whichever choice you do ultimately end up making.

The most important step is accepting that you must make this decision *on your own!* As tempting as it might be, you cannot rely on your family and friends for direction when it comes to your man. Even though you'd like to believe that they have your best interest at heart, too often they don't.

It's also imperative you understand that dysfunction should never define your relationship with a man. I know all too well that it's very easy to fall into a cycle where arguing and drama feel normal or even justifiable, but trust me, they never are.

You might have seen dysfunction every day growing up, and it might be what you've become accustomed to in your own adult life, but it's never a standard that you should be satisfied with.

If a man is stuck in that cycle and is either unwilling or unable to find the MAN-torship he needs to pull himself out, do *not* let him drag you down with him. Try to teach him the right way, but if he just can't learn, then you must let him go.

He might beg and plead with you not to go, he might even use his kids to guilt you into staying, but don't succumb to his MAN-ipulation. Even if the two of you have children together, you cannot allow that to be an excuse to stay trapped in dysfunction.

There are going to be a lot of people reading this, however, who aren't stuck in that sort of drama. Maybe you're one of them—you've got a man with good intentions and a better heart, but he still needs a little fine-tuning; a man who truly seems on the verge of undergoing that evolution we just spoke of in the last chapter.

So for you, I'll share a different message in this chapter: stick with that man. Try to weather the storms he might blow into your relationship, because unlike the dysfunctional man's, a good man's storms *will* pass.

And if you don't have a good man yet but see one out there, don't be afraid to pursue him. Rev's going to disagree with me on this one, but I believe women of today should be much more aggressive in pursuing a man they believe is going to make them happy over the long haul.

YOU MAKE THE DECISION

Whether or not that man is the right one for you is a decision you're going to have to make for *yourself.*

Period.

Yes, men can be hard to read.

Yes, they often try to obscure their true feelings and intentions.

But if you've made it this far in *Manology,* you've got a cheat sheet to help you read between his lines and even interpret what he *isn't* saying.

You need to be strong and trust *yourself* when trying to decide whether a man is a keeper or someone to throw back into the sea.

Earlier in the book I cautioned you against taking relationship advice from men, but now I have to warn you about getting it from some of your homegirls too.

That might be painful to hear, since we're talking about the friends you've grown up with, partied with, laughed and definitely cried with. But it still has to be said.

Your friends might rather see you hanging out in the club with them than snuggled up at home with your man. They might love you and truly value you as a friend, but they still love themselves more. And if they like having you as the friend who's always down to go out and hang, then they're going to promote an agenda that keeps you single too. They might not even be conscious of what they're doing, but they're still going to instinctively push you in a direction that keeps you in the role they think suits you best, rather than the one that is best suited for you. And the role they like you best in is the one that has you up in the club with them five nights a week, getting things poppin'!

Then there are the women who don't have your best interest at heart and know it, but don't care because drama is what they thrive on. I call these types of women "street bloggers," because their main function in life seems to be peddling drama. Just like whatever website you consult to hear about rumors and innuendo. Street bloggers might not be on the Internet, but they still traffic in negativity. The second anything happens in the streets—as soon as any rumors go down about who's sleeping with who, who's pregnant by who and who's fighting with who—that "street blogger" wants to tell you all about it and involve you in it too. They love taking all that negativity out of the streets and dropping it right into your lap.

Personally, I don't want to carry *any* extra negativity if I can avoid it. I don't even watch the news for that very reason. It's not that I'm promoting being uninformed; I'm simply acknowledging that I'm an extremely emotional and spiritual person, as many of us are. When I see a story about people dying in a plane crash, or a little boy losing his leg in a car accident, it affects me. I think about the pain those people's families must be going through, and it hurts me. Hard. Carrying around that pain really trips me up. So even if an event doesn't seem to touch me personally, I still try to steer clear of it.

Since it's impossible to avoid all of the negativity out there, I refuse to *invite* any into my life. I have enough problems with real bloggers trying to twist me up and pull me into drama; I don't need to allow any "street bloggers" into my space. It can be hard to avoid these types, especially since "street bloggers" can be fun to be around. They always have something provocative to say, and it's easy to find yourself drifting toward their energy, but you must never look to them for strength or guidance. You might be asking a street blogger for advice, but what you'll be receiving from them is negativity.

The next time you and your man get into a fight or are considering taking some time apart, think hard about who you're turning to for advice on how to handle the situation. Ask yourself, is that person's advice coming from a pure place? Or is that friend really just trying to keep you in a role that's best suited for what she wants? Is she truly trying to "help," or is she just looking to be entertained? Does she honestly want you to repair your relationship, or does she want you going through it because that drama creates more "traffic" for her "site"—which is her dark heart.

Remember, negative people are like black clouds in the sky. Once you push those clouds out of the way, the sun will start shining into your life again.

DON'T COMPARE YOURSELF TO *HER*

In assessing their relationships, women often make the mistake of comparing their situation to someone else's.

A woman might be going through real pain with her man, but she'll still be afraid to break things off because when she looks around, it seems like every other woman has someone to be with. So why shouldn't she have a man too?

I'm talking about smart, educated woman who are financially independent, yet stay in the *worst* relationships. They know they should break things off, but they keep hanging around because they're afraid to be alone, especially when they see so many women who they feel that they're better than that do have a man.

It's almost as if they think, *Here I am about to break it off with another dude, yet this hood rat down the block is always in a relationship. She stays triflin' with her curves hangin' out all over the place, but she's always got a man. I look good and keep myself together, but I'm still bouncin' from one relationship to the next. What's going on here? There must be something wrong with me.*

It might be easy to feel that way, but here's the thing: hood rats and hoes are *never* alone, not because they are so attractive to men but because they are willing to be with anybody who's willing to be with them.

I mean *anybody*.

You're not like that. You've got standards and preferences that can't be overlooked so easily, so if a man is not meeting those standards in your relationship and doesn't match up with your preferences, don't be afraid to let him go. Stop comparing yourself to those other women who are willing to settle, because that's not *you.*

DON'T BE EMBARASSED TO ADMIT HE DIDN'T LIVE UP TO THE HYPE

Also, never be afraid to admit that a man you thought was going to live up to those standards ultimately fell short. Too many women spend so much time hyping up a man that they're too embarrassed to admit that he wasn't really all that. *Well, I told my momma and my girlfriends that he is the man of my dreams,* they'll think. *So how can I ruin the fantasy that this is my future husband?*

Obviously it isn't easy to admit that you misjudged a man, but if your momma and your friends are being real, then they won't give you grief for having made that mistake. There probably isn't a woman alive who hasn't been tricked by a man at some point or another in her life. With so many MAN-ipulators running around out there, it's inevitable that even the smartest, strongest woman has been tripped up at least one time before. Yes, your momma has been tripped up too, maybe even by your father. So don't be embarrassed when it happens to you too.

Rather than cling to a bad relationship out of fear or embarrassment, suck up your loss and keep it moving. No matter how much the embarrassment might sting at first, in the long run leaving a deadbeat dude is much better than staying in a dead-end relationship.

BREAK THE DYSFUNCTION

Removing negative friends from the decision-making process and getting past embarrassment is only half the battle. For many women, the real war they must wage is with a man who is keeping them stuck in a cycle of dysfunction and abuse.

191

If you grew up in a household where dysfunction was the norm, this can be a very tough cycle to break yourself out of. But no matter how much your man has been through, no matter how unfair the world might have been to him, and no matter how much he might remind you of your father, you *cannot* be afraid to leave a man whose demons threaten to take over your life too.

I understand how difficult this war can be, because I've had to wage it myself. I grew up in a house full of drama, dysfunction and hostility, a house where verbal, mental, spiritual and physical abuse was normal. As a result, if a woman wasn't willing to argue and get loud with me, I'd tell myself "she must not love me." Because my interpretation of love was the dysfunction I'd been exposed to.

As I grew older and found myself in relationships that lacked those "spices," I would, frankly, get bored as hell. It got to the point where I couldn't even stay in a relationship unless my woman was constantly yelling at the top of her lungs. I needed every argument to end up with someone saying, "Really? You really want to go *there*?"

What's worse, if a woman was kind and sweet by nature, then I would try to break her spirit. I would look to spark some dysfunction just so I could feel the heat of what I considered to be "real love." I needed a woman to swear and scream like my momma used to. And if she wouldn't, then I would say something foul like, "Shut up, woman" just to force that response. I needed every woman to meet me in the darkness of my heart. And I wouldn't let up until she was there with me.

Today, thank God, the light has entered my darkest recesses. To even hear a woman raise her voice, let alone cuss and scream, makes me uncomfortable. But I needed a lot of MAN-torship to get to that point—which is why I believe that if you do not see that MAN-torship taking place in your man's life, or at least the possibility of it down the road, then you need to remove yourself from that relationship as quickly as possible.

Oh, I know it will be hard to break away, especially because those fiery, tempestuous relationships can seem so exciting, so full of passion. But as we've all seen, that fire very easily leads not only to heartbreak, but pain and even death.

ARE YOU WITH A MAN? OR IN A CULT?

You can't be afraid to leave a man trapped in dysfunction, even if it feels more exciting to stay. This is especially true if your main reason for staying is that too much of your world is tied up in that man. You see, a lot of MAN-ipulators are like cult leaders—they convince you to cut off your friends, your family and the people who truly care about you so that you'll be completely dependent on them. They always claim to have a justification for why you should stop talking to your momma ("she's disrespecting you and treating you like a little girl even though you're grown") or why you should cut off your best friend ("she's been flirting with me, trying to steal me out from under you") but it really has nothing to do with those people. It's all about controlling you and your emotions.

If you are with a man and realize that you've somehow cut off everyone you used to be close with just to be with him, then you have made a HUGE mistake. You signed up for a loving, nurturing relationship, not for a cult. Unless you are able to look in the mirror and say, "My life is appreciably BETTER since I met this man, and I know I am following my own agenda in life, not anyone else's," then it is time to go. You have lost your identity in that man's dysfunction, and the only way to find it again is to remove yourself from the situation.

DON'T LET HIM USE HIS KIDS

Another trick guys will use to keep you trapped in dysfunction is MAN-ipulating the relationship you've established with their kids.

A lot of women think they need to stay together for the kids, but I know from firsthand experience that it usually doesn't work.

I haven't shared this before, but let me put myself out there. One of the main reasons I married my ex was that she was pregnant with our daughter. In fact, I can remember the exact moment I decided to propose to her. She was eight months' pregnant, and we were lying in bed together when she suddenly turned to me and said, "Our daughter is coming into this world next month and I feel like I'm gonna be a baby momma."

She didn't say, "You better put a ring on it" or "We need to make this official." She just needed to say that she was feeling like a baby momma. When she said that, it really messed me up. Yes, we had a rocky relationship, but she deserved better. She should have been feeling excited and proud, not insecure and apprehensive.

So the next week at her baby shower, in front of all our family and closest friends, I got down on my knees and proposed. I can't lie, it was one of the most beautiful moments I've ever been part of. My ex cried with joy, and I'm sure our daughter was dancing around inside that big belly because she could feel all the happiness her mommy was experiencing.

But even though that moment was beautiful, our overall relationship was still ugly. We had too many unresolved issues, a history of nasty emotions, lying, and, yes, cheating, which the presence of a child alone wasn't going to erase. We could try to sweep those issues under the rug for a week or a month, but eventually that dysfunction was going to rear its head again.

Even though we were literally screaming and fighting with each other most days and actually said to each other, "This is so nasty. How can we get married like this?" we decided to plow ahead and tie the knot for our daughter's sake.

For a few months at least, we kept it together. Despite our drama, I did love my ex, and there were moments when I felt like we were a real husband and wife. Those moments, however, were fleeting. Most of the time we were still that arguing, dysfunctional couple, only now there was a beautiful little girl between us, soaking it all in.

I became concerned that we were creating negative standards in our daughter's life. Our example was essentially telling her, even at her young age, "This is what love is." I knew that if she grew up seeing her parents yelling and screaming, being evil, condescending and spiteful and saying devious things in front of her, that is what she would seek to replicate in her own life. When she started dating, she would think, "If he's not willing to talk to me the way I saw my father talk to my momma, then he don't love me." There's no way I could do that to my daughter.

So after just under a year together, we realized we had to call it quits. We had tried to make it work, but it was obvious that my ex and I were never going to be happy together. Rather than have our daughter grow up in a home where screaming and arguing were the norm, it was better for us to go our separate ways and be able to stay civil with each other. If our daughter couldn't see love between her parents, at least she'd be able to see respect and civility.

I needed to put that out there because I know that when some people heard I was writing this book, they probably thought, *How the hell can he give me advice about love, life and romance when he was only married for a year?*

Well, now you know why I was married for only a year. I don't expect anybody to applaud me or give me props for how things went down, but I don't have any regrets about my choice either.

Actually, that's not entirely true.

I do regret that my ex and I stood there in front of our preacher, family and friends and exchanged vows in God's name that didn't reflect what we were really feeling in our hearts. I wish we hadn't been insincere with God and used his name to make ourselves feel better about what we were doing. Because even though we might have been able to stand up there and lie to ourselves and everyone else, God always knew the truth.

The truth is that my ex and I, beautiful baby girl and all, should never have been married. I was in the wrong season, and our relationship was built on too much dysfunction for it to ever be able to withstand the pressures of marriage and parenting.

Which is why I encourage any reader who's trapped in a dysfunctional relationship to get out of it now, kids or not. Please do not raise your kids in an environment where they think "love" is defined by screaming and arguing.

As much as you might worry about your kid growing up without a mother and father under the same roof, it's better for the parents to lead respectful, civil lives apart than dysfunctional ones together. Today, I can spend an afternoon at Barnes & Noble with my daughter and my ex and the three of us can have a wonderful time together. There's no nasty words or bad energy being exchanged between my ex and me; we just have mutual appreciation for the beautiful child we created together. It might not be the dynamic that everyone dreams of, but it's certainly a healthier reality than dysfunction and drama.

CONSISTENCY KILLS
THE CAT (AND THE DOG)

So far, I've been mainly talking about flawed men in this chapter—the abusers, the deadbeats, the do-nothings, the MAN-ipulators.

But if you're with a kindhearted and decent man who just has a little bit of work to do before he's fully into that grown man season, then I'm going to offer you a different perspective. If you have a man like that in your life, I'm going to encourage you to do everything you can to stick it out with him. Give him every opportunity to figure it out and evolve into that man you want to spend the rest of your life with.

This is a message that's particularly important for African-American women to hear. Why? Because right now African-Americans are in a state of crisis when it comes to marriage. Unless we can be realistic about this situation, we're never going to be able to correct it.

Don't believe me? Think I'm exaggerating? Then let me throw some statistics at you.

- Black folks aren't getting married at nearly the same rate as other Americans. According to a recent study by the US Census Bureau, 42 percent of African-American adults have never been married, compared to just 26 percent of all other American adults.

- According to the same 2011 study by the US Census Bureau, African-American women ages thirty-five to forty-four are the only group of women in America with lower rates of marriage than men of the same race or ethnicity. African-American women are also getting married less than women from other groups. By their early forties, 31 percent of African-American women have never been married, whereas only 9 percent of white women, 11 percent of Asian women and 12 percent of Hispanic women are still single at the same age.

While everyone else runs off and ties the knot, are all these African-American women staying single because they're not interested in being married? I don't think that's the case at all. I believe many of them would love to be in a healthy, committed marriage, but they feel like they can't find the right man to do it with. Especially with the right *African-American* man.

You see, there is a growing cultural divide between African-American men and women. While African-American men continue to struggle with their validation issues, African-American women have become better educated and more career-oriented. A recent study by the US Department of Education found that more than 44 percent of African-American women graduate from college, opposed to 33.1 percent of African-American men. The DOE also found that among African-American college graduates, 66 percent of bachelor's degrees and 71 percent of master's degrees were going to *women*. Not surprising, African-American women are seeing their earning power increase, while a lot of African-American men are still stuck in the same entry-level or minimum-wage positions. Or even worse, they're looking to make a living out on the streets.

When you look at all these changing realities, what are you left with? A situation that Stanford University law professor Ralph Richard Banks has dubbed a "black man shortage." As an African-American woman making moves in the workplace, at some point you're going to look up and realize that there aren't enough "good black men" to go around. You might even feel like you have to marry "down" if you want to raise a family with an African-American man.

Professor Banks can call it a shortage, but I believe what we're experiencing today is nothing short of a black marriage crisis. There is a real gap growing between African-American women and men, and it's causing families to fall apart. Again, the numbers back this up. A recent study by the Pew Research Center found that while 21 percent of white fathers live away from their children, 44 percent of African-American fathers don't live with their children. That means an African-American child is almost twice as likely as a white child to grow up without a father in the house. If those numbers continue, we're going to be raising a lost generation.

To make matters worse, it seems like so many African-American couples that do tie the knot end up getting divorced. To me, it seems like marriages back in the 1940s, 1950s, and 1960s were built on the foundations of commitment, sacrifice, and longevity, but in modern times there's not the same expectation that a marriage is going to last. It's as if getting a divorce is actually popular because of the amount of press and media attention folks get these days when they split up. In fact, I saw a story the other day about a couple in their eighties that really shook me. When asked how they'd managed to stay together for over fifty years, the woman replied, "We were born in a time where if something was broke in a relationship we fixed it. Now they just throw it away."

How do we fix this? If you want to survive in a crisis, one of the first steps to take is making certain concessions. Think about it. When there's a financial crisis going on, pragmatists accept that if they want to hold on to that valuable job, they're going to have to accept situations they normally wouldn't put up with: working long hours for less pay, not getting a year-end raise or bonus, no acknowledgment or sympathy from the boss for all their sacrifices.

You have to suck it up and have faith that if you keep working hard, you'll eventually weather the crisis and find yourself in a better place. This comes with the understanding that the situation won't last forever. It just has to be worked through. So my prescription for working through the black marriage crisis that we are currently experiencing is for women to try to adopt a similar outlook. It is not an easy thing to do, but women need to accept that they might not get exactly what they're looking for or deserve at first. If, however, your man possesses a good heart and intentions, then you have something worth fighting for and holding on to.

If you have a good but flawed man I'm not going to call you a "lucky one," because there's nothing lucky about having someone frustrate or disappoint you. I understand that getting dumped on in a relationship is much harder to deal with than getting dumped on at work.

I am, however, going to encourage you to keep working with that man. You might not feel appreciated at first, but never lose sight of the fact that he is worth weathering the storm for. You've got to have faith that your hard work and consistency will pay off and eventually your relationship will end up in a better place. Trust me, there are a lot of brothers out there who are struggling to find themselves. They might not have graduated from college and might even have done a little time, but they are still very much worth your investment.

I know that commitment can pay off because I've experienced the effect my girlfriend's consistency and resiliency have had on our relationship. As I like to tease her, "It's consistency, not curiosity, that killed this cat." Or perhaps more appropriately for our situation, that consistency is what killed the "dog" in me.

She is certainly patient when I screw up. She doesn't jump down my throat the second something stupid comes out of my mouth, which is often.

This woman has the highest tolerance of anyone I have ever dated, and it's made a difference not only in how I see her but also in how I see myself. It's made me more optimistic about the relationship. It's caused me to stick around and try to make it work in situations where I usually would have packed my bags and left. Her consistency and patience have given me a confidence in the concept of love and marriage that I never possessed before.

Believe me, it hasn't been easy for her. I've severely tested her patience. I have tried to break up with this woman a bunch of times because her love has taken me into uncharted territory, and that's scary to me. As an African-American man who didn't have a father to show me how to navigate the difficult stretches of relationships, my instinct is to break up instead of pushing ahead into that unknown. Just recently I said some really foul, disrespectful things to her, not because I meant them but because I was trying to *make* her break up with me. I was trying to force her to walk away.

Do you know what her response was to those terrible words? With tears in her eyes she said, "Baby, what you just said to me cut me, and it hurt me so deep. No one has ever said anything that mean and disrespectful to me. But I love you. And you know what? We're going to stay in this and we're going to figure it out. Whatever it takes."

Then she said something that truly blew my mind. "I'm going to go to anger management classes with you. And after that, we're going to go to relationship counseling so we can make this thing work. I'm not going anywhere, I love you regardless of all of your flaws, your mood swings and the things you put me through. Believe me, we *are* going to figure it out."

Now you might be saying to yourself, *Whatever, this chick is trippin'. If a man goes out of his way to say some disrespectful, foul things to me, the last thing I'm going to tell him is, "Baby, it's OK."*

Trust me, my girl ain't no fool. She's got two master's degrees and a PhD, and she runs a highly successful international business. I've never been with a more educated and worldly woman.

Her attitude might appear gullible, but in reality she's operating on a different plane than the other women I've been with. She's watched her parents be together for over forty years and comes from a family where people are expected to stay together through thick and thin. Day in and day out, she has seen that consistency, patience and tolerance *can* make a relationship work, so she's not afraid to offer those qualities to me.

That's why I encourage women to have faith that there will

202

be a reward for their consistency. I know that if my girl and I end up getting married, and I believe that we will, it will largely be because she was so incredibly consistent with her love for me. She certainly didn't want to put up with the disrespect and lying that I put her through, but she did weather my storm.

As a woman, you've got to look at that man you're with and ask yourself, *Does this man have some of the respect, the decency, the energy and the consistency that I am looking for in a husband? Yes, I know he can be full of it, I know he's capable of lying and cheating, but does he have something in him that makes me want to stay with him?*

If the answer is yes, then buckle up and try to ride it out with that man, no matter how bumpy the ride might get.

And African-American women in particular, please have confidence that you *can* teach your man how to love, that you *can* keep a relationship afloat even when your man tries his hardest to sink his own ship. As African-American men, we are used to having people give up on us. Sadly, we often see it as inevitable and have made inconsistency our standard. Please don't give up on us too.

The bottom line is that almost every good man, whether he's black, white or purple, has baggage. When you find it, of course you can turn on your heels and walk away. You'll be able to tell all your friends how "independent" you are and be free to join them at the club Friday night, where you can start searching all over again for the type of man you *just left.*

Or you can stay and help him unpack it.

The choice is yours.

If you think he's worth it, then please don't give up too

quickly. Have faith that being patient with your love is extremely powerful. And then harness that power and see where it actually gets you.

PUT A RING ON *HIM*

I want to end this by encouraging you to not only stick with a good man but also to be proactive in moving the relationship forward. In other words, don't wait for him to "put a ring on it." If you think he's the man you want to be with for the rest of your life, then don't be afraid to put a ring on *him*!

Obviously, the traditional approach is that as a woman, you should wait for that proposal. If your man really loves you, then he's going to be the one to pop the question. That's as old school as Al Green's shoes, right?

But these days, women are not as comfortable sitting back and essentially asking, "Baby, do you love me?" or "Did you see their wedding pictures? Didn't they look beautiful?" No, they're getting tired of throwing hints that their men never act on.

I can understand why. Women are getting more and more responsibility in the workplace and making more and more money. And that sense of power and responsibility is carrying over into their personal lives. Instead of waiting for their men to make all the major moves, women are becoming increasingly comfortable taking the reins in a relationship.

Someone who really reflects this new mentality is Chrissy Lampkin, who is married to the rapper Jim Jones. If you watched her reality show *Love & Hip-Hop*, then you know that Chrissy was stuck in a classic situation with Jimmy; they'd been together for years, and even though he clearly loved and respected her, he didn't seem to be in a rush to put a ring on it.

What did Chrissy do? She took matters into her own hands and proposed to Jimmy. She didn't get down on one knee or hire a plane to fly over a baseball game trailing a banner that said, "Jimmy, will you marry me?" But she did show him the rock she wanted and made it perfectly clear that it was time to take their relationship to that next level.

I have no doubt that a lot of women who watched Chrissy do that thought, *You know what, I've been with my man for six years and I'm tired of waiting too. What we gone do, be living together forever? I've been throwin' hints and sendin' him messages through people, but I'm tired of all this. I'm proposing to this man, period. I'm going to be like Chrissy.*

I felt it was a great move as well. In fact, not long after Chrissy "proposed" to Jim, I can remember a friend asking me, "Well, would you be OK with it if your girl proposed to you?" "Absolutely," I said.

Truth be told, I wouldn't want to be with a woman who *wasn't* prepared to make that move if it was in her heart. Often in life you have to unapologetically invite yourself into situations. If you see a space you believe will be beneficial to you, then you must move into it, with or without an invitation. You can't waste time worrying about whether that move defies convention or breaks with tradition.

Will Smith once told me something extremely powerful on this topic. "In life, there are no rules," he said. "Two plus two are going to equal whatever *I* want it to equal."

That's an attitude that's taken Will so far in his incredible journey, and it's one that can have a similar effect on your life too. The "rules" might say you have to wait for a man to propose, but Chrissy has proven that two plus two can equal whatever she needs them to in *her* relationship. It might have taken Jimmy a little while to do the math, but eventually he figured out that Chrissy had it right, and he gave her that ring. I don't think either of them will regret how things ultimately added up.

I'm not saying it's going to be easy for Chrissy—she's going to have to exhibit a lot more consistency and patience with Jimmy, whether there's a ring on her finger or not. But at least now she has the confidence that she was able to execute a very bold plan. Now she feels like she has some control over the direction her life is taking. There's so much power in knowing that. Please try to harness some of it in your own life.

I know some of the information in this chapter might have felt contradictory, almost as if I'd been talking out of both sides of my mouth. One second I'm saying, "Break out of that relationship, no matter what it takes!" while the next I was saying, "Hold on to that man as strong as you can!" But there's simply no getting around the fact that every man is different.

As you read this chapter, you knew instinctively which sort you're dealing with. If you read the part about dysfunction and abuse and thought, *That's my man he's talking about,* then you know which advice applies to you. Just as if you read the part about Chrissy sticking with Jimmy and thought, *I can try harder in my relationship. I can be more consistent and more loving and ride this thing out,* then you received the message that was intended for you.

All I can hope is that you *received* the message and will *act* on it too. You might have been offended by what I said about women needing to be more consistent, but that's OK. You can be offended. I don't need anyone's approval. What I need is for *someone* reading this to decide that they actually love themselves enough to do things differently.

Is that person you?

REV RUN

Let me start by addressing this concept of women proposing to men. There was a time when I wasn't comfortable with it, when the concept felt backwards to me. After all, the Bible doesn't tell us that a good woman should find a man; it says that a good man should find a wife.

In Chrissy's specific case, however, I loved the moves she made. They felt very wise to me. Chrissy was 110 percent certain that Jimmy loved her, and she knew he just needed that extra little nudge. And she was right.

But not every woman is in the same situation. Remember, Chrissy didn't *chase* Jimmy, she just *nudged* him. And there is a big difference between chasing and nudging. When you chase a man, especially one that you just met and truthfully don't really know beyond the sex, you run the risk of never letting him demonstrate how hard he's willing to chase *you*. And a man's pursuit, or lack thereof, is a fantastic litmus test for just how serious he is about a woman.

Ladies, when a man really loves and respects you, he will be relentless in his pursuit of you. I'm not talking about a flurry of texts and phone calls after you guys just meet and he's trying to see whether or not he can get you into bed.

No, I'm talking about a sustained and consistent display of energy and affection even *after* you've made it clear that you're not about to hop in the sack with him.

Some women never get a proper read on a man's level of pursuit because they're too quick to take the initiative themselves. If a cute guy sends them a couple of flirty texts but then stops, they want to send him a text to get things flowing again. Ladies, I understand it can be tempting to set the pace yourself, but you've got to try to hold back.

As much as you might want to, do not pick up your phone and text that man just because you haven't heard from him in a few days. You have to be disciplined and let that man show you how much you're loved and valued.

I've taught my daughters that if a man doesn't respond to their texts within a day, he's already told them everything they need to know: no response equals no need to invest another second in him.

Of course men will try to tell you otherwise. They'll claim that they didn't get back to you because they were tied up at work, helping their mother out with something, somehow lost your information or were late paying their phone bill. Don't accept any of those excuses, because the real truth is this: when a man *really* wants to talk with a woman, nothing is going to stand in the way of his finding time to do it.

Nothing.

Even if it's just a short text like "Thinking of you," if that's what a man is doing, then he will find a way to let you know. He will sneak out of his office for a few minutes to say hello to you during your lunch break, tell his mother he needs a moment to make an important call or borrow his friend's phone if his got shut off.

If you find yourself spinning your wheels while a man tries to find a "good time" for you two to speak, or you feel like you're constantly getting stuck in the background while he "sorts some things out," then get the hint. Something in the milk ain't clean.

That man might be cute, he might be funny and you might really, *really* like him, but if his pursuit is not consistent, then he is not the right one for you. Period.

Please remember this as well: once you let him go and ignore his texts and calls, that's going to make him start pursuing you *harder.* Whereas initially he couldn't be bothered to get back to you promptly and consistently, those texts are going to start flying in your direction once he feels you're no longer interested. Don't be fooled by that. That new flurry of texts only represents what I call a "secondary pursuit." They're inspired not by true love and respect but rather by a man's need to reassure his bruised ego. You see, when you stopped paying attention to him, that was a blow to him. He won't want to believe that you're willing to let him go, so he'll actually begin pursuing you harder then he did at first. Don't fall for that "secondary pursuit," because it's not real. A man gets one chance to show you he's serious. If he blows it, move on and don't look back!

I also need to stress that a man who's truly in love *never* stops pursuing his woman, even if they've been going steady for months. Even if they're engaged. Even after they're married and have started a family. I've been married over twenty years, and I'm still pursuing my wife. And then flaunting her to the world whenever I feel I've caught up with her!

Every day I still try to make her happy. I still try to win her over to my side of things. Every day I still try to put her on a pedestal. Every day I still try to ease her mind whenever I sense that it's troubled.

One time Tyrese saw me worrying about getting home in time to talk about something with my wife, and it blew his mind. He said to me, "Just relax, Rev. Your wife loves you. You don't have to keep chasing her."

When he told me that, I had to set him straight *right* away. "Just relax? Man, listen," I told him. "You're going to have me relax myself right out of this marriage with that sort of attitude."

A lot of men make the mistake of thinking that getting married means they're allowed to downshift their energy and stop worrying about what their wife needs all the time. But that's not the case at all.

In my opinion, a married man should never want to stop chasing that woman. He should never *not* be nervous every time he thinks she might be getting unhappy or is slipping away from him. This is because a man is actually at his happiest when he's in pursuit of a woman. It's something of his natural state. For thousands of years, going out and hunting was our daily routine. Back then it might have been gazelles and lions, but we never really got the thrill of the hunt out of our blood. Today we might not be looking for that gazelle meat anymore, but we are still wired to hunt other big game, like professional opportunities or beautiful women.

To an outsider looking in—even Tyrese—that excitement might be hard to see. It might even appear that I'm too anxious or put too much energy into keeping my wife happy. I can promise you it's not the case, however. In fact, I live by the motto "Happy wife, happy life." If I ever felt my wife was feeling even a smidgen dissatisfied or unhappy in our marriage, it would make *me* miserable. Why wouldn't it? My wife is my best friend and soul mate. How could I be happy if she wasn't? So every day I wake up knowing that I'm going to have to do whatever is necessary to make my wife feel loved and cherished.

You should be looking for this same level of pursuit in your man as well, because you deserve nothing less. No matter what stage your relationship is in, never stop gauging your man's level of pursuit. Just because he starts a relationship with the right energy—phone calls, flowers, opening doors, agreeing to see chick flicks, going shopping together—doesn't mean he should begin to mail it in after a few years.

If that level of pursuit begins to taper off and you don't confront it immediately, one day you will find yourself stuck in a relationship with a man who's not doing *anything* to put your happiness and comfort first. You will find yourself dating, living with or even married to a selfish slob who only seems to care about what makes him comfortable.

You'll be scratching your head, trying to figure out what happened to that man who seemed so determined to make you happy. How could you not have seen this coming?

Well, you can see it coming, but you can't take your eyes off his "pursuit levels." The *moment* his pursuit and flaunting start slowing down, you've got your sign. You've got your clue that this man isn't everything he was pretending to be. The second you notice him starting to put you in the background or take you for granted, you need to put your foot down and say, "Sorry, but this is not cutting it. Either I start to feel wanted again or I'm gone!"

And if that man doesn't snap back to attention and start showing you the proper amount of respect and energy, then you know in no uncertain terms that it's time to go.

FROM RUTH AND BOAZ TO BEYONCÉ AND JAY-Z

If you've got a man who started pursuing you and never stopped, then congratulations are in order. You have truly been blessed in this relationship game.

For many women, however, it's necessary to make yourself as

attractive as possible in order to ensure that a man's natural inclination to hunt kicks in properly.

When I say "make yourself as attractive as possible," I'm not talking about putting on your makeup, getting your hair done, or squeezing yourself into your sexiest little dress.

No, I'm talking about doing the one thing that will truly help you not only catch but also keep the attention of a good man.

Demonstrate your independence.

Men rarely want to admit this, but an independent spirit is sexier to them than a cute butt, nice smile or provocative outfit. Nothing truly wins us over more than a woman who has a strong and steady sense of herself.

A great example of just how attractive a woman's independence is to a man is the biblical story of King Boaz and Ruth. It's one of the shortest stories in the Bible, but I believe it's also one of the most instructive.

Ruth was a widow who was sent to work in King Boaz's fields during a famine. She was a hard worker, so from the moment she got to the fields, she stayed busy harvesting the crops, digging ditches and doing whatever it was she had to do.

About halfway through the day, King Boaz showed up to see how things were going. Immediately all the other women who were working alongside Ruth dropped what they were doing and ran over to him. Basically, they were jocking the king.

The only woman who stayed focused on her work and basically didn't act like a groupie was Ruth. So out of all the women in the field that day, who do you think it was that caught Boaz's attention? Ruth, of course.

So much so that King Boaz pointed Ruth out to his servants and told them to look out for her the rest of the day. As a result, Ruth ended up getting to spend the night in his stable, and before long they were married. It was such a miraculous turn of events, a widow literally going from the pit to the palace.

It was only able to happen because of Ruth's focused independence. You see, Boaz and Ruth were from different tribes, which was a *very* big deal back then. You think interracial dating is a big deal now? It's nothing compared to the drama that took place when the king of the tribe of Judah decided he wanted to marry a Moabite widow. That was an extremely controversial move on Boaz's part, but he didn't care. He was pursuing Ruth all the way because he was so attracted to her work ethic and independence.

I see a modern parallel to Boaz and Ruth in the marriage of Beyoncé and Jay-Z. A lot of people, especially women, have wondered, "How did Beyoncé manage to convince Jay-Z to settle down?" Obviously she's beyond beautiful and talented, but there have been a lot of beautiful and talented women who've tried to pin Jay down.

To me, and this is admittedly from the outside looking in, what won Jay over was Beyoncé's independent spirit. Her total commitment to her vision for her own career. There's strong evidence to back up my theory in Jay's song "Lost One," where he rhymes: "I don't think it's meant to be, B / But she loves her work more than she does me / And honestly, at twenty-three / I would probably love my work more than I did she / So we, ain't we/It's me and her / 'Cause what she prefers over me is work / And that's where we differ / So I have to give her / Free time / Even if it hurts. . . ."

When I first heard that verse, I said to myself, *Oh, Beyoncé's got him now. He sounds confused. He sounds out of breath because he's sooooo hot in pursuit of her. And I love it!*

I'm guessing that Jay was being his usual cocky self when he and Beyoncé first started kicking it. I'll bet that he probably held back and was reserved with his texts, phone calls and attention. Then a funny thing happened. He started noticing that instead of making Beyoncé chase him, *he* was the one not getting called or texted back right away.

Not because Beyoncé was playing games but because she was truly focused on the process of being a star. I can see her telling him, "Sorry I didn't get back to you for a couple of days, baby. I was on a flight to Australia and we didn't have any reception." Or "Hey, sorry I didn't see that you called before, I was on set and we had to turn off our phones. What's up, honey?"

She was doing all the things that MAN-ipulators usually do to women, except instead of having a MAN-ipulative intention, she was coming from an honest place. She really was on that plane to Melbourne. She really was onstage, or working on a new song in the studio.

All that focus and drive probably caught Jay's attention and threw him into pursuit mode. Hard. Soon he was the one on her trail, writing her songs, letting the entire *world* know that he wanted to spend more time with his woman but was still happy to take what he could get. We're talking about Jay-Z here—Mr. Big Pimpin' himself, the ultimate playa. We're talking about a guy who never let *anyone* appear to have the upper hand over him, but even he couldn't resist letting down his guard for an independent, focused woman.

Ladies, I need you to understand that the independent mind state is the *only* one that matters. If you take only one lesson from this book, please let it be this one: independence is your most attractive attribute. It's sexier than Red Bottoms, good hair, a big butt or any other attribute you think is going to pull a man in and keep him there.

As I've said before, living and *loving* your life is always your most attractive quality. I promise that once you go ahead and start doing *you* to the fullest of your abilities, you will find that good man hot on your trail!

ALWAYS MAKE HIM *THINK* YOU'LL LEAVE

Once you're in a relationship, one of the keys to asserting your independence is making a man *think* you'll leave him if he doesn't act right. I am not saying that you should make him feel insecure, but rather that he shouldn't feel secure about the relationship when he doesn't desire to be. Even if in your heart of hearts you know you'll dang near put up with anything in order to be with that man, you can never let *him* know that.

A great example of someone putting this principle into practice is Priscilla Chan, who recently married Facebook's founder, Mark Zuckerberg. Mark and Priscilla were college sweethearts at Harvard, having met well before Facebook blew up. Mark graduated first and went out to California to work on his company, while Priscilla stayed behind at school to get her degree. They had a couple of "time out" periods during which they probably saw other people, but after Priscilla graduated and headed to med school in California, Mark wanted them to get back together. Even move in together.

Most women would have been unpacking their bags at his place the next day; of course they'd want to move in with a man they obviously loved and had invested so much time in. Not to mention the fact that he was now worth several hundred million dollars more than when they first met!

But Priscilla saw that once Facebook started getting big, their relationship was taking a backseat to his business. This might have been understandable, but it still wasn't acceptable in her eyes.

By taking her time to decide whether or not she would move in with him, Priscilla let Mark know that no matter how much money he was worth, she was still prepared to leave the relationship if he wasn't flaunting her properly. In fact, once she did agree to move in with him, it was reportedly only with a condition—Mark had to sign a "relationship contract" that guaranteed her one hundred minutes a week of "alone time," plus one date night, each week.

Why did Mark Zuckerberg agree to those conditions? Because he understands *value*. He understands it in business, and he understands it in people. When Priscilla said, "I'm not sure I want to be with you if it's going to mean always being in the background," she asserted her *value*. It could have been a bluff, but by at least giving the *impression* that she wasn't having it unless he came correct, she forced him to respect her value. As a person. As a girlfriend. As a potential wife.

That is what you have to establish in your relationship. Your value. You must let your man know that you're not disposable, that he can't just do whatever. If he can take you on an emotional roller-coaster ride anytime he feels like it, then an emotional roller-coaster ride is what you're going to get. Every day of the week.

The methodology I'm prescribing might seem cold or calculating, but as a woman you must stay in control of your heart until that man officially commits to you. I'm not saying you should be heartless, just that you should use your heart . . . less.

FALL INTO LOVE, DON'T GET PUSHED

There's been a lot of talk in this chapter about the right time to get out of a relationship, but I want to wrap things up by talking about the right time to get *into* one.

Most women get caught up with lousy, no-good men not because they can't see them for who they are but because they're so lonely that they're willing to look past those flaws.

I tell this to my daughters all the time, and I want to tell it to you too: Never let being lonely make you fall for the wrong guy. Falling is good. Just don't get pushed.

Again, it all comes back to value. After a breakup, especially a messy one, a woman often questions her value. The MAN-ipulator she just broke up with made her feel so lousy about herself that she begins to despair that she'll never find a man—forget about a good one—again. As a result, she'll give in to the advances of the type of man to whom she previously wouldn't have given the time of day.

Ladies, as you fall out of love with that MAN-ipulator who never really loved you in the first place, please make sure that you still hold on to your value. You might feel like you've lost it, but let me ask you this: if you were walking down the street and saw a crumpled hundred-dollar bill, would you pick it up? You're darn right you would!

Once you do walk away from that MAN-ipulator, please don't go back to him. Remember, missing a man is *not* an indication that you need to be with him. Let's keep it funky: you don't really miss your ex. You miss who you *thought* he was! You *thought* he was the guy he pretended to be while pursuing you, but once he "caught" you, he revealed who he *really* was. And it wasn't anything special.

Finally, don't beat yourself up too hard for having been tricked initially by that MAN-ipulator. Did you make a mistake in judgment? Well, welcome to the club. Tyrese and I are both members, and we've got a lifetime membership right here for you too. Just let go of that mistake and forgive yourself.

Whatever you do, please don't give up on love. Don't let your "ex-man" ruin it for the "next man." Never let what a few fools have done to you ruin the nice, happy and loving person you really are.

TYRESE

DON'T INDEPENDENCE
YOUR WAY INTO LONELINESS

I know I'm jumping out of order here, but before we wrap up this chapter, I have to respond to something Rev just said about independence. Yes, independence can be very sexy in a woman. My girlfriend is extremely independent, especially financially, and it has given our relationship a lot of room to grow.

But at the same time, it's often a problem when a man feels like he's not needed because his woman already has it all. It might sound twisted, but often a man's ego makes him want to feel like the "gatekeeper" of money, cars, the house, and the decisions you make as a couple. Feeling like he controls the direction of the relationship helps him *feel* like a man. Let him have that perception, even if reality is often something else.

Even if you've already established that "you can do bad all by yourself," also always try to let your man know that he is filling a *void* in your life that *only* a man can.

So while your independence is often what attracted a secure man to you in the first place, the irony is that once you have him, it is possible to go *too* far in trying to assert that independence. It's a touchy subject, but I've got to try to bring some clarity to it.

How many times have I been in a club and the DJ gets on the mic and starts yelling, "All the independent women that's got their own money, they own cars, pay they own bills and don't need a man for nothing, make some noise!!!!"?

Sure, all the women put their hands up in the air and

scream . . . but then what? When they get home at the end of the night, the only things waiting for them are their little lap poodles by the door and their "rabbits" in the drawer of the nightstand next to their bed.

Rev mentioned Beyoncé, and while it is true women love to scream "All the single ladies," most aren't truly invested in the concept. Why? Because no one wants to be lonely. No one wants to come home to poodles and vibrators nine out of ten nights. Which is why if a good man comes over and taps you on the shoulder while you're still singing, "to the left, to the left," you're dippin' off with him.

The point is, don't hold on to the "independent ladies"–themed lyrics in songs and let them twist you all up. There's no doubt that Beyoncé was a queen on her own, but she still held out for her king.

DEPENDENCE VS. INDEPENDENCE

Just remember there is a difference between *dependence* and *independence*. It's true, being dependent on a man is never healthy. If you can have a relationship without feeling like you have to rely on a man financially or emotionally, it will create more fertile soil for that relationship to grow in.

Not being reliant on a man doesn't mean that you have to aggressively be single. The goal is to have independence, but within the union of a relationship.

Finding happiness through marriage, not separate from it, should always be your ultimate goal. Which is why I keep pleading, "Ladies, please do not independence yourself into loneliness!"

Notice that the women who are trying to gas you up about "not needing a man" are always the first ones to get married and have a baby. They don't want to be alone, and you shouldn't either. It's great that your little poodle is excited to see you when you come home solo at 4:00 a.m., but I am sorry, he is not a man!

CHAPTER 8

A RING DOESN'T ALWAYS EQUAL A WIN

TYRESE

While getting married should be your ultimate goal, it's important to remember that you should never view it as the end of your journey when it comes to understanding and coexisting with your man.

In sports, after the final buzzer sounds and they give you that championship ring, that's the ultimate sign that you've won. That ring is validation that you have achieved *everything* you set out to do as an athlete. The confetti is falling, the champagne is poppin', your teammates are hugging you, people are talkin' about going to Disney Land, and you can be satisfied in knowing that you have captured the ultimate goal.

In marriage, it's just the opposite. That ring doesn't signify that you've won a thing. Instead, it signifies that the game is *just starting.*

How could that be? Your man just bought you a huge diamond, there's no way he isn't going to take care of and love you for the rest of your life, right?

Let's start by telling the truth about rings and men: some men will give you a ring just to stall. It might sound like an incredibly foolish and childish thing to do, but there are men out there who will give a woman a ring simply because they're not ready to break up—yet. For those kinds of MAN-ipulators, a ring is just another piece of jewelry, devoid of any emotional attachment.

Just because a man's wallet is in your relationship does *not* mean that his heart is in it too. I have enough money to "put a ring" on ten different women if I wanted to. But that wouldn't make me a good husband to any one of them; it would just make me someone "renting" a woman until I was ready for the next move.

When I see women flashing a huge rock like it somehow proves that their relationship is "real," I can only shake my head. If a man truly loves you, it doesn't matter how big or expensive your ring is. I have a friend who scraped together every last penny just to put a five-hundred-dollar ring on his lady's finger. It might have been a very modest ring by some people's standards, but it truly represented what he was feeling in his heart. Not surprisingly, they've been together for thirteen years and are still deeply in love.

Conversely, I've seen plenty of women go into marriages with rocks that probably cost more than a brand-new Benz yet after just a few years find themselves sitting across the table from a divorce attorney.

Again, please don't assume that because he's twenty-one that he's a *man*, don't assume that because he's capable of making a child that he's a *father* and don't assume that because he's capable of buying a *ring* that he's actually your *husband*. If I've learned anything from being MAN-tored by Rev and looking up to my pastor, Bishop Kenneth Ulmer, who has been faithful and happily married for thirty-five years, is that being a husband isn't in the "purchase" of a ring and things. It's truly in the *heart* and actions of a man that makes you a husband or father to your kids.

Never believe that the size or cost of a ring is in any way an indication of how deep a man's love is. It is an indication of how deep his funds are—no more, no less. If you think that just because a man puts a blinding rock on your finger it's OK to start coasting in your relationship, you run the risk of drifting right into some very stormy seas.

MEN NEED NEWNESS

Too many women are focused only on getting married.

Not nearly enough pay any mind to how they're going to sustain their marriage once they've got the ring. Once they've got the house, the kids and the stability of marriage, they're not asking themselves, *How can I keep this marriage interesting? How can I keep this man intrigued with me? How can I keep him here at home?*

It might sound like I'm putting all the responsibility of maintaining a marriage on the wives, but the truth is that if a woman wants her man to stay at home, she's going to have to take the lead in creating an environment he's going to want to stay in. Because on a very basic level, a woman's view of what makes for a happy marriage, especially sexually, is going to be fundamentally different from her husband's.

Women like security and routine. To most women, the idea of getting into bed with the same man night after night, year after year, sounds comforting and reassuring.

Men, on the other hand, crave newness. To most men, the idea of getting into bed with the same woman sounds boring at best, downright depressing at worst.

Or, to put the situation into even plainer terms, in a man's mind, "There ain't no woman like a new woman." While to a woman, "There ain't no man like the same consistent dude."

Yes, a woman loves to be able to say, "That thing is mine, it's not going anywhere else and it feels safe." This dichotomy is why as a wife, or even a serious girlfriend, one of the real questions you must ask yourself is, How can I convince that old dog that I'm some new kitty?

So how do you do that? You could do what a female friend of mine once told me she does with her man: she makes him think he's cheating on her with *her.*

Get it?

In a marriage, you often must recharge the energy in your bedroom in order to keep things fresh. One of the easiest ways to do it is through role playing. A female friend who's into it says sometimes she'll pretend to be a maid showing up unannounced to clean up the room. A female cop out on the beat. Or even a librarian who "disciplines" her man for an overdue library book.

I'm not saying that you need to go out and buy costumes or create elaborate stage sets in your bedroom, just switch things up enough that your man is going to feel a different energy.

For instance, another female friend created an alter ego for herself. She doesn't break it out all the time, but when she does, the alter ego is willing to do things that my friend normally wouldn't. They've been playing this game for a while, and it's gotten to the point where her man even knows not to call my friend by her real name when she's in character because he doesn't want to break the mood.

The irony is that when she initially brought up the idea of role-playing, her man seemed blasé about it. Now that they've been doing it, he fiends for that alter ego. The truth is he's never left the zoo, but when that alter ego appears, he swears he's on the plains stalking his prey!

STIMULATE HIM INTELLECTUALLY TOO

If making your man feel like he's getting new "kitty" wasn't enough of a job, here's another reality you must confront: men need to feel a sense of newness intellectually just as much as they do sexually.

If you were to ask most men to list the traits they were looking for in a woman, they would mention good looks, great sex, bangin' body, sense of humor, kind heart, being good with kids and even being skilled in the kitchen before they would get to a woman's sense of curiosity about the world.

In truth, men are dying to be around women who keep them stimulated mentally *and* intellectually. Now when I say "intellectual" I'm not talking about being a Rhodes scholar. And I'm definitely not saying you need to demonstrate that you have an opinion on every topic, because a lot of y'all confuse being opinionated with being intellectual.

I'm suggesting that as a woman you need to have a genuine

curiosity about life, both within the space that you two share and in the larger world as well—curiosity that you can then share with your man.

I've already spoken at length about how much bad sex or bad head turns me off in a woman, but the truth is that *bad conversation* has turned me off just as much, if not more so.

Many years ago I was dating a woman who certainly came correct between the sheets—but frankly, she bored me to death outside the bedroom.

It wasn't that she was stupid; she had a degree from a good school and a great job in the government, yet she never demonstrated any real curiosity about my world or made me feel like she was interested in getting to actually know me. Sure, she wanted to meet the right people and go to the right parties, but I always felt that's where it ended for her. She was content just knowing that I was a star.

I needed it to be electric. I needed to hear anything that could stimulate that space between us and give me some of the energy I needed to keep striving and growing as a man. But there wasn't anything there.

For a while, I thought maybe it was all in my mind. Then one night I was hanging out with Brandy and my girl, having what on the surface probably appeared to be a nice evening. After a while Brandy pulled me to the side and whispered in my ear, "I'm sorry, Ty, but because you're my friend, I've got to tell you that your girl doesn't know who you are. She's with you but she doesn't *see* you. She don't understand you and all the things that you are as a man. You're being underused as a man. Other people are coming around and being more impacted by your dialogue than she is!"

As soon as she said it, I knew she was right. I know some of you are thinking that Brandy was just hating or maybe even wanted me for herself, but that's dead wrong. Brandy is like a sister to me (just kidding; wanted to see if you still were paying attention), and we have been friends since we were 11 years old. I value her friendship so much precisely because she has always kept it real with me. And for what it's worth, I've given her the same sort of advice about some of the men in her life. It's just our dynamic.

Hearing Brandy's observation confirmed that my girl-friend's mentality had become "I got a man, I'm good," instead of "How can I keep this good man that I've got?" Quite simply, she couldn't, at least not with the mentality she was bringing to the table. So not long after my talk with Brandy, I did a lot of reflecting and soon the dynamics of our relationship became very different.

Listen, I understand that it can be tiring to always keep a man engaged. Sometimes we all need that dinner when we just sit there and don't say *nothing* to each other. The problem is I can't negate the relationships I've been in where exciting, inspiring conversation was the rule, not the exception. Where romantic dinners would seem to fly by in seconds, instead of feeling like they were dragging on for hours.

Obviously not every dinner and conversation will be magical, but it should feel like that's what we're capable of every time we sit down together. Which is why today when I catch my current girlfriend starting to slip into that satisfied "I got a man" mode, I quickly remind her not to get complacent.

While technically it's true that I am her man and that I am being faithful, I know that if she doesn't keep me stimulated mentally, it's only a matter of time before I start to stray. I might still be present physically, but mentally I'm going to start drifting off toward someone who *does* give me that energy. That might seem like a cold thing to say about a person you love, but as a communicator I'm going to do it if that's what it takes for this relationship to work.

ARE YOU EVERY WOMAN?

I want to throw a Chaka Khan quote at you ladies: "I'm Every Woman, It's All in Me!"

Before you accept that ring, ask yourself if you're really prepared to be *every* woman in your relationship. If the answer is anything other than a resounding yes, then you better give that ring back before it gets too comfortable on your finger.

If your marriage is going to work, you truly have to be *every* woman to your man. And the hard news is that a man needs a *lot* of different women in his marriage to make things work.

Sure, you want a man to be with you and you alone, but can you handle all of him? Can you handle all of his needs and desires being directed right at *you* and no one else? Can you handle the duties and expectations that come from being his only source of femininity?

Or are you going to buckle under that weight?

Look at me. I'll tell you right now that I'm an *extremely* complex man. When I get home from the studio at 3:00 a.m. and need some lovin' because I've been singing a sexy love song all night, or even just because I've got too much energy to fall asleep, are you willing to be *that* woman? It comes back to what I was saying about the 80/20 Rule. You've given me that 80 percent so freely, but can you give me that 20 percent at 3:00 a.m. too?

Or when you're exhausted from work but I need someone to listen to a new song and give me some feedback, are you willing to be *that* woman?

When one of our kids has kept you up all night, but I still need you to be the one that takes her to school in the morning so I can keep my appointment with my trainer, will you be *that* woman?

I know I'm asking a lot. My girlfriend once told me, "I feel like I'm in a relationship with fifteen men," because of my being *so* needy, *so* clingy and needing *so* much attention. I want lovemaking when I'm feeling horny, a shoulder to cry on when I'm feeling down, a maid to clean up my crib when I feel disorganized, a muse when I'm feeling uninspired, a cook when I'm feeling hungry, and so on and so on.

She's right. I am an extremely needy man.

Yet when she told me that, I said, "You know, I've never had another woman say that to me."

"Why, because you're Tyrese and no one ever keeps it real with you?" she asked sarcastically.

"Not at all," I said. "Because I've never been with one woman exclusively before. So anything and everything I've needed, I could get from *multiple* women. The woman who gave me lovin' at 3:00 a.m. didn't also have to give me a shoulder to cry on. The woman who was my creative muse wasn't the same woman I needed to keep the house straight. Consequently, and a lot of men can relate to what I'm talking about right now, there hasn't been a woman who's had to provide it *all* to me before. No woman has ever felt like there were ten of me because no one woman was ever getting all ten of me before. But that is what you are asking for."

"I'm not going to lie—your workload to keep me mentally, emotionally, physically and sexually stimulated is going to be tough, because as a man I am used to dealing with multiple women," I continued. "If I had all of these other side chicks I wouldn't need that much from you. But if you want me to stay here and give you everything that I have emotionally, spiritually and sexually, can you truly handle the responsibility of keeping all the different aspects of my personality satisfied? Is that just a concept to you, or are you willing to accept that burden?"

Now obviously, my girlfriend is willing to take on that burden, but let's be real, not every woman is willing to carry that much weight in a relationship. Even if you start off strong, after a couple of years it might seem like too much. The lovin' at 3:00 a.m. was sexy at first, but now that you have kids, you aren't trying to hear it anymore. Maybe after a couple of years of that, you want less responsibility. You won't mind if he's creepin' on you, because when he comes in at 3:00 a.m., he'll let you sleep like a baby.

That might sound flippant, but I'm being real. If you feel overwhelmed dealing with fifteen sides of a man's personality, maybe you'll decide you only want to hold down ten. Or even five.

Whether consciously or subconsciously, some women *do* make that choice. I have a friend who's been married for fifteen years, and he told me that without question, having a mistress is what saved his marriage. His wife doesn't know about the mistress, and if she ever found out she'd certainly be mad, but the fact is she stopped being "Every Woman" to him many years ago. And she knows it.

If not for his mistress, my friend would have walked a long time ago. He even told me, "My side piece helps keep me balanced. She makes me feel like if I can't get something from my wife, I still have somewhere else to turn. My mistress is silly, we laugh and have fun, plus I can tell her everything and she even gives me great advice about my marriage. And as crazy as it might sound, I still love my wife dearly and don't want to lose her. But if I didn't have that other outlet, I'd be gone."

Now let's be clear, that's not a situation that I'm necessarily recommending for you. If you're married, I'm sure you bristled at the very concept of a mistress giving your man advice on his marriage.

What I am trying to say, however, is that if you're not willing to be every woman in a relationship, your husband might very well turn to a mistress in order to make your marriage work.

Or he might turn to the Internet, where whatever he's looking for is only a click away. You're up against competition that women haven't ever faced before. In terms of being every woman to a man, this is uncharted territory.

This is why sexually, at the *bare minimum*, you must maintain the standard you two set before getting married. You do not want your husband asking, "Baby, is there any way I can get you to do the things that made me decide to marry you?" Because if he asks that too many times, soon he will be asking someone else to do the things you two used to do. That might not be fair, but it's the way it is.

PAMPERING IS PART OF BEING "EVERY WOMAN"

If you didn't like being told that you need to work hard to keep your man happy at night, then you're probably *really* not going to like to hear this: one of the most important parts of being "*every woman*" is pampering your man.

Yes, gaining weight or slowing down sexually is not the only way that women begin to settle. Another, and equally dangerous, mind-set that married women slip into is believing that their husbands should do all the giving, while they should do all the receiving.

So many women expect their husbands or boyfriends to constantly give them gifts, send them flowers, whisper lovey-dovey talk in their ear and open doors for them while only getting special attention themselves during the holidays or on birthdays.

Most men won't tell you this, but holidays and birthdays alone are not enough pampering for us. Nope. We need it throughout the entire year.

We might like to act tough, but never forget that at heart, men are just grown-up versions of those little boys who broke down in tears when they didn't see the Tonka Truck they wanted under the Christmas tree. Yes, we're grown, but we still love being on the receiving end of gifts. We still like getting little treats and mementos that let us know that you appreciate us and think that we're special. In fact, we don't only *like* those little gestures; we *need* them.

If you're a wife or a serious girlfriend, let me ask you something: your man might have filled your closet with Red Bottoms, Gucci, Louis Vuitton, and so much other fly stuff, but what does *his* closet look like?

If you went into his closet right now, how many shirts would you find that you bought him? Just on a whim? How many suits would you see that you picked out for him? Would you find any shoes that you surprised him with just because they were on sale and you knew they were his favorite brand?

While I appreciate that money is tight for a lot of people, I also remember those statistics I shared earlier about African-American women getting better jobs and earning more than African-American men these days. That means that while you might very well be making more money than your man, you're still comfortable letting him do the majority of the gift giving and pampering. Some of y'all will go to the mall with *his* money and on the way to *your* store walk by ties, colognes, jeans, boxer briefs, socks, haircut equipment, shaving creams, aftershaves, lotions, oils, hair care products and never once think about picking any of it up for your man. Yeah, you might stop and look at some of that stuff around Father's Day or his birthday, but the rest of the time it just doesn't seem to dawn on you that he might really appreciate you surprising him one night with a new set of clippers. Or some new boxers so he can throw those old ones out. Or even a new pair of socks! It probably doesn't even cross your mind.

Pampering doesn't even have to entail buying him something. When was the last time you just changed all of the sheets on the bed because you knew how hard he was working every day out on the job making it happen and you wanted him to come home to something comforting and clean? Or when was the last time you and the kids surprised him with his favorite dinner and a card reminding him how much y'all love and appreciate him?

When you end up buying him something, he might just smile and say, "Thanks, babe." Even if he doesn't make a big deal about it, trust me, he will love that gesture more than he ever lets on. And once you give him that little gift, don't stop there. Start booking massages for him, even manicures and pedicures. Not necessarily every week or even every month, but just enough to let him know that his needs and comfort level are never far from your mind.

You might be saying, "My man doesn't even want all that" or "My man never asks for nothin' so he must be good." Well, it's not about *asking*. It's about *needing*. And with all due respect, your man needs some pampering.

Now here's the thing: even if what I've said hasn't lit a fire under you to go out and support that man you love because you want to see *him* do better, you might want to follow my advice for your *own* benefit.

That's because the more you pamper your man and surprise him with little gifts, the more he'll do the same thing for you. I promise, if you start setting your man up for massages and pedicures, it will not be long before he's booking the same stuff for you.

As men, we know that our women want to be surprised and pampered, but we often get so caught up in our own struggles and dramas that we forget. That's why you're probably just going to make your man annoyed if you say, "Baby, how come you never surprise me with flowers anymore? How come you never pick me up a new dress just because?" He might pick you up something just to get you off his case, but he won't be doing it out of any real sense of wanting you to be happy. He'll basically just be trying to shut you up, which means that as soon as you seem pacified by whatever little surprise he brought you, he'll slip back into his self-absorbed state.

But if you keep giving him things and showing him that sort of affectionate pampering, then he's going to genuinely want to return the favor. When he walks by a new spa that opened near his job, he's actually going to think, *Oh, I bet my girl would love this place. Lemme get her a gift certificate.* Or when he sees a sale, he won't need a reminder to think, *Wow, wifey would look great in that orange dress. Let me grab it for her.* He's not even going to have to call and ruin the surprise by asking you for your dress size. It's going to be something that is at the front of his mind, instead of something he has to be reminded of. Because your giving and loving attitude will have put him in the same space.

WHAT ARE YOU GOING TO DO WITH THIS?

I know I've hit you with a lot of information. Maybe too much information.

Maybe some of it was shocking.

Maybe some of it made you mad.

Maybe some of it gave you hope.

Maybe some of it felt like it didn't apply.

Hopefully much more of it hit close to home.

I'm not looking for a perfect score with this book. I know not everyone who reads it is going to agree with what I've said. That's fine, because I don't need any pats on the back. I don't need anyone to tell me that they love me.

What I need is a reader who decides that she loves herself and her man enough to start doing things differently.

A lot of people go to church and start jumpin' and shoutin' an hollerin' and catching the Holy Ghost when the pastor gets up on the pulpit and starts preaching. Then once the service is over, they wipe away their tears, pick themselves up off the floor, leave the church, and immediately get back into the same old habits.

That's always confused me. What is the point of jumping, hooping and hollering if you're going to go home only to do the same things you came to church looking to cleanse yourself of? I would assume if you're going to jump up and down and get all fired up, it would be because somebody said something that's so raw and so bold that it couldn't help but change the way you see things.

Because no matter who you are and what you've been through, you do possess the capacity to change.

One way or another we can all get confirmation that we could be doing things differently. The question becomes, once you get that confirmation, how do you respond? Are you the type who'll say, "Man, this brother is dropping some wisdom and some knowledge, and I am soaking it up like a sponge," but as soon as the conversation is over you wring out your sponge and leave all of that wisdom and knowledge on the floor? Or are you the kind of person who not only soaks up information but then looks to *do something* with it?

I hope you're one of the latter. Between Rev and myself, I know for a fact there's a lot of wisdom that can be gleaned from this book. We've done too much living between us and witnessed too much for that to be anything *but* the case, which is why my prayer is that you go out and put this knowledge into practice, even when it feels strange or uncomfortable. Take our honesty and apply it to your own life. Don't let me pull back the curtain on my whole life, all my desires, quirks, fears and dramas, just to have you look the other way.

Take what we've given you here and then please put it into

action. Realize that while what's going on inside a man's mind isn't always pretty or even reasonable, as long as you address it head-on, you're going to be able to build the relationship you not only want but deserve.

REV RUN

It's always interesting to hear Tyrese speak on marriage, because while I know that he and I both fundamentally want the same things from the institution—namely, happiness, stability and the presence of God in our lives—we definitely have very different views on how to achieve them.

I've got issues with a lot of what was just said, but let me start by saying that I actually don't even agree with the very title of this chapter.

Tyrese might not think so, but I believe a ring *does* equal a win in life. If you can get a man to submit to marriage, then that's a win in my book (or at least my half of this chapter). Even though a happy marriage is the best thing that could happen to a man, as I've discussed, most men still do not want to commit. If you've sealed the deal and managed to tie his butt up, then you've won. Please go ahead and celebrate. You deserve it.

There is, however, one caveat: it's only a win if that man is your friend. And not even just a friend, but your *best friend.* Believe me, marrying your best friend is a huge win. It's like the Super Bowl, World Series, NBA Finals, Wimbledon, the Westminster Kennel Club Dog Show, the Oscars and the Grammies and your seventh-grade talent show all melted down into one big gold medal.

It's a win when he's the guy you want to watch movies with until you're a hundred years old, or a guy you'd be as happy with in a trailer park as you would be in a mansion. A guy that you love looking at when he's showing off his six-pack stomach or when he's hiding his gut under an extra-large tee.

Tyrese talks about the importance of remembering to pamper your man, but you won't need a reminder when you're married to your best friend. Think about it. Who's your best female friend right now? Don't you always think about her? If you see a movie you think she'd like, or go to a restaurant you think she'd enjoy, or hear about a sale she'd want to go to, don't you always make a mental note to tell her about it? Don't you actually look forward to telling her about those things? After all, it's fun to make your friend happy. It was fun to make them happy when you were five, fun when you were fifteen and fun when you were twenty-five. Making your friends happy never feels old or stale!

Friendship must be your main criterion when you think about whether a man is someone you'd want to marry. Many times relationships can start off very steamy . . . but then they run out of steam. You don't want to come to that realization *after* you've walked down the aisle. Instead, give that steam a chance to fade away and then see if you still have enough in common with that man.

I truly believe that it's much easier to turn friendship into love than to turn love into friendship. In fact, I like to say that love is actually just friendship caught on fire.

HOW TO STAY WINNING

While I do feel like getting married to your friend is always a win, I'll concede that there are several things you have to focus on with your man if you want to *keep* winning.

First, if you want your marriage to remain a happy one, you need to start hanging with other married folks. I talked earlier about how important it is for single woman to hang with married women so she could learn how to be a wife, but it's just as important for married women to hang out with each other too.

If you hang out with a bunch of single women, at best you're going to lose some of that laser focus you need in order to be a good mother and wife. At worst, you'll actually begin to resent your role in your family. I like to say that chickens hang out with chickens, ducks hang out with ducks, eagles hang out with eagles. If you're a chicken and you try to go swimming with the ducks, then you're going to have a problem.

But as important as it is that you hang with married women, it's even more important that your husband hang with other married men.

It sounds harsh, but you need to limit your husband's exposure to guys who aren't married. You don't want your husband constantly hearing about his single friends' exploits with women, or seeing pictures on Facebook of those single guys kicking it on the beach with girls in bikinis. You don't want to give the seeds of infidelity and disrespect any chance to grow in your husband's mind. Obviously you can't completely isolate your husband from the world, but you can at least be careful about who's in his inner circle.

The larger issue with single men isn't even the temptations they'll create for your husband. No, the most dangerous thing about them is that they do not see their married friends as having won. They see them as having lost. Big-time.

Having lost freedom.

Having lost good sex.

Having lost their swag.

Having lost the right to watch the game with the boys.

239

Having lost the right to stay out late or sleep in.

Even having lost the right to make their own decisions.

Single men aren't subtle with their contempt either. Oh no, they absolutely loooove teasing married men about losing. They get a kick out of rubbing those "losses" in a married man's face any chance they get. This is why single men will have the exact opposite effect on your man than a MAN-tor will.

If you hang out at a barbershop long enough, sooner or later you're going to get a haircut. You might have initially only stopped by the barbershop to shoot the breeze, but after a while you'll say, "You know what, let me get a little trim." And if you start showing up every day, that trim will turn into "Actually, take some off the sides and the top too." Until one day you're going to sit down in that chair and get your entire dome shaved!

Well, if a married man hangs out at the single guy's barbershop long enough, sooner or later he is going to get that proverbial "haircut." And as a wife, I don't think you're going to like the cut they give him at all.

I've been giving Ty a tough time in this book, but he is actually one of the rare exceptions to this rule. I know that he respects the *heck* out of my marriage and the family that I've built. And frankly, without that respect, I couldn't be such good friends with him. If Tyrese were like most single men, our friendship wouldn't last. It wouldn't even have gotten off the ground.

The good news here is that although they normally won't admit it, most married men actually prefer to be in the company of other married men. We might bitch and cry about it a bit to our wives—"I'm tired of hanging out with all these married couples. It's so boring"— but we don't really mean it. As much as we might *act* like we want to, the worst thing we could imagine would be hanging out with a bunch of single men.

It's almost like single men are a separate animal from us. Single guys start to think about going out when we're already set to call it a night. Single guys don't think twice about pounding drinks, while to most married guys (I don't drink myself) the idea of waking up with a hangover seems like the worst thing in the world. A single guy can sleep off a hangover, but there's no sleeping it off for a family man—those kids will be up at 6:00 a.m., looking for action and attention no matter how much Daddy had to drink last night!

But here's the biggest reason we actually don't like hanging out with single guys; we know they don't respect us. Sure, they understand theoretically that being married and raising a family takes a lot of work and commitment, but they don't *feel* it. In their minds, what they're doing is what's impressive. Going out, getting drunk, dancing and having sex with women, that's what deserves celebrating. Raising a family? Who cares about that? That's what their parents did. Big deal.

Believe me, that nonchalant, disrespectful attitude drives married men *crazy*. It actually ties back into what Tyrese has been saying about validation. A family man knows how much work he's put into a family—he understands that raising a family is the toughest thing he's ever done. He's going to need some validation from his peers for what he's accomplished. He's certainly not going to want to be made to feel like a chump.

A single man will *never* give him the validation he knows he deserves, while another married man will, because married men respect the *heck* out of each other. We might not talk about our families or our children with each other as women do, but the respect is always there.

Sometimes it's exchanged with only a knowing look, or a few choice words, but real family men always give each other props. I might not agree with another family man's politics or philosophies or taste in music, but if I know he's doing right by his family day in and day out, then I will always show him a basic level of respect.

This is why you shouldn't get too much resistance when you suggest that your husband make more married friends. Sure, there might be a little complaining at first, but a good man is almost always going to accept that he has much more in common with another married dude than a single guy.

DON'T PUT YOUR KIDS
BEFORE YOUR MAN

Some of you might think Tyrese went a bit overboard with the whole pampering thing, but there was an important element of truth in what he was saying about making sure your husband feels appreciated.

Now, I don't think your husband is going to resent not getting gifts or little gestures from you—after all, he knows better than anyone else in the world how hard you're working and how many other things you have to worry about.

I do, however, think there's always a danger of putting your children before your husband. I don't have to tell you what's going to happen when a marriage is resting on the skinny shoulders of a little kid, as opposed to the strong shoulders of a grown man.

As a mother and a wife, you've got to remember that just because you're giving your husband some attention does not mean that you're ignoring your kids.

A lot of women get so wrapped up in the lives of their kids that they forget about their men. When those kids grow up and move out, suddenly you have two people who don't know each other anymore, which is why so many "empty nest" couples end up divorcing.

It can be an easy trap to fall into, because while it is true, as Tyrese says, that your man won't ask for much, your kids are going to ask for *everything*. Even when they don't need nothin'.

That's why I'm always telling my kids, "Don't stress my wife out," as opposed to "Don't stress out your mother." Sometimes when I phrase it that way they'll look at me and say, "What are you talking about, 'your wife'? She's our mother." They can't conceive of a universe where Mommy and Daddy serve functions other than taking care of them.

As a parent, you've got to remind them that not only does that universe exist but it's one that the two of y'all plan to spend some time in too.

Never be afraid to put your husband's needs first. Don't think of it as depriving your kids; think of it as simply teaching your children how to wait. Trust me, kids are better off learning how to wait in line for some attention from two happy and functional parents. They might get mad or impatient, but in the long run they'll thank you.

THE BEDROOM AND THE BOARDROOM

There's also important truth to what Tyrese says about a man needing to feel like his woman is his most fervent supporter. And perhaps the place he needs to feel that support the most is in the bedroom.

For a married man, there is a connection between how you perform in your career and whether or not you're getting to put on any performances in the bedroom. If you pour all of your effort and hustle into providing for your family yet still hear no too often in the bedroom, it is going to affect your swag; when it's time to ask the boss for a raise, or pitch a new client or present a new proposal, you're going to go into those meetings expecting to hear no. And of course when you go into a meeting feeling like that, you already know what the outcome is going to be.

Having said that, I do understand that sometimes as a woman you are going to feel like you have to say no, even though, as we discussed in "*Manology* after Dark," the Bible instructs us otherwise. This is why I try to encourage Tyrese that he needs to ease back a bit on his "Every Woman" ideal. It sounds nice, but he should realize that part of being married is understanding that just because he might *want* some nookie when he gets home from the studio at 3:00 a.m., he very well might not *get* it. If that means he has to lie in bed reading a book for an hour until he falls asleep, then hey, so be it. Going to bed feeling a little frisky never killed anyone. But *refusing* to go to bed frisky has certainly killed plenty of relationships.

I try to tell Tyrese to imagine if the tables were turned and he was dating a female R&B singer who wanted to climb on top of him every time she got home from the studio at 3:00 a.m. Sure, it would probably be sexy as heck the first ten times it happened; after that, not so much. Soon Tyrese would be saying, "Come on, baby, I've got a big day tomorrow. I need my sleep." And after the first couple of times he was late or tired in a big business meeting because his lady needed some nookie at 3:00 a.m., it would become a real sticking point in their relationship.

That's why in a marriage a man needs to understand that, to paraphrase the old Rolling Stones song, "You can't always get what you want, but you can usually (so long as you took out the trash) get what you need." As a wife, your goal should be to help him find that balance between getting what he truly needs and what he only wants.

BE A PROFESSIONAL FORGIVER

The most important thing I can tell you about marriage, however, doesn't have to do with who your man hangs out with, how much sex y'all have, who buys who what, or even what sort of pecking order you establish with your children.

It has to do with forgiveness.

At the end of the day, I really believe that a great marriage is just two people who are dedicated to forgiving each other. In fact, when people ask me what my most important role as a husband is, I always say—before provider, lover or even friend—"professional forgiver."

I use the term "professional" not because I'm getting paid for it but to emphasize just how serious a job it is. You can't forgive haphazardly, part time or only when you feel like it. No, you have to be a *professional* forgiver. You have to wake up every morning knowing that you're going to be forgiving *at least* one thing that day.

And to be extra clear, when I say be a professional forgiver, that is not code for "let your man cheat" or "look the other way while he does dirt." You already know that I don't cosign that sort of behavior.

Instead, I'm talking about forgiving the little day-to-day mistakes, misunderstandings, miscommunications and resentments that on their own don't seem so serious but collectively over time can seriously erode the foundation of your relationship.

It's not the big, serious, hurtful transgressions you need to forgive in order to make a marriage work; it's the silly aggravations and arguments that you need to learn to let go of.

If Justine and I have a disagreement, there's something really deep that I do. When I'm thinking one way and just know I'm right but she's *still* thinking another, I'll pick being *kind* over being *right*—not because I don't care about the point I was trying to make but because

Jesus has shown me that there's no victory in proving that you're right all the time. God has let me know that I'm not going to sleep better if I go to bed feeling like the victor every night. That's just stupidity!

This applies to both husbands and wives: no matter how aggravated or mad you might get, think of your mate as a little kid. Do I get frustrated when Miley asks for another bowl of cereal but then doesn't eat it? Sure. Do I get ticked off when I warn her not to run while she's carrying a cup of juice, but she does anyway and spills it all over the floor? You better believe it. But do I carry those annoyances around with me for the rest of the day, or even into the next one? Of course not. I forgive her and keep it moving, because I know that she's just a little kid and that little kids, no matter how many times you warn them, are going to make mistakes.

Well, you've got to treat your husband or your wife the exact same way. If you see your wife struggling with a weight issue, you shouldn't get frustrated and then tell her she's not working hard enough to lose it.

A husband should show his wife so much love, support and compassion that she wants to put in that DVD not because she's scared she'll lose him if she doesn't but because she wants to reward him for being such a loyal friend and partner.

I know that these lessons can often sound easier said than done, but I promise that I try to live them as much as possible. If my marriage does look pretty decent on *Run's House* or in these pages, it's really only because I've embraced forgiveness. Trust me, when you hold on to pain, issues, drama and disappointment, it is like having bad plumbing in your marriage: the love can't get through! But when you learn to let go of those things, the love between y'all will start flowing properly once again.

Allow me to share one final thought: I don't want to undercut the messages of this book, ladies, but you'll never fully understand your man perfectly, just like he's never going to understand you perfectly either. And you know that's OK, because your only real duty as a wife is just to care for and love your spouse. And when you can do that, no matter what obstacles or setbacks you encounter during your journey with your husband, you'll know that you have what it takes to get past them.

MANOLOGY: RELOADED

As I mentioned before, I wrote *Manology* because I have a problem with what women don't know.

That's not to suggest, however, that I don't have a big problem with what men don't know too.

Or more specifically, what men won't *admit* to themselves.

I initially had planned to address men directly throughout *Manology*. Then I was told, by people allegedly "in the know," that men don't read books like this.

I took their advice, but I should have known better. Because if men don't read books like *Manology*, then how do you explain this message I received from a fan named Mark not long after the book was published:

Tyrese: Someone left this book *Manology* in the barbershop and I can't lie, the way you and Rev put it together about love, life, and men made me really open my eyes. It was like, "Whoa, there are a lot of young guys running around clueless about life. I hope that *Manology* gets to the streets here in Philly ASAP! It could save some brothers the way it's saved me."

I'm so thankful that I received Mark's message, because it reminded me that no matter what conventional wisdom might say, brothers out there *are* looking for this sort of information! Which is why I have a responsibility, one that I take very seriously, to share it with them.

Remember, this book wasn't written as a gimmick. Rev Run and I did not go through this process, which was very intense and grueling at times, just so we could grab a check and walk away. No, we're in this for the long haul, because as Mark reminded us, this sort of information can save lives! Which is why I'm always going to speak my truths, no matter how uncomfortable they may be.

So without any further ado, fellas, let's get into some real talk!

BREAK THE CYCLE

The first thing I want to discuss is our tendency as men to self-sabotage when it comes to our relationships. So many times, when we are in a beautiful relationship with a woman and we are experiencing the *blessings* that come with a good woman, we start looking for ways to ruin it.

We might not even be conscious of this tendency, but it's very real. Yes, at the very same time that we are celebrating this great presence in our lives, part of our subconscious mind is looking for ways to get rid of it.

We also do this with our careers and our friendships from

time to time, but our greatest tendency is to do it with our romantic relationships.

Now, you might be saying to yourself, "Nah, homie. That's not me you're talking about; why would I do that?" But please, don't make a fool out of yourself as a man by assuming that you are not suffering from self-sabotage and self-defeat. Because this tendency strikes all of us. It has certainly touched me.

I spent many years being blessed time and time again—with acting roles, business opportunities, and beautiful, intelligent women who wanted to love me—but I wouldn't let those blessings stick. It's almost like I got bored with my blessings. Because when those blessings started rolling in, something inside of me wanted to figure out a way to sabotage them. To lose that role that had been written for me. To make a deal disappear. To chase away that woman who was beautiful and had a pure heart.

For a long time I thought it was just me, that I was the only one who operated this way, but then I watched a documentary about Marvin Gaye.

Now, if there was ever a brother who seemed to be extremely secure in his blessings, it would have to be Marvin. Not only could Marvin sing like no other, but he was also extremely intelligent, he was a world-class athlete, and, of course, women loved him.

But according to this documentary, Marvin tried his best to ruin every one of those blessings. He started cheating on his wife and chasing prostitutes, missing his appointments in the studio, and doing all sorts of drugs.

On the surface it just seemed like another rock-star story, but I remember that they interviewed one of Marvin's closest friends and he said something very interesting. The friend said that despite all the great things Marvin had in life—beautiful women, fame, selling millions of records—subconsciously he was afraid of that sort of success. He was afraid that if things got *too* good, he'd lose touch with his roots.

He'd lose touch with the pain that he'd felt as a youth, the pain that motivated him to sing so soulfully and reach the heights of the music industry. Marvin needed some type of drama, some type of conflict that allowed him to stay in tune with his pain. Because that's where his art came from, a real place.

Now, to some of y'all that might sound crazy, but I get it. Obviously, as a singer, I'm going to relate to Marvin better than most, but I believe in my heart that as men we all posses this self-defeating gene.

Because as men, we're all more comfortable striving for blessings than actually *resting* in those blessings. So we work so hard for something good, then ruin it. We start working again, get blessed again, and ruin it again too. And rinse and repeat. Rinse and repeat.

Which is why I'm here to say, "You *can* break that cycle!"

I know this because I did it myself. The key is simply being conscious of the fact that you're stuck in a cycle in the first place.

In my own case, I wasn't conscious until my mentor got tired of watching me block blessing after blessing. Finally he pulled me aside and said, "You know what your problem is, Tyrese? You need to get out of your own way!"

When he said that to me, it was like a light went on in my head. It hit me so powerfully that years later I ended up writing a book with that very title (and now that you're almost done with this one, you can read that one next!).

So, fellas, please Get Out of Your Own Way!

I can't share all the steps you need to take—you're going to have to wait for *Manology 2* for that—but there are a couple of key points that I want to share right now.

PRIDE AND EGO

One of the simplest steps you can take to getting out of your own way is letting go of your pride and ego.

We already discussed the tendency of a lot of men to self-sabotage, but the other side of the coin is that there are a lot of men out there who won't fight hard *enough* for a good woman. Instead of chasing a good woman away, they won't chase her at all!

I know a guy like this, an entertainer whom I'm mentoring. He's a very bright and charismatic guy with an incredible future ahead of him.

One day I saw all these blogs writing about how he and his fiancée, who was also a public figure, had just broken up. The blogs were calling it a "mutual decision," but something in the stories didn't feel right to me. So being a mentor, I grabbed my phone and texted him:

"Are you kidding me?" I asked him. "You are going to just let this woman pass you by?"

A few minutes later he hit me back with:

"Aye, man, you know our schedules got busy. She's off doing her thing, know what I mean? It just didn't work out."

Talk about self-sabotaging! You're in a power couple with a beautiful and successful woman and you just let her go because your schedules are too busy? Sorry, I can't let that slide.

"Dog, go get your girl!" I wrote him back. "Go do what you have to do. You need to be desperate, you need to be thirsty, you need to do it by any means necessary! Do, and this is *key*, do anything that she needs you to become in order to get her back into your life!"

And then I hit him with a scenario that he probably wasn't even conscious of. "You and your boys are probably celebrating that you are single again. Am I right? Well, let me tell you the *real* reason they're so happy. It's not because they're happy to see you out of a bad relationship, because that was a great relationship. They're happy because when you were with her, you stopped clubbing, you stopped hanging out. And since you're the star, when you were out on the scene, life was good for them. They were getting that free bottle service, they were getting all the chicks that were hanging around to meet you, but couldn't get close enough. And once you were gone, all of that was gone too!

Do you think they are going tell you, "Listen, man, fight to get her back. She was The One." Hell no! They say they want the best for you, but they want that bottle service and those groupies even more. Trust me: yes, they are celebrating, but it's not for what happened in your life. It's for what they think is about to happen in theirs!"

Now, granted, that might be an extreme situation. Obviously, not every man brings the kind of star status and access to the table that my friend did. But that scenario does play out to one degree or another in a lot of situations.

I already told the ladies to be careful of their friends' true motivations when it comes to their romantic relationships, and, fellas, it's no different for you and your boys. You can't let your ego trick you into thinking that they want the best for you in your relationships. No, they want their meal ticket back. Or maybe they want you back because you're the one with the nicest car. Or you've got the most comfortable crib to hang out in. Or that you bring a certain kind of energy to the crew that they miss. Whatever the reason, they will encourage you to stand there and let a great woman just walk out of your life because it's beneficial to them.

They're not going to tell you the truth, but I will. If you have a great woman in your life, do not just let her walk away. Go get her, dog! Your boys will be fine without you on a Saturday night in the club or watching the game. But you will be miserable without that woman in your life.

LOOK PAST THE SEX

We can talk about breaking the cycle, letting go of pride, and standing strong in the face of criticism, but the real truth is the biggest obstacle we have to overcome collectively as men is looking past the sex.

Fellas, you know I'm speaking every last bit of the truth right now.

Because I'm speaking the truth, this is going to be a very bold section, one that will likely make women a little uncomfortable. I apologize for that, but there's no way I can get through to these men if I don't speak in a language that they understand. So if some of the things I'm about to say sound like I'm talking about women as if they are objects instead of humans, trust me: that's not how I truly feel. But the truth is this *is* the kind of language men use when they speak to each other, so it's the kind of language I'm going to use here.

For example, I can't tell you how many conversations I've heard between men that go something like this: "Lord, she got a fat one. Plus she light skin and got good hair. Watch, I'mma put a baby in her." A lot of African-American men really think that way. A beautiful dark-skinned sister with natural hair can walk by them and they won't even give her a second look. But let that light-skinned chick with good hair stroll by and they're already talking about making babies. Simply because they want their kids to have light skin and "good hair" too.

Remember how I talked about "compartmentalizing" earlier in the book? How men could use it to justify cheating? Well, this mind-set is another example of our ability to compartmentalize. We're so focused on the validation that comes from having sex with and knocking up a certain kind of woman that we never think past that. We never think, *OK, she looks good, but will she be a good mother?* Or, *Yes, she got a great butt and nice hair, but is her relationship with God the same as mine? Are we going to want the same things? Will we approach the world the same way?"* Men rarely ask themselves those sorts of questions. Instead, they're out for the sex and the validation, and anything beyond that, the attitude is, "We'll cross that bridge when we come to it."

That's why now I want to flip it, and talk about how we can use compartmentalization in a *good way*. How we can say, "Yes, I'm horny. Yes, I want to smash that," but not let that desire bleed over into the rest of our thoughts. So that "Yes, I want to smash that" doesn't quickly turn into "Yes, I want to put a baby in that," or "Yes, I want to wife that."

So instead, let's use the ability to compartmentalize to say, "Yes, I love how you go down in the bedroom, but that's it." To be able to tell ourselves, "Let's not get things twisted and think just because this head compartment is so great, all the other ones will be too."

And let's keep it real: Some of you take it even further than validation. Some of you get so wrapped up in the sex you're having with a woman that you try to get her pregnant so you won't lose her. Forget about good hair for your kids, you're so afraid to lose that sex that you'll try to knock her up so that you can keep her in your life forever!

We've all been there. You're with a girl and it's the best sex you have ever had in your life, but you're still insecure about the relationship. Every time you leave your home, the idea of one of your boys stopping by while you're out and maybe having sex with your girl starts to drive you crazy.

So first, you don't let your boys come around anymore, just because you want to protect that good you-know-what. And then you take it a step further. Even though all the signs are there that this relationship is no good—would you ever worry about your boys doing something behind your back in a good relationship?—you decide to take the ultimate precaution against this woman leaving you: you decide to put a baby in her.

Some of y'all even act like it wasn't a *decision*, but that it just *happened*. Well, maybe you can lie to yourself, but I'm not buying that. Don't tell me you slipped up and forgot to pull out in a moment of passion. No, you got her pregnant on *purpose*. Because you just couldn't live with the idea that one day she'd break up with you, that one day all that flirting you've been noticing would actually lead her to have sex with one of your homies. So in your mind, whether it's the conscious or unconscious one, you told yourself, "I'm going to get this woman pregnant so that I always somehow have access to this woman. Because even if we break up at some point, I really believe I will get her back because we have a baby together."

Fellas, no matter how great the sex is, do not impregnate

someone because you're afraid to lose them. You have to get past that motivation! You have to learn to separate having good sex today with wanting to be in a relationship with someone forever. It might sound very simple, but this is an issue that trips up so many men. And then, by extension, so many women and innocent children as well. Children who get born into terrible, dysfunctional situations simply because a man couldn't look past good sex.

So what I'm saying here is, if you think that woman is beautiful and great in bed, then try to understand that might be all it is. Just because she gives great sex does not mean she should be your wife and the mother of your child. If you think this woman goes down on you and gives you the best head you have had in your life, that's OK. Enjoy it while it lasts and then move on when that moment is over.

A boy clings to great sex. A seasoned man knows how to enjoy it until it has run its course and then says, "This is where it stops."

DON'T RUSH INTO A RING

A lot of *Manology* might have felt as if it was aimed toward helping women find the right guy to marry, but it also needs to be said that men should not rush into that relationship if they are not ready!

Should marriage be your goal as a man? A resounding yes. But should you rush your way into it if you're truly still not ready for it? Of course not.

I've seen too many relationships like the one I described in the last section, where the sex is great but everything else is difficult, and the man still takes that as a sign to move forward! Because in his mind he thinks, *Well, maybe getting married will get rid of all these conflicts and insecurities that she had. And once we're under the same roof, and have little kids running around, then I'll be more focused on this relationship. I won't want to hang with my boys as much and I'll cut out all the creepin' I've been doing too. And then this thing will be better.*

Sorry, man, but I've got some very sad news for you. In a situation like that, marriage will actually make your relationship *worse*. Instead of going away, all those insecurities and dramas are only going to get heightened once you're on the other side of marriage. You know how you leave the toilet seat up in the bathroom? Or how you act like you're still in kindergarten and don't shake your thing properly, so all the pee ends up on the floor when you go to the toilet in the middle of the night? You know that? Well, your woman will tolerate that when you're *dating*. But when you're married, when she thinks she's going to be stepping in your pee every night for the rest of her life, that's going to drive her crazy. And a million other little things like it. This sweet, kind woman will turn into something that you won't even recognize.

Trust me: the last thing you want to do is hurry up and get married only to discover that you drive each other crazy on the *other* side of marriage. Because when you are married, and especially when you have kids, there is no out. Or certainly not any easy ones.

You see, a lot of men are starting to get the wrong idea about marriage. Unfortunately, they see so many celebrity divorces in the headlines that they think divorce is an acceptable, maybe even a popular, thing to do. But you must remember that for every high-profile split, there are many more celebrity couples out there who have been married for ten, fifteen, twenty years, but aren't getting any magazine covers for that accomplishment.

Yes, if one of those celebs file for divorce then they will be on every tabloid, every blog, every website, and every magazine there is. But let them celebrate their twenty-fifth wedding anniversary at a party with their kids? You won't hear much about that.

As a man, you should be holding yourself to those standards. Not the standard you see on one of these *Housewives* reality shows. As a man, you have to be prepared to hulk it out through the inevitable difficulties and disappointments that are going to arise in a marriage. Not run away at the first sign of trouble.

If you're going to let your impression of marriage be informed by what you see on TV, make sure you go back and watch Rev Run on *Run's House*. Really take notes on how he and Justine throw themselves fully into dealing with every difficulty that comes their way, no matter how trivial or major the situation may be. That's the standard you want to be holding yourself to, not the dumb, empty standard being presented on so much of reality TV.

LIVE TOGETHER FIRST

I want to end this with a final piece of advice: don't be like me.

And by that, I mean really know what you're getting into before you get married. I didn't do my homework, and I paid the price as a result. I wouldn't change having my daughter for ANYTHING in this world, but I would change the path I took toward marriage.

And if I could do anything over, it would be this: I would live with my fiancée first.

Remember, experience is your highest truth. So if you have the ability to get a heads-up about what's around the corner before you get there, who wouldn't want to take advantage of that information?

Consider a happy, stable marriage as Disneyland and living together as a navigation system. Now, if you're not from L.A., you're going to need directions in order to find Mickey Mouse. You'll need to know when to make a left turn. Which expressways to avoid and which shortcuts to take. You're going to want to consult your road map and GPS system; otherwise you're going to get lost and stuck in traffic jams. You might even run out of gas. So by the time you finally pull up into Disney World eight hours later, you're going to be so tired and annoyed that you're going to have lost most of your passion before even getting on the rides.

But if you consult that navigation system, you're going to save yourself a lot of headache. Maybe you'll go over the map and see that no matter which route you take, there is still going to be a lot of traffic. So instead of forcing it, you'll say, "You know what, maybe Disney World isn't the best trip for us," and call it a day. Or maybe you'll see all that traffic and say, "We don't care how long it takes, we just want to do this together," and then make the trip.

That's the advantage you'll get from living together first. You'll have all the information in front of you to make an educated decision, instead of *assuming* that everything is going to work out once you put a ring on it. Because no matter what fairy tales you read, I am here to tell you that having a good marriage is going to be work!

In fact, while I will never EVER question God—I repeat, I will never ever question God—sometimes I do wonder: If God was still here on earth, would He update what marriage is? Would God redefine sex since there are now gays and lesbians who are getting married? Would God redefine who we are as men and women and how we should go about our lives? Would

God give me advice on how to deal with a marriage that is now broken because I got caught cheating and lying through messages on Twitter and Facebook? Would God update the Bible based on modern-day dramas, issues, and conflicts that didn't exist fifty years ago, let alone five years ago? Would He? I often wonder.

Again, I am not questioning God, but rather trying to give you some insight into just how powerful the emotions that are created by a marriage are—for better or for worse. A failed marriage can affect you so deeply that you might catch yourself thinking, as I have, that maybe this whole system is broken, that maybe there is a better way to do this.

That's why even though I know—and Rev Run has reminded me of this so many times—that we are not supposed to sleep with women before we are married, I believe from personal experience that you never know anybody until you *live* with them. If you're not living with someone, your relationship is like one long, never-ending date. Everyone can have a good time when a relationship consists of sleeping in your own bed, then meeting someone you're attracted to in the afternoon for some sushi. Sure, you're always going to have butterflies in your stomach living like that.

But when you live with somebody, and you gotta roll over and walk around in the same house and you're seeing this person for twenty-four hours a day, seven days a week, it becomes very, very different. You don't miss someone when you see them every day. Those butterflies get harder and harder to find.

So if you have the opportunity to collect information on this woman that you're about to spend the rest of your life with, take advantage of it! See if this woman has the spirit, the intelligence, the integrity, the understanding, the consistency, the persistence, the determination, the independence, the love, the loyalty, and most important the patience to spend the rest of her life with you as your wife.

And if you can identify most of those qualities after a year of living together, then by all means wife her up!

But if she seems to be lacking in some, or even most of them, then it might be time to move in a new direction before you invest too much more in that relationship.

Now, some of y'all are reading this thinking, *Hell, after you said all of that, I don't even know if I ever want to get married!* But please don't take that away from this section, because that's not the point I am trying to make. The point is that if someone had said these things to me, if someone had given me that heads-up and given me things to consider and think about before I got married, one could argue that things would have turned out differently. In fact, I might still be married to this day!

I know I gave you, both men and women alike, so much advice in this book, but if you can take one final nugget with you from these pages, let it be "live together first." Not because I'm trying to steer anyone away from marriage, but because I want to see each and every one of you who is reading this book enter into the happy and fulfilling marriage that you deserve.

Rev, I know you strongly disagree with me on that one, which is why I snuck it in there as the final word. I guess we'll just have to take it up in the next book!

ACKNOWLEDGMENTS

Rev Run

I'd like to thank everyone on the team who helped that initial conversation between Tyrese and me evolve into *Manology*. I'd also like to thank all the people I've met over the years, both in person and online, who have introduced themselves and let me know that I inspire them. Whether it's through my music with Run DMC, *Run's House* or my *Words of Wisdom,* it means so much to know that my words and prayers have impacted you. It's an honor to have met each and every one of you and I hope that this book will bring a little bit of light into your life.

TYRESE

This is always the hardest part, because there are so many inspiring people who have impacted my life and have been a direct extension of my success and a part of making me who I am today. I wanted to shout out a few of those who helped me with this project:

Joey "Rev Run" Simmons: My family, my brother, my mentor, and now my partner in *Manology*. Of all things we know that our friendship and relationship is waaaaaaay beyond this book, and if we had written out all of the inspiration and insight that we have shared between us over all these years, we would be at twelve books by now. You are a fearless man of God, a family man, and true friend of substance. You're an honest, sincere, and honorable human being. I want to thank you not only for myself, but for all of your millions of Twitter followers who are inspired by your daily messages. You brought integrity and family values back to television in *Run's House* and reminded us that "family" still exists in the world. I am honored to know you and I feel like God sent me a family cause he knows I was missing one . . . !

Jillian Manus, Matthew Benjamin, and my entire Touchstone family: Thank you for believing in our vision and for being boldly honest and staying the course to get us here! We salute you!

Chris Morrow: A bold and consistent writer who has the patience of a true vet; thank you for staying the course! I hope and pray that we create a shift in the universe with the message in *Manology* part 2, coming soon!

Bishop Kenneth C. Ulmer: It's because of you that I feel closer to God and have grown closer to him and his word. You are the most articulate and passionate man of God I have ever been in the presence of. I can't put everything you mean to me into words. People can only hope that they come across a man that represents for the kingdom of God the way you do, so that they can be inspired to further their walk with God. Bishop, thank you from the bottom of my heart. I love you. You never know—one day I may just step up to that podium, and it will be all "your fault for sure"...

Will Smith: One word comes to mind when I think of you: selfless. Being around your passion for life, knowledge, awareness, and heart has made me a better man all across the board. I feel not only lucky but honored to consider you a friend and, more important, a mentor who I know genuinely believes in me and wants the very best for me. I've said this to you before: After putting so much of myself out there it makes me uncomfortable at times to have it come back my way in the form of you having my best interest at heart. I can only say thank you.

La Tasha Mason and Marvenus Daniels: You two ladies are the truth. From my fan club to my book club to transcribing on this book, it's safe to say I for sure found my number-one supporters and I am so grateful for you both truly. Thank you for everything!

Jerome Martin: From the beginning you have always been there, and that story hasn't changed. You have become at this point more of a therapist and ear when I'm going through any and everything that life throws at me. You are a star. I love you and thank you for enduring this ride with me throughout all these years, first representing me at Ford Modeling agency and now as my personal A-list Hollywood agent. My life has been transformed—pun intended! You literally always have my back and I can't thank you enough.

Isabella Castro: My "Queen of Execution" aka "The Gate-keeper"! Everyone you interact with will agree that you are a "force of nature." Your plate is so full—how is it possible for one woman to handle so much detail with such grace? I am screaming "thank you" and the people of the world echo that same feeling! There is so much more to do, so stay sharp! And stay on your path of greatness, little Valentina is here! I love you both!

Adriana: You have a little angel in Marley. Our family is growing as a team and I hope and pray you stay on your path cause your presence is felt and welcomed always. We have a lot to do so let's keep grinding! Bless you!

Gayle Atkins: I love you. I just want to remind you that my career and everything is all your fault. Thank you for taking my call when I was only fourteen and believing in me; I can only hope I continue to make you proud . . . I love you forever!

Greg Parks: GPeeezy! Your name should be "Loyal for Life" because that's what you are. I got your back forever and that will never change.

Gerald Jackson: You are one of my best friends and have held me down for ten yeaaars! As my head of security you have a clean record. Let's keep rocking another 10+.

Reggie Andrews: I don't know where to start. I never knew what a father figure was till I met you. Every morning when I walked in that music class at Locke High School my life felt different because I was evolving and learning something new and you made it fun to learn. I only wish there was a class on "How to Be the Greatest Teacher of All Time" because you would for sure be the star of it!

To my team of agents, lawyers, managers, business managers at GSO, and staff: It's pretty much impossible to get to another level of life and or your career without having an incredible team in place and I can only thank you for everything you do from day to day. Every email, fax, letter and call, all in hopes to move the needle forward! Let's keep plowing because the top is near. May God continue to protect and bless my team.

And to my little angel Shayla Gibson, my lovely, powerful, smart, and beautiful little girl: When you get older you're going to read and understand this. It doesn't matter where I am in the world, my heart still pumps for you. Just know that I will never leave your side. I am out here making it happen so that you will never have to live and be exposed to the many things I grew up in. You are the best of me and your mother and I love you both with all our hearts. Forever! I am so proud to be your father! You will be a step above the rest and I and your mother are gonna see to it! I love and adore you!—Your Proud Dad!

Every person on this list has in some way, shape, or form made me into the man that I am today. In this world one can only hope to come across someone who can help him along the way and have a genuine support system of powerful and inspirational people. I send my love to all of you. Even if you don't see your name on this list, know that you have contributed to my life and journey. I love you, too!

Brandy Norwood my best friend for life! John Bryant, Lala, Avi Arad, Andrew Young, Anita Baker number 1 for six weeks with "Lately," I'm honored! Dexter King Bernice King and Martin Luther King III, my new extended family! To my amazing agents and team, ICM Joanne Wiles, Lorrie Barlett, Dana Simms, Michael Bay, T4 lets get it, I'm ready! Barris Bolton, A. J. Brandenstein, Bill Braunstein, Ian Bryce, a real *gem*! Lisa Callif, Sean "Diddy" Combs, Biff Warren, always on your A-game!! Thank you! Karen Curry and family, I love the Currys! Lee Daniels and Leah Daniels, Teddy Pendergrass is up next! Mike Le, Eugene and Eddie K-Town is changing the game! The *best* cast in the *world*! George Daniels Julius Denim, Ananda Lewis, Lorenzo Di Bonaventura and Vin Diesel, thank you for showing me the ropes big, bro. F6 and beyond! Samantha Vincent, send my love to the new little one! Tony Dixon, Josh Duhamel, Salendra Durham, Herman Flores, Brad Furman, Savon Gibson, BayBay, Shonta Gibson, Tyrone Gibson Sr., Tyrone Gibson Jr. My real family I love you all! F. Gary Gray, Lyndsey Green, travel agent greatness! Shannon Hefferon, Taraji P. Henson, I adore you forever! ICM, T. D. Jakes, Andrew Jones, Quincy Jones, Mark Kaplan, Todd Keith, R. Kelly, Gayle King, Robert Kondrk, Kurupt, Shia LaBeouf, baby bro for life!! Elva LeMasters, Raymond Lewkow, Cheryl Coleman, Justin Lin you are a pure genius I trust you with my life and future! Fast King! Sue Wishengrad, QD3, Scott Mantell, James Llewelyn, Janine Rayburn, Lynise Levine, Ben Lyons, Anthony Mandler, Brett Mayo, Barbara Wintroub, Lil Ronnie congrats on the big move! Kate McGregor, Priscilla Murray, I love you mother! Truly! President Barack Obama and Michelle Obama, two terms! I'm so proud!! Robert Offer, Jeff Johnson, congrats to you and your wife! So proud!! Charlie Mack, my guy for life! Omar Rambert, Vicki Palmer, Teddy Pendergrass—rest in heaven, special love to the Pendergrass family, Joe Puleio, Larry Khan, Brian Relyea, my dear Maya Saif were still going strong! Stix, Jerome Spence, Sam Kling, Peer Music, Jill Scott, Ed Shapiro, Afeni Shakur, John Singleton, Scooter, Clinton Sparks, Steven Spielberg, T-Neal and the Core DJ Family, Tim Story, Joanetta Stowers, Tim and Bob,

Steve Harvey, Brad Swart, Kiarash Behain, G. Flowers Paxton Baker, Matt Alonzo I salute you! Tommy Garcia, Bill Brown, Dennis Ashley, HJ, Alan Foster, Yvonne Faison , Grammy Academy Los Angeles Recording Chapter, Uncle Craig Davis, Deepak Chopra EMI Label Services/Capital, my family my music life! Happy one-year anniversary! We did it! Michael Harris, Leota Blacknor, Jesse Flores, Matt Sawin, Richard Furch, Mike B, Richard Nash, Tara Razavi, Darrell Thompson, Iyanla Vanzant, Ron Waldman, Lizzy Moore—LA Chapter Grammys, Eric Dawkins, so proud of you and your wife! Paul Walker, my brother of ten years we're still laughing! Rolo Hendricks, Tikiya Crawford, Tom Walper, Denzel Washington, I still won't feel like I made it as an actor until I work with you! David Webber, Marcus "Siege Monstrosity" White, Coach Al, you are a great man of God, thank you for training me! Marvin Brown, Carol Lehmann, Oprah Winfrey, Elaine Wynn, a true gem!! Jordan Zimmerman, Zimmerman Agency, Doris Tan, Meek, Eugene Luckett, Chris Herche, Robert Zuckerman. And to all my nieces, nephews, cousins, and extended family—I love you all.

To my number-one *Open Invitation* album dream team. We are now celebrating the one-year anniversary of this album, with almost 500,000 records sold. We did it independent, and it would not be possible without you! You showed up for me and I'm lost for words!

Brandon "Bam" Alexander, you genius and for sure one of the great producers of the future; thank you for trusting me! Lil Ronnie, Stuart Schenk, G. Flowers, Aaron Sledge, Asaleana Elliott, Berris Bolton, Cedric Smith, Chris Lacy, Cliff Jones, Donald Atkins, Elva LeMasters, J Tarin, James "J-Doe" Smith,

Acknowledgments

Kendall Nesbitt, Richard Furch, Kendrick Dean, Kiarash "The Rundown" Behain Lashawn, Daniels Leon, Timbo, Michael Harris, Isabella Castro, Nick Roach, Richard "Scooter" Sledge, and Dan Hook.

Double album and book *Black Rose* is up next; get ready!

And finally, five years ago we had a vision to become one musically, so we formed TGT: Tyrese, Ginuwine, and Tank. Atlantic Records backed us and now it's here, it's no longer just a vision or an idea; it's real. I love you both as brothers and true R&B Kings through and through! History in the making! Let's go *get it*!

ABOUT THE AUTHORS

TYRESE GIBSON, also known simply as Tyrese, is a dynamic figure in entertainment today who has had huge success as a multi-platinum and Grammy-nominated R&B singer, songwriter, actor, bestselling author, and television producer. After the release of several critically acclaimed and award-winning albums, he transitioned into films, including *Baby Boy*, *2 Fast 2 Furious*, *Fast Five*, and the Transformers trilogy. Gibson also created the bestselling comic book *Mayhem!*. His most recent music endeavor, *Open Invitation*, debuted at number one and included the hit single "Stay," which remained number one for eleven consecutive weeks. Gibson's first book, *How to Get Out of Your Own Way*, was an instant *New York Times* bestseller.

REV RUN, aka Joseph Simmons, is one of the founding members of the pioneering hip-hop group Run DMC, which was recently inducted into the Rock and Roll Hall of Fame and hailed by

Rolling Stone as the biggest rap group of all time. His hit MTV show *Run's House* aired for six seasons. Starring alongside his wife Justine and their six children, Run became America's favorite father and a model of family values, humor, and spirituality. He is the author of *Words of Wisdom* and the coauthor, with his wife, of *Take Back Your Family.* Run's daily inspirational words of wisdom are followed by nearly four million people on Twitter and have established him as a thought leader in the world of social media.